Providing Effective Library Services for Research

Jo Webb, Pat Gannon-Leary and Moira Bent

facet publishing

© Jo Webb, Pat Gannon-Leary and Moira Bent 2007

Published by Facet Publishing,
7 Ridgmount Street, London WC1E 7AE
www.facetpublishing.co.uk

Facet Publishing is wholly owned by CILIP: the Chartered
Institute of Library and Information Professionals.

Jo Webb, Pat Gannon-Leary and Moira Bent have asserted
their right under the Copyright, Designs and Patents Act 1988
to be identified as authors of this work.

British Library Cataloguing in Publication Data
A catalogue record for this book is available from the British
Library.

ISBN 978-1-85604-589-6

First published 2007

Typeset from authors' files in 11/15 pt Bergamo and Chantilly
by Facet Publishing.
Printed and made in Great Britain by MPG Books Ltd,
Bodmin, Cornwall.

Contents

Acknowledgements

Writing a book like this was never going to be easy: it was our first collaboration, and this is a huge and complicated topic. We would like to thank all of those who helped us along the path to completion.

First of all our gratitude to those who helped us to develop the concept of this book, in particular Rebecca Casey, formerly of Facet Publishing, and Professor Sheila Corrall. Later on, the endless patience and support of Sophie Baird, our Commissioning Editor, and other members of the Facet team, enabled us to complete the work.

Next we must acknowledge all the researchers with whom we have worked through the years, especially those who gave up their time to be interviewed. We have learnt so much from you all.

We would also like to thank our colleagues, especially the ResIN team at Newcastle University, as we have drawn on their good work for many of the practical examples through the book. Clare Powne and Robin Green were valuable sources of information, and prompted many of our ideas for Chapter 9.

Naturally any list of acknowledgements would be meaningless without listing our family and friends. Pat would like to single out Mike McCarthy, and Moira thanks Adam, Simon, Alex and Caitlin for allowing her the time and space to work on the book. We would all like to thank Chris Powis for his practical support in filling in some of the gaps at the end of the writing process.

Acronyms and abbreviations

ARL	Association of Research Libraries (USA)
AUUC	Association of Universities and Colleges of Canada (Canada)
BL	British Library
CERL	Consortium of European Research Libraries
CoP	community of practice
CRS	contract research staff
CURL	Consortium of Research Libraries of the UK (formerly Consortium of University Research Libraries)
CVCP	Committee of Vice-Chancellors and Principals
DENI	Department of Education for Northern Ireland
EARL	Electronic Access to Resources in Libraries
EEBO	Early English Books Online
EIS	electronic information services
ETD	electronic theses and dissertations
FAIR	Focus on Access to Institutional Resources
FHE	further and higher education
FOI	freedom of information
FOIA	Freedom of Information Act
FOISA	Freedom of Information (Scotland) Act
HEFCs	Higher Education Funding Councils
HEIs	higher education institutions
ICTs	information and communication technologies

IFLA	International Federation of Library Associations and Institutions
IR	institutional repository
IT	information technology
JANET	Joint Academic Network
JISC	Joint Information Systems Committee
JISCPAS	JISC Plagiarism Advisory Service
LIS	library and information services
NSS	National Student Survey
OA	open access
RCUK	Research Councils UK
RIN	Research Information Network
RLN	Research Libraries Network
RSLG	Research Support Libraries Group
RSLP	Research Support Libraries Programme
SCONUL	Society of College, National and University Libraries
TOCs	table of contents (services)

Glossary

alerting services: these send regular e-mails to provide updates on new publications. Once the alert is set up, it happens automatically, so the researcher does not have to engage with the publication regularly unless they wish to. *See also* **current awareness services**.

andragogy: term, coined in 1833 by Alexander Kapp, to distinguish the teaching of adults from the teaching of children (pedagogy). The term implies self-directedness and an active student role.

archives, rare books, special collections: terms variously given to the valuable primary resources held by many university libraries. They can include original manuscripts, collections of letters, early printed books, maps, scientific notebooks and any other rare and often unique materials deemed by library staff by virtue of their age or rarity to be deserving of special treatment.

bibliometrics: the application of mathematical and statistical methods for measuring quantitative and qualitative changes in collections of books and other media, e.g. to measure the scattering of articles to different journals or the growth and obsolescence of literature in different subject areas.

blogs: short for weblogs, these are journals/diaries available on the web for general public consumption.

Business Source Premier (EBSCO): combines a database with some full text access, mainly in business and management topics.

carrels: originally small rooms within a library where researchers could work in comparative quiet and privacy, sometimes being lockable or containing lockable drawers or lockers in which researchers could leave their papers. Now the term is often used for enclosed desks which afford more privacy than more standard library furniture.

CD-ROM (Compact Disc Read-Only Memory): an index or reference work stored on a compact disc and accessed via a computer.

citation analysis: involves examining an item's referring documents, thereby gauging the popularity and impact of specific articles, authors and publications. Citation analysis is a significant part of the tenure review process in countries such as the USA.

communities of practice (CoPs): these describe the process of social learning that occurs when people who have a common interest in some subject or problem collaborate to share ideas, find solutions and build innovations. CoPs may be real or virtual. The latter use online discussion, collaborative blogs, wikis, chat and mailing lists.

Concordat: this is aimed at improving the career management and support of research staff appointed on fixed-term contracts. It was agreed, in 1996, by the Committee of Vice-Chancellors and Principals (CVCP), together with major sponsors of research in universities and colleges.

contract research staff (CRS): university staff on research grades with a fixed-term contract.

current awareness services: these are of two types. The first deliver current information about journal articles to the desktop via e-mail. The second comprise **CD-ROM** or web-based **databases** containing recent journal articles which have to be accessed by the researcher. *See also* **alerting services** and **table of contents services**.

Data Protection Act 1998: UK Act of Parliament giving people the right to access information held about them by organizations.

databases: collections of information stored in a computer in a systematic way, so that computer programs can consult them to answer questions.

DIALOG: a business of The Thomson Corporation providing information from scholarly publishers along with tools to search that information.

dissertations: *see* **theses**.

e-books: in the 1990s these were, typically, large reference works (e.g. XRefer, Wiley Encyclopaedias) with purchasing models driven by the print environment. Although some of these collections offered a replacement for the printed works, they were in general not well used by researchers. The new interactive reference books, such as Knovel, may offer more of interest to research. More recent developments are concentrating on textbooks, with a few notable exceptions relevant to research.

electronic information services (EIS): online information services including online databases, full-text journal services, etc.

e-mail alerting services: *see* **alerting services**.

Endnote: software tool for publishing and managing bibliographies.

e-science and datasets: e-science involves the use of large datasets, often by groups of scholars simultaneously around the globe. Improved technology allows collaboration and communication and sharing of information and resources in new ways. Researchers are increasingly using IT for data mining, modelling, simulation, analysis and data collection and are familiar with interactive tools and resources which are often instantly and freely available across the world wide web.

FirstSearch: from OCLC, a collection of **databases** taken from many subject areas which can be searched individually or together.

formative assessment: developmental and usually used for feedback only, whereas **summative assessment** counts toward a final mark.

Freedom of Information Act 2000: UK government legislation defining what information public sector organizations are obliged to provide on request.

Funding Councils: the Higher Education Funding Council for England (HEFCE) in partnership with the Office of Science and Technology (OST) grants project-based funding for commercializing university research and has impacts in terms of infrastructure for these activities (Higher Education Innovation Fund, HEIF). The Scottish Higher Education Funding Council (SHEFC) has created the Knowledge Transfer Grants scheme to help universities invest in infrastructure for knowledge transfer activities. The Higher Education Funding Council for Wales (HEFCW) operates its Knowledge Exploitation Fund with similar objectives. There are also several UK-wide programmes through OST to promote knowledge transfer activities of HEIs, such as the Science Enterprise Challenge Fund and the University Challenge Fund.

grey literature: any written material which has not been published commercially; it has often been produced 'in house' and typically includes resources such as technical reports, working papers and other documents, often written as the outcome of a specific project.

hard science/soft science: Storer's (1967) differentiation between hard sciences and soft sciences and those in-between. For example, Storer categorizes physics, chemistry and biochemistry as 'hard', botany, zoology and economics as 'medium' and psychology, sociology and political science as 'soft'.

information literacy: the ability to access, evaluate, organize, manipulate and present information (including electronic information) in a wise and ethical manner.

institutional repositories (IRs): these capture and make available as much of the research output of an institution (e.g. a university) as possible. Output includes material such as research papers and electronic versions of theses, but may also include administrative documents, course notes or learning objects.

Intute: a free online service providing access to web resources for education and research. All material is evaluated and selected by a network of subject specialists to create the Intute database.

JISC: in the UK, many resources are provided through the Joint Information Systems Committee (JISC) Collections Company, and the JISC Collections Portfolio of Online Resources is a good starting point for identifying key **databases**. The JISC also provides a model licence agreement and guidance for both librarians and publishers, and it works with librarians to identify new resources to add to the JISC portfolio.

JISCmail: a UK-based service whose mission is 'To facilitate knowledge sharing within the UK centred academic community, using e-mail and the web, through the provision, support and development of specialist mailing list based services, enabling the delivery of high quality and relevant content' (www.jiscmail.ac.uk/).

learning outcomes: these comprise the specific information/skills that are the focus of student learning during a given lecture. They are presented in module/course handbooks and give a series of statements indicating what students should know, understand and be able to do at the end of the module/course.

LibQual+™: a survey tool that libraries use to solicit, track, understand and act on users' opinions of service quality. These services are offered to the library community by the Association of Research Libraries.

LISA (Library and Information Science Abstracts): an international abstracting and indexing tool designed for library professionals and other information specialists.

personal library update sessions (PLUS): can be popular with older researchers embarrassed about admitting they are falling behind in information skills.

PhD: degree of Doctor of Philosophy, a higher degree than a bachelor's or master's degree, involving at least two and a half years of supervised research resulting in a thesis. PhD graduates may call themselves 'Dr'.

ProCite: a software tool for publishing and managing bibliographies.

rare books: *see* **archives**.

RDN: *see* **Intute**.

records management: systematic control of all records, regardless of format, from initial creation to final disposition.

Research Assessment Exercise (RAE): an attempt by the UK government to evaluate the quality of research undertaken by British universities. Each subject, or **unit of assessment (UOA)** is given a ranking by a peer review panel. The rankings are used in the allocation of funding each university receives from the government. The RAE exercise was last conducted in 2001 when UK HEIs were invited to submit selected academic researchers for assessment under 68 subject-based UoAs. For each UoA a panel was established.

research selectivity: funding allocations to different universities are based on the research outputs and success at obtaining outside research grants.

Research Support Libraries Programme (RSLP): aims to make primary material more readily accessible by supporting subject-specific project work.

Roberts Review: following the outcome of the 2001 **Research Assessment Exercise (RAE)** a review of research assessment was launched in June 2002. The review was owned by the four UK HE funding bodies and was led by Sir Gareth Roberts.

RSS feeds: can be used to have the TOCs (tables of contents) of journals automatically sent to a personal webpage or RSS reader. RSS feeds can be more convenient than e-mail alerts, such as those from ZETOC, as they have direct links to the full text of some articles. RSS feeds can also be set up directly from websites.

SCONUL Research Extra (SRX) (www.sconul.ac.uk/use_lib/srx/ scheme): permits reciprocal borrowing for researchers whose home library is a member of SCONUL vision 2010.

social computing tools: tools such as wikis and blogs are now in common use and some libraries are adopting these as methods for communicating with researchers.

soft science: *see* **hard science/soft science**.

special collections: *see* **archives**.

summative assessment: counts toward a final mark as opposed to **formative assessment**, which is developmental and usually used for feedback only.

table of contents services: are e-mail alerting services which deliver tables of contents of recently published journals in a researcher's field to their e-mail inboxes. *See also* **alerting services** and **current awareness services**. Such services include the Emerald Alert Service, IngentaConnect, Kluwer Alert and Taylor & Francis's Scholarly Articles Research Alerting (SARA) service.

theses (UK) and dissertations (USA): a very valuable source of research information.

third strand activities: activities involving university relations with business, industry and the regional agenda.

unit of assessment (UoA): a subject area. *See also* **Research Assessment Exercise (RAE)**.

Web 2.0: web-based services like **wikis, blogs** and other social software that emphasize collaboration and sharing.

wiki: a type of website which anyone can edit. Since it is interactive it is an effective tool for collaborative authoring.

1

Supporting research and researchers: some perspectives

Introduction

In the five years since its original conception, this book has undergone substantial changes in both aims and content. Rather than being an academic treatise, it has been written for practitioners from the perspective of practitioner-researchers. In terms of suggested readership, we think it will be of particular value to newly qualified and practising liaison and research support librarians. Although written from the perspective of a UK academic library, the content should be appropriate to a wider audience.

Our principal objective has been to provide a practical starting point for those of us who work directly with researchers. We are not being prescriptive – although we may have some strong opinions – but we very much hope to stimulate debate and the development of your own ideas. This book is not a comprehensive summary of every single aspect of research support. Although we agree such a *vade mecum* may seem appealing, in practice it would be impossible to produce such a work, for it would never be absolutely current, nor applicable to your own particular circumstances.

We hope that there will be ideas with which you disagree and perspectives that you question; if we have made you think, then this book has achieved its aim.

Context

We wish to provide a practical introduction to the ways that library and information services can support researchers and research activities. Why do we need to do this at all? Since research is about the discovery and communication of knowledge, surely it is obvious that libraries play a significant role in this process? After all, libraries are gateways to academic knowledge via stewardship of their own collections and by facilitating access to other material. Supporting research is one of the core purposes of library and information services in education and other sectors. Our role in supporting research is self-evident, and cannot be questioned.

The ways in which the quality of information provision can be enhanced for researchers has been a focus of attention nationally and internationally, for example through the Research Support Libraries Programme (RSLP) and the Research Information Network (RIN), as well as the international open access (OA) and institutional repository (IR) movement.

Research productivity and quality enhancement are major priorities for higher education. The Research Assessment Exercise (RAE) in the UK has reshaped higher education, intensifying competition between institutions, reinforcing and redefining distinctions between elite research-intensive universities and others, changing the nature of academic publishing and shaping academics' lives and career prospects. The same processes are also taking place in other countries (for example Australia's Research Quality Framework), with tenure decisions determined by publication and research quality assessment.

So how does this actually influence our work as information practitioners? We are aware of national programmes and projects, ranging from collaborative access through SCONUL Research Extra, special purchases by the Joint Information Systems Committee (JISC) of key research resources like Early English Books Online (EEBO), and development projects in special collections, archives and in enhancing catalogues. What has been the impact for us within our services, beyond promoting yet more new services to people who are busier than ever?

Are we actually facing significant challenges to our central role as intermediaries in providing information to researchers? What can and should libraries contribute – or are we simply a bureaucratic obstacle? Individual researchers can trace the details of publications through Google Scholar and then order books and articles directly from the publisher or another third-party supplier without needing to follow our protocols. How do libraries add value to the research process? If our libraries follow cost-recovery models to finance their operations, we are in competition with commercial suppliers: can we actually guarantee that our services are faster, more effective and of higher quality than our rivals?

In the UK we do not have the assurance that, come what may, we will always have excellent collections; at the time of writing at least, there are insufficient financial resources in the university sector to fund systematic collection building. Collaboration and shared access at a national and regional level are priorities. It is possible that the changed funding environment with student fees paid from 2006–7 may alter the resource base for many universities, but it is likely that enhancing the quality of taught students' experience will be given higher priority.

There has been much recent discussion about the future of subject librarians in the UK, threatened with downgrading and redundancy after job evaluation and service reviews at some institutions. By contrast, in Australia subject staff are more numerous and the centrality of their role is acknowledged across the institution. In the past, we had a schizophrenic attitude to our users: craving and creating dependency in some aspects of our services, yet remaining aloof in others. Is this still the case? We have much greater access to high-quality information than ever before, and although we maintain that there is a key role for us in developing the information literacy of all our user groups, it is clear that we are supporting people who seem much more information-savvy than they were 15 years ago. Perhaps we have mixed attitudes to researchers, jealous of their elite status, irritated by their single-mindedness, affection for awkward aspects of the collections and perceived disdain for us? What can we do to change this kind of attitude, among both librarians and researchers?

Also, we suggest, although we have directed much attention to research support at a policy level, at practitioner level in the UK at least we have spent less time reflecting on our role in supporting research than we have on other areas of our work. We have focused much of our professional development on challenging issues in other areas, most particularly on providing services for undergraduates and taught postgraduates. Within the profession much of our research is focused on e-learning and information literacy development work. We have explored questions of access and equity for distance learners and disabled users. We have redesigned our buildings to create vibrant learning environments and developed innovative online resources and services to enhance the student learning experience. But are we ignoring other user groups in our innovation and development?

Let us tell you some stories . . .

We conducted a number of searches for this book, exploring the literature of library and information science in respect of academic research support, and also some educational theory about researchers' learning needs and behaviours.

Having read and shared our thoughts on the secondary sources, we felt that we needed to introduce something else, so that the book would not only combine a synthesis of previous findings with some practical hints and tips but also include another, more personal, element. We decided to add in the authentic voices of researchers, in the UK and more widely, to explain some of the points, to colour and enrich our accounts, and to find ways of sharing more effectively our lived perspectives of working with them. We are also sharing some of our own experiences, and thought you might be interested in some of our personal motivations for working on this book.

Jo's story

Like many of us working in library and information services, Jo did not choose libraries: they seemed to choose her. She studied and worked at Oxford, becoming familiar with the huge wealth of library and information resources and services. Several of her friends as undergraduates became research students and academics, and for a time this had seemed like a potential career path for her as well before she was claimed by libraries. While studying at Aberystwyth she encountered theories about the structure of knowledge, information-seeking behaviour and information retrieval.

Jo then started her first professional post at Cranfield University where she was involved in the introduction of formal information skills teaching to master's and doctoral students. In preparation for this teaching, she started to read more about researchers as library and information users, and reflect on her encounters with the exclusively postgraduate and research community in which she worked. In particular she came across a book by Ernest Rudd, *A New Look at Postgraduate Failure* (Rudd, 1985). She found this an illuminating work, providing case studies of why and how postgraduate students failed to complete their degrees. Many of the accounts and discussions in this work have remained with her, and she still recommends it to colleagues if they want to understand the research student experience.

At De Montfort University Jo worked with researchers in faculties and in particular taught on the university's research training programme. She is also involved in advocacy work for the institutional repository. More recently she started to realize the differences between research and scholarly activity and the time pressures on researchers as she began some research of her own, as well as writing for the professional literature and taking on greater managerial responsibilities. These experiences have all shaped her perspectives: recognizing the passion and professionalism of researchers, and the constraints and the stresses they face.

Pat's story

Pat was motivated to work on the book because, when working as a researcher, she was surprised by how little some of her fellow researchers appeared to use libraries. Also, several of them seemed unaware of how to conduct searches using electronic information services available via their desktops. On reflection, this was perhaps not so surprising. While she was working on doctoral and postdoctoral research, library and information service staff never approached her with an offer of input or assistance. She was lucky in that she had an information background anyway, but perhaps too many library and information service personnel assume that, having reached or passed PhD level, researchers are competent in information seeking.

Pat also found working on the book very helpful because she was doing work-based research on the teaching–research nexus at the time and working on the two projects concurrently helped her to look at the bigger picture.

Moira's story

Working in public, hospital and polytechnic libraries meant that Moira had not had to think seriously about library support for research until she took up her current post at Newcastle University. At that point, she realized that she really knew very little about what was expected of her in this role and she started to ask advice from her more experienced colleagues. She felt she needed to know what the library did to support researchers and what she should be doing in her own post. She didn't even know what an impact factor was! Although she had successfully supported teaching for many years, Moira was unclear how support for research was different.

It soon transpired that, in company with many other libraries at that time, the library had no clearly written policy for research support; it was seen as an integral part of 'what the library does', so there had never been a need to articulate it more specifically. Once discussions had started, however, it was felt that this would be an appropriate time to explain more clearly how the library supported research and, at the same time, find out how this mapped across to what researchers felt they needed from the library. You will discover later in the book how this activity crystallized into the ResIN project, which allowed Moira to study in great detail just what was involved in research support (and exactly how useful, or otherwise, impact factors can be).

Moving from a new to an old university library allowed Moira to widen her understanding of the different and varying challenges faced by libraries in these sectors in balancing the needs of teaching and research, dealing with issues of prestige, preservation of collections of national importance and managing expectations of researchers.

More recently, as a researcher herself, Moira participated as a student in a research training programme, which gave her valuable insights into the priorities of beginning postgraduate students. She also has an interest in the relationships between supervisors and postgraduate students and the opportunities for collaboration and communication which this relationship can offer to librarians.

So, as authors we have been motivated by experience and reflection on practice. Each of us, in various ways, has engaged in research support and training and has been directly involved in research. We can offer experiences based in old and new university libraries and from the perspectives of library staff and active researchers. As service providers and service users we have questioned the effectiveness of library services, while being aware of the constraints in which we operate. We strongly believe that libraries and information professionals can enhance the quality of research through the provision of both resources and services.

Stories from researchers

We approached researchers who were early career stage, research students or new academics; others were more senior – deans of research, internationally known and respected. We interviewed people by telephone and face to face, writing up the results and sharing them between ourselves. Of course, if we had been working on this full-time rather than as something that we have been fitting in during evenings and at weekends, we would have conducted more extensive interviews and surveys but, nevertheless, we found we had a wealth of information from the interviews, much of which served to triangulate the other information which we found from the secondary literature.

This triggered a third stage of data gathering. We realized that there was an emergent theme – how researchers' information and learning needs shift during their careers. We then decided to run a workshop at a UK learning and teaching conference in 2006 on 'Researchers' learning lives', exploring with researchers what they understood by research, and how this conception and the necessary skills shifted as their careers developed.

Researchers' learning lives

So what did we find out from the conference workshop and our interviews? The fundamental discovery was that we rarely step back and reflect on what we understand by research and what being a researcher means. This is in contrast to another professional model in higher education where we reflect more often on what it means to be a 'teacher'.

Many of those we interviewed and worked with defined themselves as researchers, but when we asked them what this meant, we got a range and variety of answers. It was acknowledged that there are different levels, grades and career stages of research. School students might describe themselves as researchers when preparing projects, and family historians spend large amounts of time working in archives, finding new (and to them, significant) material. For the purposes of this book, we have restricted our definition to academic research taking place at postgraduate, doctoral level and beyond. We found common agreement that a researcher is someone who seeks answers by finding things out, reflects and takes action. Many of the people we worked with were social scientists and others working in applied areas, so it was not surprising that many of them felt that researchers were people who extended boundaries and who might make connections, working within and between disciplines.

We also explored what was understood by the term 'research'. Research was seen as discovering or perhaps describing original and/or new knowledge, but beyond this it soon became clear that this was a disputed concept. Some argued that research was theory-led, others that it was data-led. There were significant differences about whether research was an individual activity or a collaborative one, undertaken either in groups of researchers or between researcher and participant(s). All agreed that research included investigation and gathering evidence in a purposeful enquiry leading to interpretation and analysis. There was a strong feeling that a key part of university research was linked to communication, sharing knowledge, making it available in the public domain, and being willing and able to defend the research publicly.

We also asked what researchers saw as their learning needs – and how these evolved by career stage. Political skills – described variously as 'the tyranny of realism', 'learning how to play the game' and 'changing the world versus paying the bills' – featured substantially. Other skills listed included bid writing, research methods skills and research ethics. There was some support for library and information training, both formal and informal. There were also suggestions for support and development in the wider information domain, in particular understanding how to get published and facilitation of a community of practice.

How this book is organized

As you will see, the book is organized informally into three parts. The next two chapters are about researchers: who they are, the economic and employment context and what we know of their interaction with library and information services. In Chapter 2 we set the context, outlining current issues in the research community. This discussion includes an overview of current developments in scholarly communication and open access, and in other policy priority areas. In Chapter 3 we move on to a consideration of what we understand by research and what it means to be a researcher: just who are these people we call researchers? We illustrate the discussion with case studies of four not very typical researchers, suggesting that generalizations are often dangerous.

The next section of the book is a review of what services and generic resources are required to support research. After reviewing different experiences of the challenging area of collection management (Chapter 4), we have written two very practical chapters (Chapters 5 and 6) covering the researcher's toolkit – resources and services. As you would expect from a team which has been very involved in research training programmes, the next chapter (Chapter 7) is on the information-literate researcher, illustrated by case studies of teaching at three different institutions.

The two chapters in the final section are more reflective. Chapter 8 discusses the role of the library in supporting research activity and some of the present and future challenges. Chapter 9 concludes the book, with a discussion of some of the key principles of library support for researchers.

So, read on, and we hope that you too will start out on our journey, and end by being enthralled and engaged by the ways in which libraries support scholarship and enhance research activity.

2 Current challenges for libraries and research support

Introduction

In this chapter we intend to provide a summary of current issues within the research community that are of particular relevance to library and information services. This chapter should be read in parallel with Chapter 3. The latter considers researchers and the nature of research; this chapter looks at policy issues at the interface between research activities and the library and information domain.

Issues facing researchers in the current higher education environment are many and varied. Those highlighted here include ideas relating to scholarly communications, academic freedom, financial interests, ethical issues, freedom of information and knowledge transfer. The last-mentioned has implications for the research–teaching nexus, covered in Chapter 3: knowledge transfer approaches and activities occur within and across institutions and across disciplines. Knowledge transfer does not just focus on research and research-related knowledge but also links to the teaching and extension missions of higher education institutions (HEIs). Other important issues affecting researchers are workforce planning, performance management and the position of contract research staff, which is also discussed in that chapter.

Scholarly communication

The study of how scholars in any field . . . use and disseminate information
through formal and informal channels.   (Borgman, 1989)

What is the main reason for academic publication? Is it truly scholarly communication? Is it to satisfy the RAE, to gain promotion or tenure? Job opportunities, tenure, promotion, rewards and recognition tend to be dependent on the attention received by papers which researchers publish and therefore impact can be more important than royalties (Cronin and Overfelt, 1995; Walker, 2002). It is clear that for the researchers that we interviewed communication was a critical element of their research activities, making their work available and engaging in scholarly debates. Equally, as tenure decisions and careers are based on publication, researchers *must* publish.

The RAE has had a substantial impact on the nature of academic publishing and academic careers, but it has not been the only driver in changing our focus on scholarly communication. Slow dissemination of research results via scholarly journals coupled with serials pricing issues and easier access to technology have encouraged the emergence of alternative publication models in the form of e-prints and self archiving. An e-print is 'a digital duplicate of an academic research paper that is made available online as a way of improving access to the paper' (Swan et al., 2005).

E-prints may be listed on the web pages of an individual or a research group, but equally they may be located in a digital repository – which we will discuss below. There appear to be substantial differences in how readily e-prints are adopted in different subject areas. Barjak's study (2006) of European scientists' use of information and communications technologies for scholarly communication mentions that the disciplines of chemistry and psychology are more hesitant than some others, namely astronomy, computer science and economics, in adopting electronic manuscript repositories. A study reported by Antelman (2004) found that open access publishing created a higher degree of research impact across the disciplines of philosophy, political science, electrical and electronic engineering and mathematics.

Open access

Of course, the easy availability of technology and the cost of journals are not the only forces behind open access. Many open access (OA) advocates believe that since much research is publicly funded there should be an obligation to make the work available without restriction. Many will argue that the current funding model for much research is flawed: researcher receives state grant – researcher publishes results – researcher's institution (publicly funded) has to pay a private sector provider to access it. Champions of open access argue that as content originators, the academic community has the potential to transform paradigms of academic communication, democratizing and liberating access to knowledge for all. McCulloch (2006) describes how the OA movement attempts to reassert control over publicly funded research in order to achieve 'the best value' and make such research output transparent and freely accessible. It is rapidly transforming established models of scholarly publishing deemed at best imbalanced and, at worst, flawed (Friend, 2002; Johnson, 2004; Prosser, 2004, Joseph, 2005).

In practical terms, there are two ways for researchers to provide open access for their work, according to Swan et al. (2005): first by publishing articles in OA journals, and secondly by self-archiving e-prints of their subscription journal articles in IRs.

These options offer alternatives for authors unable or unwilling to satisfy output demands via traditional journal publishing and involve electronic publication of author-supplied documents on the web without commercial publisher mediation. Scholarly articles can be made freely available to potential readers by self-archiving papers in electronic repositories or by publishing in OA journals, e.g. *D-Lib Magazine*, which make their quality-controlled content freely available to all comers, using a funding model that does not charge readers or their institutions for access.

Pinfield (2005) discusses how OA also creates greater impact potential for research, citing research evidence which backs up this claim: first that, over a number of disciplines, OA tends to produce more citations and papers, and secondly that open access results in more downloads.

Nicholas et al. (2005, 503) looked at the progress towards OA on a country by country basis, finding that 'authors based in Asia, Africa,

Eastern Europe and South America were about twice as likely to publish in OA journals compared to those based in Australia, US and Western Europe'. They also found that attitudes differed depending on disciplines, with those publishing in biochemistry, neuroscience, mathematics and material science being more knowledgeable about OA than those based in the arts and humanities, social sciences, economics and business, which was partly attributed to the fact that scientists are more active in journal publishing.

McCulloch (2006) refers to some country-specific and European agreements in support of the OA movement including the Declaration of the *Budapest Open Archive Initiative* (2002), the *Charter of European Cultural Heritage Online* (ECHO) (2002), the *Berlin Declaration* (2003) and the Open Access Team for Scotland *Declaration* (2004).

At the Electronic Theses and Dissertations (ETD) 2006 symposium, according to Reeves, Hagen and Jewell (2006), Peter Suber defined open access literature as digital, online, free of charge and free of most permission barriers, such as copyright and licensing restrictions. ETDs are ideal candidates for open access, given the rigour to which they are subjected, the fact that their content is frequently cutting edge, comprehensive, highly specialized research and their potential as resources to researchers. However, they can be difficult to locate and to access.

It became clear in the late 1990s that the usefulness of separate e-print repositories would be enhanced by the development of the interoperability between them. The Open Archives Initiative movement addressed this issue (Correia and Teixeira, 2005). Other UK projects include the ePrints UK project, which is developing a series of national, discipline-focused services for e-prints from compliant open archive repositories, particularly those provided by UK institutions of further and higher education, and the SHERPA project, which is initiating the development of openly accessible institutional digital collections of research output in a number of organizations.

There are several other research projects set up to address barriers to the success of e-print archives – copyright, peer-review and quality control, long term preservation and cultural issues. These include:

- the FAIR (Focus on Access to Institutional Resources) programme, funded by the UK Higher Education Council's Joint Information Systems Committee (JISC) (2002–5) to investigate e-print repositories, e-theses services and intellectual property rights
- the California Digital Library eScholarship Repository (http://escholarship.cdlib.org)
- the DARE (Digital Academic Resources) programme (www.darenet.nl/en/toon), which involves collaboration of some 20 Dutch universities and research organizations including the National Library of the Netherlands.

These projects are discussed further below.

Electronic theses and dissertations

The implementation of electronic theses and dissertation programmes may involve home-grown, open source or commercial systems and may use a consortium-based approach. JISC Focus on Access to Institutional Resources (FAIR) is one such programme, designed to open up access to institutional assets. The project, led by the Robert Gordon University, involved an assessment of existing best practice relating to the production, management and use of e-theses. This was run in parallel with related projects at Glasgow University and Edinburgh University,

The synergy of open access and open source has been used at Edinburgh University Library to design and implement an e-thesis service. The Theses Alive! project was set up by Edinburgh University Library, to investigate the technological and cultural issues involved for UK higher education (HE) institutions wishing to attain electronic theses as part of the above-mentioned JISC FAIR programme. The Theses Alive Plug-in for Institutional Repositories (Tapir) was developed as part of this project. Southampton's TARDis project sits alongside other e-prints and e-theses FAIR funded projects and involves the development of a multi-disciplinary institutional repository.

The JISC-funded EThOS project is taking forward many of the recommendations from the Electronic Theses project. This aims to create a service so ETDs can be deposited in a central repository at the British Library. The data derived about the UK approach towards the management of e-theses may be of use in countries which have not yet made their theses available in electronic format. Of course, many countries have the equivalent of the EThOS and SHERPA projects, e.g. the Theses Canada Portal provides access to over 47,000 ETDs. In the Netherlands, universities are collaborating on an initiative known as Digital Academic Repositories (DARE) to develop an infrastructure and services to store, preserve, provide access to and distribute the scientific output of the Netherlands. DARE provides a distributed network of institutional repositories. In the USA, the eScholarship program enables the low-cost publication and widespread distribution of the materials that result from research and teaching at the University of California (UC). A free open-access infrastructure, the eScholarship Repository, offers UC research units direct control over the creation and dissemination of the full range of their scholarship and makes materials freely available to the public online. The program also produces eScholarship Editions, digital scholarly monographs on a range of topics, access to which is free for all UC staff, with selected monographs being freely available to the public.

In the UK, Cranfield University has introduced mandatory submission of electronic theses, while the University of Waterloo is the first Canadian university to mandate electronic submission of theses and dissertations. A number of issues need to be addressed from the points of view of librarians, academic staff and registry staff. One effective method of managing the process is to set up a working group with all stakeholders in the process. There is a clear need for administrative procedures to be discussed in detail and a recognition that the time involved in changing regulations may be significant. A concern not just for electronic theses and dissertations but also for all genres of digitized material is that of long-term preservation and the need for electronic archiving.

Institutional repositories

Academic institutions worldwide are developing IRs. In the UK such development has been encouraged by the Science and Technology

Committee report (Great Britain, 2004) and funded by the JISC under the Digital Repositories Programme. Pinder (2005) notes the focus on IRs in the aforementioned report from the Science and Technology Committee and argues that the best way to achieve major improvements in scholarly communication is, as the report suggests, making it mandatory to deposit research papers in open access IRs. In Australia, Mercieca (2006) points out how the OA publishing movement, coupled with open source 'off the shelf' software that facilitates the establishment of digital scholarly content, has fostered more independence in publishing resulting in the establishment of e-presses. This movement has afforded Australian academic and research libraries an opportunity to test and experiment with alternative forms of disseminating scholarship, especially that created by their own institution.

As Rumsey (2006) points out, even putting the publishing arguments to one side, there are other drivers prompting organizations to develop IRs, concomitant with the library's function of collecting, managing and curating materials:

- the management of digital objects and long-term preservation of research, which may not occur if output is posted to personal or departmental websites that may lack stability
- the need to provide mechanisms for dealing with different publication types, multiple versions and relationships (IRs may include datasets, slides from presentations and other media types and need to ensure that metadata for such types complies with international standards to facilitate discovery)
- branding and increased visibility, because an IR is searchable and registered with search mechanisms, e.g. OAIster and Google Scholar
- compliance with requirements of external bodies such as HEFCE submissions.

At the ETD 2006 symposium, Jean-Claude Guédon, discussing examples of the open access movement, pointed out that academic staff at universities and research institutes, while having the opportunity to deposit their work in an IR, fail to realize the benefits since they feel their work does not receive a high enough profile in a mixed content institutional repository. Guédon recommended putting all peer-reviewed papers and articles in one section of the repository and ETDs in another, suggesting that the latter could be a test bed for academic submissions, i.e. if the use and citation of ETDs improves, then academics will come to appreciate the impact and value of institutional repositories and make contributions.

Digital archiving

One example of digital archiving is the National Digital Heritage Archive (NDHA) of the National Library of New Zealand, whose librarian, Penny Carnaby, expressed feelings common to cultures around the world:

> Significant amounts of our thoughts, writing and publishing as a nation are now only ever in the electronic form – which is no less precious and no less fragile than its print counterpart – and it would be a real tragedy for this country if it was lost for the want of somewhere to store it.
>
> (Carnaby in Reid, 2006, 430)

Issues of digital archiving were raised in Canada in 2004 when Anderson et al. produced a report on a Canadian national research strategy and discussed digital archiving as one of the key themes, highlighting the importance of conducting research on the systems and protocols necessary to ensure long-term accessibility of electronic forms.

The fact that the thoughts, writing and publishing of all nations are now produced in electronic forms gives a sense of enormous e-information overload and the daunting task facing librarians and researchers in trying to keep up to date with developments and attempting to facilitate/initiate searches. The better the information available, in terms of metadata, full text, citation data and authentication of information, the better the searching tools can be.

Google Scholar

Google Scholar (GS) is a search tool, launched on 18 November 2004, that attempts to link to scholarly research materials (e.g. peer-reviewed papers, theses, books, preprints, abstracts and technical reports) on the web. At the time of writing it was in beta version, meaning it is undergoing continual improvements and revisions. In theory GS should be useful for beginning-level researchers who want a few articles on a topic rather than serious scholars who need to do thorough research using a variety of resources, especially those journal article databases that provide advanced search features allowing researchers to focus narrowly on the aspects of the topic they really need. In practice, it is the starting point for many researchers, offering clear and easy access to secondary sources, in contrast to many library-provided gateways and portals.

Researchers should find it easier to locate the text of articles through some of their academic library's general databases and electronic journals. Adding OpenURL linking to Google Scholar is a value-added feature that libraries can provide in order to link their researchers from references they find to the library's own extensive electronic and print collections, with clear identification of their ownership to highlight to researchers the value of the library service.

Google Scholar has a number of positive features: it provides a one-stop shop; it is multidisciplinary in coverage; it is user friendly (since its use of a unique algorithm orders search results by their relevance to the search/query); and it includes a number of resources from grey literature which might be difficult to obtain via traditional indexing and abstracting tools.

GS also has some disadvantages. It lacks sufficient advanced search features and its presentation of results is counterintuitive and illogical. Its poor design means some search results are inaccurate, e.g. the number of articles found in some searches increases rather than decreases when the range of years is limited, and it lacks transparency in terms of its content, compounded by its refusal to publish either a list of the journals crawled or its updating policies. Its coverage is uneven and includes many resources that would not be considered scholarly. It is stronger in the sciences – especially engineering and health – and in the social sciences than in other areas but holes in its coverage are not obvious.

Issues for consideration by researchers include the following:

- Will we want to continue to publish in expensive scholarly journals with limited subscriptions?
- Will the growing strength of Google Scholar skew impact factors of journals so that those ranked more highly in GS are favoured?

Issues for consideration by librarians include the following:

- Will GS drive our users away?
- Will GS become researchers' main source of research information?
- Will our role as intermediaries and facilitators be superseded by GS?
- Is there room for both GS and traditional library databases?
- How should GS be integrated into the academic library's repertoire of collections and services?
- Should libraries put their funding into secondary indexing and abstracting tools or rely more on resources such as Google Scholar?
- What can libraries do to make their expensive resources as user-friendly as Google Scholar?
- Are other tools like Google Scholar down the road? (e.g. Elsevier's SCIRUS?)
- Can libraries also be involved in portal development such as the United States' Agriculture Network Information Center, a collaboration between the National Agriculture Library, university libraries and other partners that deliver selected, quality agricultural research information?

The language of scholarship

> Universities are unified by the language of scholarship. We speak the same language in different dialects. . . . There is a mother language of scholarship.
>
> (Ayers, 2005)

Linked to our discussions of scholarly communication is the real and genuine debate on the language of scholarship, and knowledge transfer across nations and cultures. An examination of the history of scholarship demonstrates that the status of English as a world language and international communication system is comparatively recent. Until the 18th century Latin was the language of scholarship, but the rediscovery of the classics during the Renaissance led to an information explosion in academia. Latin was the language of culture and power but not the language of home, community or commerce. Although Latin gradually lost its place in the school curriculum, the fact that it was the language of scholarship in the dawn of modern science in the sixteenth century means that many scientific words, such as the chemical elements, have Latin as their source. Latin is also prevalent in the language of law.

In the sixteenth century, English became established as a literary medium although Latin was still the language of scholarship and the 'grammar' schools founded in England at that time existed mainly to teach Latin grammar. Attitudes changed in the second half of the century when literary criticism developed and scholars began to consider matters of pronunciation, spelling and expression in English.

The origins of formal scholarly publishing date back to the mid-17th century when works such as the *Philosophical Transactions* of the Royal Society of London appeared in print. Russell (2001) describes how scientific journals evolved at a time when it was no longer practical for members of erudite scientific societies to communicate their work through private letters. Over the next three centuries a huge international scholarly publishing industry was built up, with the research journal as the prime means of communication between researchers.

Since English was originally a Germanic language, subsequently influenced by Norman French after the Norman Conquest of 1066 as well as by Latin, it has a much larger vocabulary than either the Germanic or Romance languages. The capacity of English to accommodate foreign words and to absorb vocabulary from a large number of sources has contributed to its development as an international language, and to the dominance of English-language publishing in many disciplines. It is becoming more used in European universities, especially in highly international fields such as the hard sciences and business studies. It is less used in social sciences and humanities where more 'nuanced' expression is required. It is worth noting that many secondary sources index only a limited number of non-English language titles, restricting access to material published outside Anglophone countries. Archambault and Gagné (2004) conclude that this English-language dominance is less problematic in the sciences, where English is the de facto international language, but in the social sciences and humanities there can be difficulties, especially when research selectivity has led to an increased emphasis on bibliometric assessment.

Actually the language of scholarship could now be described as 'Standard American English' and clearly the fact that one of the great powers – and one of the great producers of scholarly publications – uses English as its means of communication has influenced this evolution. The economic expansion of India and China raises the question whether this will continue to be the case – in China at least, English being one of the official languages of India. The global popularity of institutional repositories, Google Scholar and other internet services is extending access to research published in languages other than English.

However, consideration needs to be given to what constitutes a unit of communication for today's researcher. This could in fact consist of data, data sets and software. The researcher as a communicator may be presenting such information in the light of how it will be approached by its users, and for what purpose. Wittenberg (2004) discusses the changing role of the author in the digital environment and the necessity of giving more consideration to matters that usually concern the publisher, e.g. the layout, which may not necessarily have to be linear as would be the case with paper-based text.

An example of this is the FAME (Framework for Multi-agency Environments) project at Newcastle University, funded by the Office of the Deputy Prime Minister. For this project the research team initially produced a series of documents about ten pages in length, each termed 'white papers'. Subsequently a website was developed, as was a readiness assessment tool known as the RAT. This tool was based on information derived from case study research and was originally developed via Excel. Also, for the website, the research team had to 'deconstruct' their white papers so that the relevant text from different papers could be matched to potential users, forming 'pathways' through the literature depending on their point of need. Different potential users included IT managers, practitioners and service users.

Academic freedom, funding and research ethics

The principle of academic freedom enshrined in the Education Reform Act (1988) is that 'academic staff have freedom within the law to question and test received wisdom and put forward new ideas and controversial or unpopular opinions without placing themselves in jeopardy of losing their jobs' (Great Britain, 1988).

Some academic researchers have been subject to self-censorship in terms of their research work because of commercial or institutional pressure. Cases are reported by the media, e.g. two *Times Higher Education Supplement* (THES) pieces in 2006, and discussed on a JISCmail list. In some instances this may be because the researchers are aiming to give a voice to disenfranchised 'players', in others it may result from partnerships with industry. Because of funding allocation models, costing and pricing of necessity affect research strategies and, inevitably, the person or institution holding the purse strings has some influence over how the research is disseminated and used.

Generally researchers in universities are expected to maximize the prospects of their research being taken into practice through the commercial route by protecting intellectual property. It is the responsibility of the principal investigator or research manager to ensure that all involved with a research project are aware of the terms and conditions of contracts with commercial and industrial organizations and the implications of these in relation to their project. There are commonly ethics committees within higher education institutions which have approval procedures to ensure that issues such as informed versus passive consent of participants are fully addressed, especially in cases where those participants may be especially vulnerable.

Maximizing research impact is also dependent on dissemination of research via conferences and authorship of papers. Ethical procedures here require that anyone listed as an author should accept responsibility for ensuring their familiarity with the contents of the article and should be able to identify their contribution. Universities generally disapprove of the practice of 'honorary authorship'. In addition to intellectual property issues, there are further issues relating to information security and freedom of information. These are covered later in this chapter.

Dissemination of research and knowledge transfer plays a role in several areas of university activity, not only in institutional marketing and positioning, but also in the classroom and the lecture theatre: how far do active research staff choose to share their findings with students? Practitioners have been encouraged to make use of research in their own practice in the form of evidence-based practice and pedagogical research. Engagement of staff and students in and with research and research-informed teaching are issues which have been foregrounded in the UK in 2006.

In terms of being awarded research funding, collaborative projects are looked upon favourably by research councils. Such collaborations may be on an international scale and may be multidisciplinary in nature. Multidisciplinarity highlights the fact that research takes many forms and that new methods of producing, preserving and accessing research must take into account the points of origin (Anderson et al., 2004). Information and communication technologies afford the opportunity of representing diverse forms of knowledge, and mechanisms must be found not only to preserve such forms but to integrate them into the existing system of resources (Shearer and Birdsall, 2005).

Ayers describes librarians as the 'heroes' of the digital revolution in HE while academics are seen as resistant to the potential of information and communication technology. In his view, 'Information technology has not made the impact on higher education . . . that it has made on many other aspects of society. We've built a great infrastructure that has transformed many social and business aspects of our work and our libraries, but teaching and scholarship have been relatively little touched' (Ayers, 2004, 62). Lyman and Varian (2003) estimate that information produced in a digital form has increased by about 87% per annum, while the percentage increase for print production is 36% p.a. The increasing access to – and potential to repurpose – digital information has highlighted the importance of our next key area.

Copyright and plagiarism

Copyright and intellectual property are key issues affecting knowledge dissemination, particularly in the digital environment. As discussed below in relation to freedom of information, there is a need to maintain a balance between the rights of the author of an original piece of research and the rights of the public interest. Changes in the scholarly communication system wrought by ICT developments have rendered this a more complex issue.

The scholarly publication system is unique in that researchers generally do not expect financial rewards for their output but wish their research to be disseminated as widely as possible. This runs counter to the publishing model where the publisher is assigned copyright of an article emanating from the researcher's work and then licenses access to the article back to the research community.

Courant (2005) has pointed out that the majority of scholarly publications have little or no street value but copyright safeguards those researchers – mainly in the sciences – who may be able to generate income from their output. Courant contends that copyright goes against scholarly notions of sharing ideas and he advocates experimentation with new forms of publication such as digitization. He believes that demand for services such as Google Scholar will help to shake up the system.

The concepts of copyright and intellectual property underlie other issues, e.g. rights management, open access (knowledge/data storage and retrieval); commercialization and institutional incentive/reward systems (knowledge production and the social contract); and institutional repositories (knowledge systems) (Shearer and Birdsall, 2005).

The availability of textual material in electronic format has facilitated plagiarism. Most academic staff are engaged in advising their students how to avoid plagiarism, such as copying and pasting sections from electronic text, and therefore are well aware themselves of potential pitfalls. At the level of scholarship at which most academic researchers are operating, it is hoped that plagiarism is unlikely to occur. However, as Kock and Davison (2003) have pointed out, academics – especially those new to research – can be under pressure to publish, to get their RAE quota or to obtain tenure, which can lead them to resort to plagiarism. As Hannabuss (2001) emphasizes, under contract law an act of plagiarism by an academic may be regarded as a failure to perform 'substantially', resulting in loss of livelihood. Certainly most universities publish a code of good practice in research for their academic staff in which they stipulate that plagiarism, deception or the fabrication/falsification of results are activities regarded as serious disciplinary offences by the institution.

Plagiarism by researchers is less likely to involve claiming authorship of an entire piece of work and more likely to take the form of misattribution or insufficient attribution of sources. The ease with which electronic formats can be cut and pasted and the need to be highly disciplined in recording web sources can exacerbate this problem. One concept of concern to researchers is that of self-plagiarism (Hexham, 1999). This may seem tautological, but it can occur when a researcher reuses previously published work/data in a subsequent article without notifying readers that the material has appeared elsewhere.

Publishers, editors, peer reviewers and librarians may all perform a gatekeeper role in respect of intellectual property for the sake of their own, their institutional and their professional associations' reputations. Librarians can collaborate with academics to ensure that research students – and newer colleagues – have the necessary skills to cope with a variety of formats in both the paper and digital environments; to understand the research process in which they are engaged; to appreciate the level at which 'idea-borrowing' is acceptable; to adopt appropriate citation methods; and to conduct such processes in an ethical manner.

In the UK the JISC Plagiarism Advisory Service (JISCPAS) serves the academic community providing generic advice and guidance on all aspects of plagiarism prevention and detection. The holistic approach of JISCPAS is unique although organizations such as SURF in the Netherlands, an HE and research partnership, negotiates ICT deals with institutions in their country and, in the USA, the Center for Academic Integrity offers a forum for the identification, affirmation and promotion of the values of academic integrity and promotes honour codes.

Copyright legislation can be a barrier to the dissemination of information not only with print material but also with digital media. In order to submit an article to a repository, researchers must first ensure that they are entitled to self-archive and do not breach copyright restrictions imposed by the original publisher of the work. The policies of individual publishers can be consulted via the SHERPA/RoMEO project.

Freedom of information

Section 22 of the Freedom of Information Act 2000 (FOIA) (which applies to England or Wales and Northern Ireland) provides that any information to be published by a university will be exempt from disclosure providing certain conditions are satisfied. Section 22 (1) states that information will be exempt from disclosure if the institution intends to publish the information at some future date, whether or not this date has already been determined. The Freedom of Information (Scotland) Act 2002 (FOISA), however, is more prescriptive, stating that information is exempt only if it will be published 'at a date not later than 12 weeks after that on which the request for information is made'. This could have implications for English universities conducting joint research with a Scottish higher education institution. However, there is a section (27(2) of the FOISA) which states that information obtained in the course of, or derived from, a research programme is exempt if the programme is continuing with a view to a report of the research being published *and* disclosure of the information prior to publication would be likely to prejudice substantially the programme or interests of participants.

If the higher education institution does not intend to publish the information requested there are other exemptions, set out in the following sections of the FOIA, that may apply to information arising as a result of research.

Section 36 Confidentiality (FOISA)
If a public authority has received information in confidence from another person and the disclosure of such information would give rise to an actionable breach of confidence, the information may be exempt from disclosure.

It is common to find that institutions have created intellectual property as a result of research produced as part of a collaborative agreement with other institutions. These collaborative agreements often contain confidentiality agreements or clauses which, on the face of it, prevent the publication of the results of the collaboration.

The absolute exemption from the obligation to disclose information provided 'in confidence' applies only to information received from another body or person in confidence and does not apply to information which the institution generates itself, although this may be covered by Section 43 Commercial interests (see below) (Section 33 FOISA).

In fact the exemption is much narrower than it initially sounds as it applies only in circumstances where a legally actionable breach of confidence might arise. There is always a risk to an institution relying on a Section 36 (FOISA) exemption that a court will decide that the underlying duty of confidentiality should be overruled in the public interest (see below).

Section 43 Commercial interests

Information which constitutes a trade secret or the disclosure of which would prejudice the commercial interests of any person may be exempt from disclosure.

This is not an absolute exemption and so, in applying it, an institution must apply the public interest test (see below).

Section 21 Information otherwise accessible

Any information published in the publication scheme is absolutely exempt.

The university may want to publish information about research projects, future procurement plans, successful tenders, etc. in their publication scheme to gain the benefit of not having to respond to individual requests.

Section 40 Personal information

Information covered by the Data Protection Act 1998 is exempt under the FOIA.

Sections 24 & 26 National security & defence and Section 38 Health, safety & the environment

These exemptions might be useful in cases of defence-related research and animal rights campaigners' requests respectively.

'Public interest' is not defined in the FOIA, and 'in the public interest' simply means something which serves the interests of the public.

It should be borne in mind that:

- the courts have often made a distinction between things which are in the public interest and things which merely interest the public
- competing interests to be considered are the public interest favouring disclosure against the public interest (not the private interest) favouring withholding information
- if the university fears that the information is too complicated for the applicant to understand, this is not an argument for withholding and the solution is to supply contextual information.

FOI, intellectual property right and copyright

Complying with an FOI request cannot be an infringement of copyright held by a third party in the disclosed documents. There is a statutory defence to copyright infringement where the publication of copyright material is in order to comply with a Westminster Act of Parliament such as the FOIA. It is important, however, that, when such material is disclosed, the recipient is clearly notified that further copying or reproduction is not allowed and that they should contact the copyright holder for permission if they wish to exploit the disclosed material further.

When receiving a request which could require the disclosure of the university's own intellectual property or that of a third party, the following FOIA provisions should be considered:

1   Who owns the intellectual property in the information?
2   Is it owned by a third party If so, is there an existing licence to use the intellectual property and what are its terms of usage?
3   When copies of information are provided, is the recipient clearly warned about any copyright restrictions in place?

4   If a disclosure is being made, is the copyright of a third party clearly marked?

5   Who requires to be consulted if the intellectual property is subject to research criteria which are then subject to a collaborative agreement (and therefore owned by a number of parties)?

6   Do any other FOIA exemptions apply?

Working away from the university

Research staff may work away from their home institutions on an occasional or regular basis. They may be part-time workers or they may be engaged in fieldwork which demands that they travel a great deal. One of the major issues for such researchers is having desktop access to the necessary information resources. Another important issue is the fact that the paper and electronic information such researchers receive and create as part of their employment with the home institution comes under Acts such as the Data Protection Act 1998 and the Freedom of Information Act 2000. Primary copies of such information should, ideally, be stored on site at the home institution. Care should also be taken about storing confidential research information on the researcher's private PC. Research staff may also use university laptops when they work away from home and, again, care should be taken in storing information on laptops where it is not readily accessible and is vulnerable to loss or theft. Arrangements should be made to back up such information and appropriate security measures should be taken to prevent unauthorized access to that information. These issues may come under the auspices of the library or may be dealt with by another section of the university responsible for data protection, freedom of information and records management.

RLN, the British Library and national libraries

The Research Libraries Network (RLN) – subsequently the Research Information Network (RIN) – was set up following the recommendations of the Research Support Libraries Group (RSLG) chaired by Sir Brian

Follett. The RSLG was established in 2001 by the four UK HE funding bodies,[1] the British Library (BL), and the National Libraries of Scotland and Wales, and endorsed by the House of Commons Select Committee on Education and Skills. It is accountable to its funders, namely the aforementioned funding bodies, the BL, the two National Libraries, and Research Councils UK (RCUK) on behalf of the Research Councils.

The RIN, which started operations in February 2005 for an initial three year period, aims to:

- provide strategic leadership for collaboration between publicly funded research information providers and their users in the development of effective, efficient and 'joined-up' information services to support UK research
- co-ordinate action to propose and specify solutions to meet researchers' changing information needs, building on the earlier studies carried out by the RSLG
- act as a high-level advocate for research information, across the UK and internationally.

Dr Michael Jubb as Director of the RIN addressed a meeting of the Consortium of Research Libraries in the British Isles (CURL) in 2005 and posed some challenging questions:

- How do we ensure that the research community is effectively involved in decision-making?
- How do we lever more resource [sic] into the development of the information infrastructure? Will the shift to a full economic costs regime have a positive impact, or are other measures required?
- Have JISC, the BL and others already taken effective charge of all the key issues? How can the RLN maximize its own added value?
- What should the RLN aim to have achieved by 2008
  — for researchers?
  — for libraries?

It was apposite that a former Board member of CURL, Jan Wilkinson, should be appointed Head of Higher Education at the BL at the time when it embarked on a new collaborative enterprise with universities through the RIN. It was envisaged that the BL would develop services and products to support the needs of students, university teachers and researchers, and continue to underpin research and HE in the UK. According to the BL website (www.bl.uk), over 60% of the BL's business is conducted with the HE sector.

E-science

As Michael Jubb posed some challenging questions to CURL members in respect of the RIN, so did Reg Carr in terms of e-science. Dr John Taylor has described e-science as being 'about global collaboration in key areas of big science and the next generation of infrastructure that will enable it' (Carr, 2004). E-science, therefore, is about large-scale, collaborative global research activities which will rely very heavily on access to large data collections. E-science will not only use large quantities of electronic information but will also generate large quantities of electronic information. This poses challenges for librarians in terms of handling and management of what Tony Hey, Director of the e-Science Core Programme, has termed the 'data deluge' (quoted in Carr, 2004). Such data will be produced in a variety of formats, e.g. raw data, which will provide taxonomic and semantic challenges for librarians.

Carr's questions were as follows:

- Are CURL members, as major research libraries, going to get involved in the support of e-science? Or are we just going to let it happen without us?
- Are we all going to try to get involved, or just some of us?
- And if some of us are going to get involved, are we going to do it collaboratively, in the context of CURL for example, or are we just going to plough our own individual furrow?
- And, if we do seek some kind of involvement in the support of e-science, can we afford it? Or, to put that same question the other way round: Can we afford not to be involved?

Conclusion

As this book was going to press, UK Research Councils were beginning to issue self-archiving mandates for all the research papers they funded. So far, the Biotechnology and Biological Sciences Research Council (BBSRC), the Economic and Social Research Council (ESRC), the Medical Research Council (MRC) and the Natural Environment Research Council (NERC) require that copies of peer-reviewed papers resulting from new funded awards be deposited at the earliest opportunity in an e-prints repository. It is anticipated that the other four UK Research Councils will follow suit. Updated tabulations of the position are available from the SPARC Europe website.

It behoves librarians and information managers to keep up to date with all these developments in order to influence scholarly communication for the benefit of their own organizations and the wider scientific and scholarly community. Katsirikou (2003) and Correia and Teixeira (2005) suggest that librarians can achieve this by:

- establishing institutional repositories
- helping researchers archive their papers within IRs
- ensuring researchers know how to find OA journals and archives in their fields
- setting up tools to allow researchers to access OA journals and archives
- promoting high level discussions with their institutions about the advantages of OA deposition
- supporting SPARC Europe in its encouragement of OA models that better serve the international researcher community
- cancelling over-priced journals that offer poor value for money as OA journals proliferate, and as their usage and impact grow
- producing meaningful performance indicators (PIs) on downloads and citations.

As Ponsati and Baquero (2005) have pointed out, statistics on e-journal use available from publishers' systems enable librarians to find out more about the use of journals and researchers' habits than was possible with text-based journals. Citation analysis and bibliometrics are tools for examining scholarly communication processes and patterns. They enable librarians and information professionals to gain improved understanding of research needs; to fine tune their management policies for paper and electronic collections; and to support their institution's research endeavours. Obviously citation analyses and bibliometric studies are supplemented by continuing collaboration between library and academic staff since it should be borne in mind that changing research interests and composition of academic staff necessitates periodic review of collection management and access policies.

The need for collaboration between librarians, academics, publishers and IT organizations in developing resources to serve scholars and their disciplines is discussed by Wittenberg (2004). She stresses the focus may need to be less on ICTs and more on changing organizational structures and on recognizing scholars as active collaborators in the creation of resources, as mentioned above in connection with the language of scholarship. Librarians as collaborators in that process can advise on information architecture, cataloguing and indexing, content management, preservation, access and user needs. Nancy Lin of the American Council of Learned Societies (ACLS) believes there is a need for more focus on user needs and user training in order to capitalize on digital developments, especially in the social sciences and humanities (Lin, 2002).

Note

1   The four UK HE funding bodies are the Higher Education Funding Council for England, the Higher Education Funding Council for Wales, the Scottish Higher Education Funding Council and the Department for Employment and Learning in Northern Ireland.

3 | Defining research and researchers

Introduction

We will now move on from the discussion of current issues to examine what we understand by research and the people we describe as researchers. We will also look at some of the key developments in the nature of and environment for research, especially in the UK. We have included four case studies of very different researchers to illustrate the diversity of career paths, status and reasons for undertaking research, as a way of illuminating these discussions of definitions, history and policy. These are based on real researchers, but their names have been changed to preserve their anonymity.

The aims of this chapter are:

- to define research and researchers
- to examine the history of the PhD
- to consider the impact of the Roberts Review, the Concordat and the RAE on research in the UK and on researchers, making international comparisons where possible.

What is research?

As a starting point, we felt that it was important to actually uncover and unpick what we meant by the term *research*. We searched a selection of resources to explore the different dimensions of our definition. The main phrase which recurred during this examination was 'systematic investigation'. Such an investigation is made to discover, interpret or revise facts or theories. Another recurring description of research is that of developing or contributing to 'generalizable knowledge'. So research activity primarily involves the discovery of knowledge not previously known or understood or the development of a new way of organizing or structuring known material that provides a new understanding about its subject matter. Scholarly research, therefore, is systematic or methodical, involves the discovery and interpretation of facts or the revision of accepted theories in the light of new facts. It may also involve the practical application of new or revised theories.

Although many students undertake research projects during the course of their academic careers and there are many researchers outside formal education – ranging from passionate amateurs to literary biographers – this book has restricted its consideration to scholarly research in academia. We define this as commencing with the doctor of philosophy (PhD or DPhil) degree, widely recognized as the most important postgraduate qualification for graduates wishing to pursue academic and research careers.

Case study 3.1   Motivation for research: the part-time student

John is in the second year of a part-time MPhil/PhD in history. He works at a university as a senior manager. He studied history for his first degree. 'I got a 2.1, which is what I expected to get. I wasn't mature enough to get a First. If the subject bored me, you could tell pretty easily.' History was always his passion. 'I loved the subject all through my childhood. I used to listen to my Grandpa's stories about the First World War and read history books all the time.'

He always envied those who stayed on and continued their studies, taking master's and research degrees. 'I didn't really see that as my future. I desired to do that, but I wasn't actually sufficiently confident in my abilities to take the risk of staying on.' On the other hand he wasn't sure what he really wanted to do, spending three years doing a succession of low-paid jobs in industry before getting a job in a university.

John then went on to take a postgraduate professional qualification and became a manager at a university. Nevertheless he carried on reading widely in history, and kept looking for a part-time MA in the subject. 'I realized that I wanted to be able to describe myself as a historian, and to do that I needed to take an MA. I didn't want to be a distance learner. I wanted to go to seminars, discuss the subject face to face with other students and my tutors.' Eventually, a master's course was validated at one of the universities in the city where he lived and he registered straight away.

The course wasn't entirely as John had imagined. 'To be honest I wasn't impressed by the quality of the teaching, nor the student experience. I had to try quite hard not to be an over-opinionated mature student, but I got quite cross, particularly about the quality of administration.' Nevertheless, he really liked the opportunity to study history again, and thrived academically, getting a distinction and an extremely high mark for his dissertation.

'I had been wondering for a while about whether I wanted to do a PhD and by the end of my MA studies I was pretty sure that this was the next step for me.' He registered at the beginning of the next academic year.

'I chose to stay at the same university, despite my irritation, because it had a good RAE rating, and I had identified a suitable supervisor. This person had been my MA dissertation tutor, and he was competent, but he left me to my own devices, which is what I wanted.

'It's a bit of a rip-off being a part-time student. Everything at my university for research students is based around the assumption that you are full-time. I can't get to training sessions or meetings because everything is held at lunchtime. If I wanted to attend them, I'd have to take a day off work and I'd rather spend those days doing my research in archives and special collections. So I pay £1600 a year for a couple of meetings with my supervisor and a library card.

'I'm not interested in all the training and career development stuff. I'm bringing a lot of skills and expertise into my research work already from the rest of my life. After all, I'm a senior manager, have written and presented extensively in my professional area, and have spent a lot of my time reading and researching my topic. The only course I attended – on advanced academic writing – focused on how to use commas. I could only assume that the previous session was on how to use full stops.

'In truth I am really motivated and happier working on my own. I am expanding on my MA dissertation topic for my current research, and the work I did originally was very extensive – I was told that my bibliography, for example, was doctoral level.

'I realize now that I would have been very well suited to working in a university about 30 years ago, when your career wasn't defined by how you performed in the RAE. I would have made a really good university history teacher. I also recognize that I am a better academic now than I would have been straight from my first degree – I suppose you could describe me as a late developer. I'm still passionate about my subject and am really enjoying the opportunity to do research. If all goes well, I've even got a working title for the monograph I want to publish from my thesis.'

And where does John see himself after completing the PhD? 'I don't know what I will do. I keep hoping that I will get the opportunity to do some part-time teaching and get engaged in the academic life of the department, but I don't think that I will change career. It's the learning and discovery – the research itself – that matters.'

History of the PhD

We will start by exploring the professional models underpinning the development of research degrees, as this has shaped the research environment and most particularly the career development of academics. The doctorate's special status as a research degree originated in Germany and was imported to the USA in the mid-19th century by new scholars taking up faculty positions in American academic institutions and bringing with them the German research ethos (Cude, 2001). Yale was the first American university to adopt the PhD in 1860. Other universities in North America followed suit and, by the turn of the century, the degree was available in academic institutions across the continent.

Although UK universities had research qualifications such as the Cambridge Certificate for Research, with the establishment of the PhD in North America and Europe, UK qualifications began to appear inadequate. Shortly after the First World War the degree was adopted by the universities of Oxford and Cambridge (although Oxford calls the qualification the DPhil). Australian universities adopted the degree after the Second World War, the PhD being introduced to the University of Melbourne in 1947.

While there is some variation between disciplines and between institutions, the PhD requires around three to four years' full-time scholarly endeavour, a thesis exhibiting original research and a public oral defence of research. The length of the thesis may vary according to the discipline, with the humanities generally requiring the 'magnum opus' (Monaghan, 1989). There has been some debate about the necessity for this, given the proliferation of peer-reviewed journals which publish students' research. There has also been a trend recently for PhDs to be awarded on the basis of public output. This involves a candidate submitting a portfolio of their public outputs and supporting their submission with a discussion of the contribution of that output to the advancement of the field of study.

The latter part of the last century was a time of rapid growth for higher education institutions (HEIs) and it was at that time concerns emerged about the period of time required to attain the PhD. Time and financial concerns could deter candidates from completing the degree and, in consequence, could impact upon academic staffing of HEIs, teaching and research quality. The Roberts Review of 2002 concluded that academia was not an attractive career path for many of the brightest PhD graduates, and that this was harming the UK's research base and causing recruitment and retention difficulties for universities.

Case study 3.2   The international student

Ahmed is a computing research student who is halfway through his studies. He is originally from Egypt. 'I work as a university lecturer in my country, and I would really like to progress my career. The subject of my research is not taught to a significant extent at home, and I really wanted to work with Professor X and his research centre as it has such a high international reputation.

'I moved to the UK 18 months ago with my wife and our children. My wife is a doctor and she is studying for the MRCS (Member of the Royal College of Surgeons) qualification. Our son and daughter started at a local primary school.

'We are happy here – I have always wanted to spend some time in England, and our children love their school. However, we miss our families very much: we are used to seeing our extended family very often, and we have been struck by how different society is in this country. The weather has taken some getting used to as well. We have had to buy lots of new clothes – and you can never predict what the weather will be like from one day to the next.

'I need to make progress with my research so I can complete my thesis and return home. My subject has a strong research culture and there is a real sense of community in my research group. As well as the compulsory research training the university organizes, there are weekly research seminars and a reading group where we critique research papers. I have co-authored a journal article with my supervisor which has been accepted for a good journal and I am working on a conference paper with him as well.

'My research is very much like a regular job. I come in the early morning, work on my research, have lunch and leave at the end of the day. I tend not to work on Fridays, but I come in on Sundays instead. Sometimes I come in during the evenings and on Saturdays if I want to do some experiments. I do this less than some of my colleagues – my friend in the chemistry department seems to be in six days a week, every week.

'I've made a big investment coming over here – taking time away from my main job and moving the family so far from home. I must complete my research within the time allocated, so I can go back and resume my career.'

Training and skills of research students

Another concern that had been running in parallel with those issues of the competitiveness and attractiveness of research degrees was the skill level of research students, and their employability in academic and other occupations.

In 2001 the UK Research Councils (including what was then the Arts and Humanities Research Board) in collaboration with UK GRAD (the graduate student training agency) and the HE sector developed the Joint Statement of Skills Training Requirements of Research Postgraduates. This identified the competencies that a postgraduate researcher should have or develop during the course of their PhD degree programme. It has been used as a framework for the development of the personal and professional skills of postgraduate researchers within institutional provision for research degree programmes, in the following ways:

- for training needs analysis (TNA) on induction and throughout the course of the PhD studies
- as a basis for tools for personal development planning (PDP)
- to map their provision of training courses against the Roberts recommendations.

The skills were clustered and identified as follows.

1　Research skills and techniques – to be able to demonstrate:
　　— the ability to recognize and validate problems
　　— original, independent and critical thinking, and the ability to develop theoretical concepts
　　— a knowledge of recent advances within one's field and in related areas
　　— an understanding of relevant research methodologies and techniques and their appropriate application within one's research field
　　— the ability to critically analyse and evaluate one's findings and those of others
　　— an ability to summarize, document, report and reflect on progress.
2　Research environment – to be able to:
　　— show a broad understanding of the context, at the national and international level, in which research takes place
　　— demonstrate awareness of issues relating to the rights of other

researchers, of research subjects, and of others who may be affected by the research, e.g. confidentiality, ethical issues, attribution, copyright, malpractice, ownership of data and the requirements of the Data Protection Act
— demonstrate appreciation of standards of good research practice in their institution and/or discipline
— understand relevant health and safety issues and demonstrate responsible working practices
— understand the processes for funding and evaluation of research
— justify the principles and experimental techniques used in one's own research
— understand the process of academic or commercial exploitation of research results.

3 Research management – to be able to:
— apply effective project management through the setting of research goals, intermediate milestones and prioritization of activities
— design and execute systems for the acquisition and collation of information through the effective use of appropriate resources and equipment
— identify and access appropriate bibliographical resources, archives and other sources of relevant information
— use information technology appropriately for database management, recording and presenting information.

4 Personal effectiveness – to be able to:
— demonstrate a willingness and ability to learn and acquire knowledge
— be creative, innovative and original in one's approach to research
— demonstrate flexibility and open-mindedness
— demonstrate self-awareness and the ability to identify own training needs
— demonstrate self-discipline, motivation, and thoroughness
— recognize boundaries and draw on/use sources of support as appropriate
— show initiative, work independently and be self-reliant.

5   Communication skills – to be able to:
 — write clearly and in a style appropriate to purpose, e.g. progress reports, published documents, theses
 — construct coherent arguments and articulate ideas clearly to a range of audiences, formally and informally through a variety of techniques
 — constructively defend research outcomes at seminars and viva examination
 — contribute to promoting the public understanding of one's research field
 — effectively support the learning of others when involved in teaching, mentoring or demonstrating activities.

6   Networking and teamworking – to be able to:
 — develop and maintain co-operative networks and working relationships with supervisors, colleagues and peers, within the institution and the wider research community
 — understand one's behaviours and impact on others when working in and contributing to the success of formal and informal teams
 — listen, give and receive feedback and respond perceptively to others.

7   Career management – to be able to:
 — appreciate the need for and show commitment to continued professional development
 — take ownership for and manage one's career progression, set realistic and achievable career goals, and identify and develop ways to improve employability
 — demonstrate an insight into the transferable nature of research skills to other work environments and the range of career opportunities within and outside academia
 — present one's skills, personal attributes and experiences through effective CVs, applications and interviews.

The Research Councils emphasized that training in research skills and techniques is the key element in the development of a research student, and that PhD students are expected to make a substantial, original contribution to knowledge in their area, normally leading to published work. These skills may be present when the student begins a course of study, explicitly taught, or developed during the course of the research. It was expected that different mechanisms would be used to support learning as appropriate, including self-direction, supervisor support and mentoring, departmental support, workshops, conferences, elective training courses, formally assessed courses and informal opportunities.

For library and information services, the development of much more explicit training and development programmes has provided a major opportunity for formal involvement in research training programmes, a point we will return to in later chapters.

The Roberts Review, the postdoctoral student and CRS

The Roberts Review covered the supply of science, technology, engineering and mathematics skills throughout the education system. In terms of research it highlighted two major issues. First, the fact that, in the short term, PhD study was financially unattractive, as were careers in academic and industrial research for which scientific PhDs are required. Secondly, that PhDs did not prepare people with transferable skills appropriate to academic and business working environments. This finding echoed the Research Councils' Joint Statement of the previous year. The Roberts Review recommended that HEIs take responsibility for ensuring that all their postdoctoral researchers had a clear career development plan plus access to appropriate training opportunities. It further recommended that all relevant funding from HEFCE and the Research Councils be made conditional on HEIs implementing these recommendations.

The Roberts Review also discussed the problems affecting postdoctoral and other contract research staff (CRS). Among these were the lack of a clear career structure, low levels of pay and unsatisfactory training. Work on a short-term contractual basis is a major barrier to the recruitment and retention of researchers. There is no clear career structure and little possibility for salary progression within contract research. Salaries compare badly with those of scientists and engineers so that HEIs cannot compete in the job market. PhD students and CRS may receive little or no training in transferable skills or continuing professional development, leaving them inadequately prepared for potential careers.

The Roberts Review believed that two things were critical to improving the attractiveness of PhD research. First, enabling the development of individual career paths geared towards different career destinations, and secondly, making opportunities matched to funding open to postdoctoral researchers.

CRS and the Concordat

The number of contract research staff (CRS) in HEIs increased significantly between the 1970s and the present day and there are now over 30,000 employed in UK HEIs. A number of studies (Department of Trade and Industry, 2002; HEFCE, 2003; Treasury, 2003) have shown that key concerns of CRS include job security, lack of a career structure, low status and under-resourcing of research.

In 1996 the Committee of Vice-Chancellors and Principals (CVCP), together with major sponsors of research in universities and colleges, agreed a Concordat aimed at improving the career management and support of research staff appointed on fixed-term contracts. The Concordat provides a framework of principles on which institutions employing CRS are expected to build their own policies.

An opinion piece by Meis, Carmo and Meis (2003) refers to the 'research treadmill' and how economic globalization and the shortage in (in this case Brazilian) government funding for science have led to increased competitiveness. Concomitant with this increase in productivity is increased use of postgraduate and postdoctoral students in many countries. As Cássia et al. (2003) and Lawrence (2003) point out this increased competitiveness can be seen in the insecurity and instability felt by many CRS and in the predominance of scientometrics over knowledge. In the UK, research selectivity results in an institutional emphasis on research productivity combined with explicit, independent and standardized monitoring and evaluation of research output, which fails to create a culture advantageous to a broad range of CRS staff (Harley, 2003).

Case study 3.3 Being a contract researcher: a personal account

Helena is a contract researcher at a new university. She has held her post for a year now. She began on a nine-month contract, which terminated at the end of last July. Shortly before it was due to terminate her contract was renewed for a further five months pending funding. She has recently heard that her contract has been renewed for a further two and a half years. This is only the second time in her research career that she has had such a lengthy contract.

Helena came late to contract research. She had worked for a number of years in universities and studied part-time for an Open University degree, a master's degree and, finally, a PhD. She had no particular career path identified in pursuing her studies: she just caught the studying bug. While undertaking her master's she was in a dilemma over which topic to choose for her dissertation. She decided that one topic had more meat to it than the other so:

'I refrigerated that one and then defrosted it so I could use it for my PhD.'

During one of her posts in another new university, Helena was asked to help run some focus groups with service users. She greatly enjoyed this and she and two of her colleagues presented a paper based on their work at a conference. During a social event at the conference Helena engaged in conversation with a head of school from another university who described the research they were undertaking there. Helena was unaware previously how much research of this nature was being conducted. However, she began checking the websites of universities to see if there were any job vacancies in this area and subsequently she was successfully appointed as a research assistant.

The duration of Helena's first research post was one year so she took a gamble giving up a permanent job for it. However, she no longer had a family to support so felt that she could take the risk without detriment to anyone else. If nothing came of it at the end of the year she had the freedom to move to wherever she found work.

Helena felt she had made the right decision. She thoroughly enjoyed the work, travelling around the country meeting and interviewing lots of interesting people. Again she was conscious this was something she could not have done so easily if she had had strong family commitments. However, as the end of her contract neared, the question remained as to what she was going to do next. Her university was submitting several bids, with her name and CV attached, to Research Councils and other funding organizations in the hope of securing further research work. Her contract was extended for a further three months or so in this period as her institution wanted to retain her. She was funded partly from a 'slush fund' and partly by being seconded to other services within the university to undertake research on their behalf, e.g. during this time she did the background research for one academic's keynote conference presentation.

Just when it looked as though none of their bids was going to be successful, Helena and her colleagues heard that they had been awarded a prestigious three-year project. This meant that she could have a three-year contract. On the strength of this Helena moved out of rented accommodation and bought a house. Once again she immersed herself in fieldwork and travelled widely. On several occasions she was living out of a suitcase. Since there was now something of a research culture within her university department, Helena was sharing an office with other researchers and found this stimulating. Her numeracy skills were less strong than those of one of her colleagues, who was able to give her valuable advice on SPSS.

'Generally I found I was never taught how to use statistical packages or software analysis tools like NUDIST: it was just a case of "Here is this project and you *will* use this package". You were teaching yourself how to use the tools while you were conducting your analysis. You probably didn't always use them in the most effective way. It was just a case of learning enough to get by and produce reasonable bar charts, etc.'

Since she was being paid from the project funding, it was possible for Helena to attend events such as conferences and workshops at which she was disseminating the results of her research, but it was less easy to attend training events other than those offered by her institution. Pressure of work meant it was also difficult to make time to attend in-house training.

As the end of her contract neared, Helena was once more engaged in writing research proposals to try to get further funding. This was on top of fieldwork, dissemination events and report writing.

'Every time I get near the end of a short-term contract I go into panic mode and start looking at job adverts. I know I could probably get a teaching job – I do several sessions teaching research methods – but teaching is not what I want to do. I love research and want to stay in it if I can.'

On at least one occasion in her research career Helena has had to step out of the research arena and take an administrative post in a university until a research post was advertised for which she applied.

'I have to constantly update my CV and I have a file of responses to "person specifications", "comments in support of your job application" etc. to hand, in readiness for the next round of job applications when the latest research funding dries up.'

Helena has moved between the old and new universities in her area and undertaken research in a variety of fields, some of which were more familiar to her than others. Each project has involved a very steep learning curve requiring Helena to immerse herself in the associated literature and get up to speed with the topic in hand. Her shortest contract has been three months, her longest three years. She is only now earning the sort of salary she was earning some 15 years ago in her pre-research days. A lot of the time she is working alone, as the sole researcher in her department. She admits it is quite stressful and demanding on occasion but says, 'Despite all the uncertainty, I love what I am doing. I feel I am learning all the time. I particularly enjoy the fieldwork, the meeting people and the writing side of things. For me it is the perfect job, especially now I have the luxury of a three-year contract!'

Research selectivity

The UK higher education system has suffered large cuts in public funding since the 1980s. Concomitant with this change there has been an expansion in student numbers and an increase in non-government resources. The grant allocation process has included peer-review judgement largely through the Research Assessment Exercise (RAE), which takes place every four or five years and is the basis on which funds are allocated selectively to universities for their research.

Selectivity has been used both to allocate grants to research and, allegedly, to protect research against the large cuts. The RAE has measured universities' performance in the market in order to distribute research grants. Research support from HE Funding Councils, research grant and contract-awarding is often based on hard-nosed assessments of whether or not a higher education institution can deliver high-quality work. Without that support, in some cases, the ability of a university to deliver high-quality teaching and research would be undermined, as would the infrastructure – in support services such as libraries, computing and laboratories – needed to sustain its work.

As the number and range of higher education institutions achieving the designation of 'university' increased in the 1990s, and as public funding for HE became more restrictive, there has been increasing competition among universities for continually reduced funds. The notion of selective support for research excellence to particular departments or institutions has been challenged. Challengers to research selectivity argue for a more 'egalitarian' system of funding with the more successful departments and institutions being penalized to ease the finances of others that are less successful. However, opponents would counter with the argument that any watering down of selectively backing excellence could progressively weaken the ability of the successful institutions to attract public and industrial support based on the quality of their work.

With growing demands for accountability of public funding of higher education through the 1980s, there was a call for an evaluation of the effectiveness of research activities in the form of a research assessment programme. Such programmes have a significant influence on the type and nature of knowledge being created.

The latest RAE exercise was conducted in 2001 when UK HEIs were invited to submit selected academic researchers for assessment under 68 subject-based units of assessment (UoAs). For each UoA a panel was established which had the responsibility of providing a single rating for each institution's submission to that particular UoA. Every institution provided data including details, at the individual researcher level, of up to four works (published between January 1996 and December 2000) as evidence of research quality.

Ratings in the 2001 RAE were awarded on the seven-point scale shown in Table 3.1.

Table 3.1 RAE rating scale 2001

Grade	Description
5*	Quality that equates to attainable levels of international excellence in more than half of the research activity submitted and attainable levels of national excellence in the remainder.
5	Quality that equates to attainable levels of international excellence in up to half of the research activity submitted and to attainable levels of national excellence in virtually all of the remainder.
4	Quality that equates to attainable levels of national excellence in virtually all of the research activity submitted, showing some evidence of international excellence.
3a	Quality that equates to attainable levels of national excellence in over two-thirds of the research activity submitted, possibly showing evidence of international excellence.
3b	Quality that equates to attainable levels of national excellence in more than half of the research activity submitted.
2	Quality that equates to attainable levels of national excellence in up to half of the research activity submitted.
1	Quality that equates to attainable levels of national excellence in none, or virtually none, of the research activity submitted.

The impact of research selectivity (in the form of the Research Assessment Exercise) on knowledge creation strategies and academic work in UK universities led the Higher Education Funding Council for England (HEFCE), along with its fellow funding bodies, to decide to review the RAE's 'continuing fitness for the purpose'. The new policy directions on research in the White Paper (DfES, 2003) were perceived as a threat by many disciplines.

Some issues of particular concern involved the concentration of research funding in large 'excellent' departments; steering non-research active institutions towards parts of their mission other than research; and rethinking PhD training with larger graduate schools in fewer universities.

One proposal is the creation of a 6★ category to reward submissions which scored 5★ in each of the last two RAEs. It is feared by some opponents of the White Paper's increased selectivity that much research of national significance could be lost (e.g. that scoring a 4 or 3b rating).

Increased research selectivity could, it is argued by such opponents, cause negative effects beyond the loss of the research itself. These include loss of motivation and incentive, of role models to students and staff, of research culture, and of many features associated with a university experience. Research funding in the UK is already highly concentrated by international standards. If funding is focused too narrowly on a small elite, there is a danger of ossification and lack of competition.

Groups of universities (e.g. 1994 Group) made collective responses to the White Paper as did learned societies and professional associations expressing some of these concerns.

One proposal made by the White Paper is to restrict postgraduate degree awarding powers to successful research consortia. HEFCE recently proposed that such a restriction would limit PhD teaching to departments scoring an RAE rating of 3a or above. The Roberts Review also made the suggestion that institutions should have PhD awarding powers removed from them. This could have severe consequences for poorer students who cannot afford to leave their home town to study for a PhD, yet have no local institution that can meet their needs. To ghettoize certain universities and the staff within them so that they have no opportunities to make links between their teaching provision and emerging research would not send a positive signal about the importance of teaching, but would downgrade it.

The preparatory teams working on the RAE revision have indicated that forthcoming changes will remove the currently perceived disincentives for practice-based research. However, from past experience the practical realities of evaluation have changed little despite changes in the guidelines. It is possible that a broader cultural change in academia is necessary before the RAE undergoes a sea change. Until this happens, 'third strand' activities requiring considerable time commitment from academics may lose out as time and energy are devoted to increasing the outputs recognized by the RAE.

As this book was going to press, the Department for Education and Skills (2006) launched a consultation exercise on the use of metrics to rank research outputs. Responses to the DfES document on the reform of higher education research assessment and funding were to be received by 13 October 2006.

Research and teaching

Higher education's research base distinguishes it from other spheres of education. Teaching and research at HE level are mutually beneficial. While not all staff need to be active researchers, the environment in which students learn should be underpinned by active research, and all students should have access to staff who are practising researchers in order to impart 'cutting edge' knowledge (Breen and Jenkins, 2002). Teaching also benefits research since imparting their knowledge to others clarifies the research for the researcher.

Financing research through funders such as Research Councils is a competitive source of support for those demonstrating excellence or innovation, identified via peer review. Unfortunately the degree of selectivity is already crippling many institutions, especially newer universities: figures from the 2001 RAE show that 75% of HEFCE research funds are allocated to fewer than 20 HEIs.

Increased research selectivity risks stifling small centres of excellence or dispersed and single scholars. Further concentration of research funding would also have an adverse effect on the development of practice-based and hence industry-linked research in new universities, contrary to the desire expressed in the White Paper to increase such links.

Case study 3.4   A research and teaching career

Sue Brimmacombe is Professor and Head of Research in the Arts Faculty at Welford University. She has published nine books, some of which have crossed over into general interest, and spoken at many conferences. She is also featured regularly in the media.

'When I was a child I wanted to be a novelist – preferably a member of the Durrell family. I didn't work very much at school after I was 13 and got a job in publishing straight after my A-levels. I always intended going to university, but because I didn't get very good grades and there were family issues, I decided to work until I qualified as an independent student. I spent three years full-time in publishing, working my way up to Editorial 2, which was mainly copy-editing. After I left the publishing house I was always able to get jobs as a freelance proofreader, copy-editor or copywriter.

'I went to Plateglass University and read English – the Open Day was good, I liked the student who took me round on the tour and the course was interesting. I didn't really know about its reputation. They were also happy to admit me as a mature student. I found the course and the other undergraduates a bit dull. I was saved by hanging round with some really interesting and interested postgraduates. By the middle of my second year I had decided to do an MA in Critical Theory – for which I got British Academy funding. I shopped around a bit and decided to go to Russell University. The course wasn't based in the English Department, but instead was run by passionate and committed people from European and American Studies. While I was working on the MA, the tutors did what I do to good students now, and encouraged me to stay on to do a PhD.

'I got British Academy funding for my PhD as well, shifting my focus to feminist thought – what some people might see more as social policy. I was quite lacking in confidence, and found I largely had to teach myself and construct all the knowledge and theory, as no one was working in this area anywhere else. My PhD took a long time, perhaps laziness, but also the lack of a community and the scale of the work. I shared a house with two computing science research students at the local polytechnic, and I wrote up much of my research on a spare computer in their office. I didn't have any proper space or access to a computer at Russell University – research students had two spaces – a (literally) empty room and a TV room where we watched *Neighbours*. Not like now.

'It took me eight years to finish my PhD, three years of which were funded. I started teaching part-time when the money ran out and then a year later got a full-time job at Welford Polytechnic. By this stage I hadn't published very much – just one article, and didn't have any influence or networks. I think it's different now, it's much easier to find out about calls for papers and so on, so although to get a job you need to have published, it's more accessible to start out than when I was beginning.

'In the first years at Welford, teaching took up so much time I just left the thesis, although I had secured a publishing contract to write a book (one of two proposals I had made). I used to teach 15 hours a week, a mixture of service teaching to all sorts of students, ranging from pharmacy to engineering, as well as on our Combined Arts degree. I really liked the poly teaching. It wasn't necessarily easy, and I worked in a very male-dominated culture, but the students were so politically sharp, really engaged learners. I thought the curriculum was exciting. We used to teach English, politics, history all together. If we taught the history of the Russian Revolution, the students had also read Tolstoy. I'd taught at Russell University as well, but the teaching and the students were stale and staid by comparison.

'There wasn't a research culture at Welford, and I didn't see then what it meant to be a teacher–researcher. I hadn't learnt from my other degrees very much about research. Welford (now a university) changed quite a lot and suddenly there was an English Department and an influx of English lecturers who had all been to Oxford. I kept being told I wasn't any good, I didn't have a PhD, hadn't been submitted for the RAE and so on. I got a month off and wrote and submitted my thesis. It went straight through. I then got study leave and turned the thesis into a book a year later.

'I carried on doing loads of teaching, in many different subjects, ranging from Shakespeare to media studies as well as feminist theory and women's studies. I was also subject leader and Head of Quality, so had major administrative responsibilities too. Around this time I started to collaborate with other people, and published with them on literary adaptation. I learnt and developed a lot through collaboration, and continue to work closely with one of those colleagues.

'The RAE and the introduction of subject benchmarks for teaching have changed the environment so much now. We have a standardized curriculum, and the subject boundaries are much more rigid – none of this interdisciplinarity I used to love in my early days at Welford. It's less interesting now. Teaching is different these days too. Research is a priority for all of us in the School and we do an average of six to eight hours a week. I mainly teach final years and postgraduates. As a researcher, the difference is that I know how to do the research and I'm connected in to the networks: I have really good contacts and I get invited to speak at conferences. I still want and need to write and publish.

'I got a Leverhulme major fellowship and took the year off to write the other book I'd wanted to do back when I was a PhD student – though it's not the same book as it would have been back then. The discoveries of that year weren't just about the time to write the book, but the opportunity to work in archives – the range of material available on British and American feminism, the scale of output from the alternative press. I'm torn about whether to write a history of feminism or try to set up a major digitization project next.

'I got my Chair in 2003. I was two months shy of 43. I reckon with two kids as well that was quite good going (before I had children my target was 40). The professor thing was the second best day of my professional life (the first being getting the PhD and the third being opening the Leverhulme letter). When the interview panel chair rang me after my interview and told me I was unanimously considered professorial material it was as much a shock as when, eight years on, my supervisor told me I'd always been writing at PhD level. The Leverhulme changed my life and I told them so. The year's absence from work decoupled me from that association with heavy admin. I know I'm doing a big administrative job now, but at least it's research related and I don't get quite so many digs from colleagues about my work. But to be fair to the children, having them also gave me, amazingly, time to think. Especially when I had Justine. I used to bundle her in the pushchair, walk up to town and think, think, think. That's the thing you don't have time for at work – allowing your mind to range freely.

'If I'd been to the same secondary school I don't think I'd get on as well today. I think it's harder to make good at a later stage because of the assessment climate – actually A-level results in some contexts still count more than degrees! I was at a big grammar with a six-form intake which had a huge change in the staff base the year after I got there because it stopped being a grammar and lost its sixth form. The culture was anti-intellectual from both teachers and students and you could get away with anything – we spent a lesson sitting on our chairs on top of the desks to see if the maths teacher would care or try to teach us. The sixth form college was better but grades weren't great even for my hardworking friends – and my personal life was complicated then and by that time I was pathologically lazy. I read lots, but probably only half the set texts.

'Basically I used my three years at Welford to catch up – to read books, understand literature and its industrial context particularly and obviously meet authors and people interested in poetry and creativity. At Plateglass I honed my politics because some of the postgrads were Marxists, some were embryonic post-structuralists and I read Sartre and de Beauvoir for the first time. I did philosophy in my first year and also read Kierkegaard, Camus, etc. In fact I had a friendly argument with my tutor because he didn't regard de Beauvoir as part of existentialism and it was quite normal then to exclude her. So I was ahead of my time.'

Third strand activities

Research selectivity policies mean continuing pressure on academic researchers to acquire a reputation in their field by publication and other forms of self-presentation. Pressure on the institution comes in the shape of accountability and the RAE, along with pressures for relevance and for 'wealth creation' in relation to the third strand activities (OECD, 2002, 153).

A UK government aim is to create a culture in which academic researchers and universities collaborate more closely with government and business in identifying future directions of research and in various stages of the production of knowledge and its conversion into marketable outcomes. While teaching and research are clearly central to the idea of a university, the importance of 'third strand' activities involving university relations with business, industry and the regional agenda is being increasingly recognized. Initially, third strand activities were defined as anything other than the universities' core business of teaching and research. However, an integrated third strand programme can complement a university's established teaching and research activity. Hatakenaka (2005) points out the benefits to the educational experience of students, especially PhD students, and the relevance to societal needs, 'when taught by academics who are themselves working with real world issues. . . . Ph.D. students who are trained through industrially relevant research will know how to take into account industrial needs in their future research and are likely to be more employable for industry.' Third strand activities are now becoming embedded and sustained within university culture.

In the UK, Funding Councils are making money available for third strand activities, with recent funding opportunities promoting universities' reach-out to businesses. Arrangements for this vary in the different parts of the UK. The Higher Education Funding Council for England (HEFCE) in partnership with the Office of Science and Technology (OST) grants project-based funding for commercializing university research and has impacts in terms of infrastructure for these activities (Higher Education Innovation Fund, HEIF). The Scottish Higher Education Funding Council (SHEFC) has created a Knowledge Transfer Grants scheme to help universities invest in infrastructure for knowledge transfer activities. The Higher Education Funding Council for Wales (HEFCW) operates its Knowledge Exploitation Fund with similar objectives. There are also several UK-wide programmes funded by OST to promote knowledge transfer activities of HEIs, such as the Science Enterprise Challenge Fund and University Challenge Fund.

In respect of third strand activities, universities are increasingly appointing non-academics with experience in industry or other relevant external employment sectors. Such trends may ameliorate the situation where many of the best PhDs are leaving their discipline for other careers or, indeed, leaving the country to conduct research or to work elsewhere, for example the USA. As Robert Freedman commented: 'We should promote the necessity of a joined up education, research training, and academic career pathway strategy to the government to ensure the continued supply of quality people into university and industry sectors' (Freedman quoted in Withnall, 2000).

In North America academic entrepreneurship is perhaps more typically an extension of an HEI's mission. The Association of Universities and Colleges of Canada (2005) reports how universities in Canada are responding to the growing demand for their research services by establishing strategic research plans, strengthening their research administration process, increasing inter-university collaborations and facilitating both cross-sectoral and international research efforts. European faculty members are more removed from entrepreneurship than their American counterparts and in Europe third strand activities are only recently emerging as an academic mission on a par with teaching and research at some universities. In Finland moves have been made in this direction with regional engagement of the universities being seen as part of their third strand activities and included in the new Universities' Act (Goddard et al., 2003). In some Eastern countries similar moves are happening. In Japan, organizations such as the Japan Science and Technology Corporation (JST) have started sponsoring programmes aimed at national universities and national laboratories to encourage the development of research into marketable products with university administrators acting as liaison between the faculty members and JST (Pechter, 2001).

Research issues and what they mean for libraries

One message that emerges from the literature on research and researchers in HEIs is the importance of the culture (Campbell et al., 2003). Stress is laid on the need for supportive environments, access to information and advice and integration of research staff (especially CRS) into institutions. This is where the library and information services staff have a role, especially in relation to induction and skills development. Library and information services staff can play a part in making researchers feel more valued and, thereby, better motivated when they receive integrated and formal support and access to information and facilities.

In addition to the findings from the interviews we conducted as part of our research for this book, the value of the library in the lives of HE researchers is illustrated in case studies from HESDA (2003). For example Louise, who moved from HE to a marketing management post, refers to the 'challenge' of not using reference and textbooks to back up her knowledge and says she misses 'the library being on hand'. Another case study researcher now working outside academia, Elizabeth, misses the 'pure' values that academic work places on reading and learning.

Another issue with an impact on libraries is the importance of investment in research infrastructure. Operating and maintenance costs of state-of-the-art equipment (which can rapidly become obsolete) need sustained support. In an internationalized research environment, a country's ability to attract and retain leading researchers is dependent on the research infrastructure. Collaborative engagement in international development research and knowledge transfer enhances collective understanding of global issues and is critical to the realization of technological solutions.

Conclusion

This chapter has tried to give a flavour of what it is like to do research and of the context in which researchers work and study, in order to illustrate some of the pressures, constraints and opportunities in their lives. Following on from this, it has highlighted what some of the research issues discussed mean for libraries. Now that the context has been presented and the background explained, the book's focus will shift slightly to a more practical approach in order to answer the question, 'How may libraries best support scholarly activity?'

4

Collection management

Introduction

In previous chapters we looked at the background and context for research support. We will now turn to a more practical review of how library services and librarians should support the scholarly activities of their users. This chapter explores some key themes and concerns relating to the management of collections to support research. After summarizing surveys on researchers' use of collections and reviewing influential reports and strategies, we use two fictional case studies to put the issues into focus. A detailed discussion of what comprises a 'collection' is followed by some suggestions on how to deal with collection management challenges. Our starting point is a fundamental one: without collections, either physical or virtual, our role is meaningless. We suggest that in the UK we have three key drivers for much of our service innovation and development:

- the fact that we no longer have sufficient resources in terms of budgets and physical space to acquire and store all the material that may be required
- the need to promote and exploit the resources which are available, making them accessible to users both in physical terms and through developing understanding and knowledge of how to maximize the value of resources

■   the potential offered by technology and collaboration to address these first two issues.

Researchers' use of libraries and information

I like libraries to have a commitment to my field.

(Professor, Economics, UK)

The importance of physical libraries is minimal; I might visit one two or three times a year, but I depend heavily on electronic journals.

(Professor, Social Sciences, UK)

As always we need to remember that researchers are not a homogeneous group. There are many different patterns of library use, depending on individual differences, preferences and disciplinary perspectives, and we need to think about our own user community first of all. Nevertheless there are some very helpful studies of researchers' use of libraries and information services which indicate how these have shifted over time.

The impact of funding and resource availability was raised as a matter of serious concern in the 1980s, for example in the interesting research study by Pocklington and Finch (1987) which explored whether the research process was being damaged by the effects of constraints on funding and, if there was damage, its nature and effects. This has continued to be a cause for concern.

Although there have been many changes since this research took place in 1995, some of the key questions and discussion points in Erens (1996) remain of value. This work is an analysis and review of a large-scale survey, itself modelled on an earlier survey of 1989. It was one of the additional research projects prompted by the Follett review of 1993 (Joint Funding Councils' Report Group, 1993).

Erens found that 75% of academics responding to the survey identified their own university library as being most important for research and a similar proportion said that their university library met their research needs for UK books either well or fairly well. About one-third of all respondents were dissatisfied with their local library provision. The vast majority of academics considered that it was important to have access to good book and journal collections (96% for UK journals; 84% for UK books). Access to journals was identified as a significant problem. Academics from Oxbridge were the most satisfied; those from new universities much less so.

The survey also identified some significant changes in behaviour. Half the respondents indicated that they now relied less on browsing the shelves than before, with one-third saying they used their own library less. One in four used libraries other than their own university library more often. It was also clear from this survey that the access to electronic information services was starting to have an impact with half the respondents stating that they used electronic collections.

A smaller project in 2000 CORSALL (Collaboration in Research Support by Academic Libraries in Leicestershire) involved De Montfort University, Loughborough University and the University of Leicester (Bloor, 2001). Its purpose was to investigate ways in which the libraries of the three universities might collaborate more closely in the services they provided for their researchers (i.e. research-active academic staff and research students). The project was commissioned by the three libraries in response to interest from researchers and senior management at their respective universities.

Nearly 1000 researchers responded to a questionnaire survey and around 27,000 interlibrary loans were analysed. The main findings of the report were that the level of reciprocal access between the three libraries was low. The main barriers were lack of knowledge and lack of time, with researchers reluctant to use one of the other university libraries, even if the required material was available. Some subject strengths were identified, particularly complementary collections across the libraries in psychology and business.

The analysis of interlibrary loans revealed however that the combined resources of the three libraries would only be able to satisfy 11% of requests. At current price levels use of a national document supply service was more cost-effective. Opportunities for collaborative acquisition policies were also limited. It was noted that there was potential for shared access to databases, although subscription licence agreements prevented this.

One of the key findings was that the levels of use of e-resources varied significantly between subjects and institutions. The generally neutral conclusions of the report were that current reciprocal access arrangements should continue (these have now been superseded by the SCONUL Research Extra scheme) and that training and awareness-raising of e-resources was required (Bloor, 2001).

Although with a different scope, a recent study by the Research Information Network provides some interesting insights into how information needs and behaviours have shifted. This study explored researchers' use of what it defined as discovery services, that is, search engines, gateways, library catalogues and databases (Research Information Network, 2006). It found general satisfaction with discovery services especially in the sciences, although researchers could not always access the material they found. Searching was seen as an integral part of the research process and results were refined down from a large set of results. So in general, recall was preferred to precision (an important point to remember when advising researchers on retrieval strategies). Many different discovery services were used, although many of them were used only by a small number of searchers.

Key findings

In terms of relevance to the focus of this chapter, there are some key considerations from these three reports.

First of all, researchers need to have access to the kinds of material which are important to them and the best library and information services are those which provide the most comprehensive access. The legal deposit libraries, with their comprehensive collections of UK material and substantial heritage collections, are obviously the greatest resource in this country, but there are many examples of excellent collections across a very wide range of institutions. We should remember though that in terms of access to current journals and shared discovery tools, all libraries can enhance their services, and though unable to match a copyright library we can make significant progress in meeting the needs of our researchers, especially if we are committed to digital delivery. Therefore we need to ensure that we focus on ways of enhancing resource discovery and access through systems and service development.

Secondly, collection management activities should recognize and accommodate diversity and change. Not only did researchers use a very wide range of discovery tools, they also had heterogeneous information needs and adopted very different approaches to finding what they needed. Many researchers only used a very small number of discovery tools. Gaps in provision were noted: access to foreign language material, backfiles of electronic journals, effective ways of identifying chapters in multi-authored works and limited secondary source coverage in some disciplines. Some of the issues in the RIN report echo Erens' work more than a decade ago; other concerns have emerged more recently. We need to be conscious that there are no single solutions to collection management across disciplines and that the issues and solutions shift over time.

Thirdly, as librarians we need to consider the information universe from the perspective of our users. We can underestimate the importance of peers and networks in making information available. Many researchers would contact colleagues directly for copies of papers or research articles. Of course, if we reflect on this, it is standard information-seeking behaviour to use your social network to find something rather than struggle to work out where and how to find something. After all, how often do you ask a friend or family member for a piece of information rather than researching it yourself?

Reports, programmes and networks: the strategic background

Before focusing on current approaches to effective collection management, it will be helpful to review some of major reports which have influenced the development of collections and collaborative development in recent years.

The Anderson Report

The Working Group on National and Regional Strategies for Library

Provision for Researchers (chaired by Professor Michael Anderson) was established in 1994 following concerns identified in the Follett report over the capacity of UK libraries to support research. The Group was given the following remit:

- to survey the issues involved
- to identify areas where more detailed work was needed
- to recommend what further work should be undertaken.

The report (Joint Funding Councils' Libraries Review, 1995) highlighted some specific problems:

1   The increasing volume of published material and above inflation prices meant that libraries were finding it more difficult to maintain collections.
2   The shift from library services predicated on holdings to those built on access still required that the holdings were maintained somewhere. There had been no attempts to ensure that this was the case.
3   There was a clear need to preserve non-print materials.
4   Better ways of managing and collecting grey literature were required.
5   The success of non-formula Follett funding for special collections and archives highlighted the need to develop longer-term strategies to continue this work.
6   There was a lack of co-ordinated national collection and access policies.

The report also identified issues in relation to research support for higher education, national, research council, public and independent libraries. Two possible solutions were considered: either focusing on remote and electronic delivery, or shifting core provision to a national network of 'hyperlibraries', funded separately from the institutions in which they were based. The first was thought to be a model that would suit researchers in science, technology and medicine, but it seemed unlikely that the range of material required by humanities researchers would be available in digital form. The second option was felt to be unsatisfactory and uneconomic for many reasons, including the related reduction of services at all other libraries, tension in the governance of the 'hyperlibraries' with divided remits and the uncomfortable truth that there were few libraries with uniformly excellent holdings, and acknowledged pockets of excellence in many. Instead the Group decided it would be most effective to build on the strengths of dispersed collections in the UK and hence stressed the need for all major libraries in the UK to co-operate to ensure that researchers had adequate support. The report made a number of specific recommendations including:

- that universities should address the issue of library support for research in their information strategies, in their submissions under the Research Assessment Exercises and in bids for research funding made to the Research Councils
- that universities should consider making funds available to allow their researchers to travel to significant collections as an alternative to their own collection building
- that a national retentions policy be created
- that collaborative arrangements between universities should be encouraged
- that there was a need to explore whether a system of recompensing those universities which faced significant additional costs in providing library services to researchers should be introduced.

One of the outcomes of the Anderson Report was the establishment of the Research Support Libraries Programme (RSLP).

The Research Support Libraries Programme

The RSLP was a national initiative, funded by the four higher education funding bodies and co-ordinated by the Research Support Libraries Group. It brought together both traditional and new forms of access to library information, with specific reference to support for research. It started in the academic year 1999–2000 and finished on 31 July 2002, with funding totalling almost £30m awarded during the lifetime of the Programme.

The Programme funded three strands:

- collaborative collection management projects (in any subject area)
- projects that provided support for humanities and social science research collections
- access funding to compensate major holdings libraries for costs incurred in providing facilities for visiting researchers from other HEIs.

£11.4m was made available for 53 projects, as well as a number of other activities. A further £15m was disbursed over three years to 48 higher education libraries under the Access strand. An additional £5 million was subsequently made available by the funding bodies for an extension to the Access strand to compensate higher education libraries for the use made of their facilities during academic year 2002–3 (see the RSLP website www.rslp.ac.uk for full details).

RSLP projects mainly dealt with traditional library materials but, in almost every case, also created an electronic resource. These took the form of bibliographic and archival records, collection descriptions, digitized images and texts, and web directories and portals. The Programme also funded, or co-funded, a number of studies and other pieces of work.

Most of the projects funded by RSLP were discipline-oriented, although one or two focused on a format. These included projects on archaeology, non-European languages and area studies, theology and church history. Other projects sought to map research collections in UK regions: RASCAL (Research and Special Collections Available Locally) recorded resources in Northern Ireland, while Mapio Cymru, a project led by the University of Wales, Aberystwyth, mapped the library and archive resources of the Principality. Among other activities, SCONE (Scottish Collections Network Extension) identified research collections in the newer universities as well as in other higher education institutions in Scotland, and consequently extended the Research Collections Online

database to include information relating to them. There were major collaborative collection management projects for Asian studies and for Russian and East European studies, and projects that sought to facilitate access to such diverse materials as pamphlets, aerial photographs, early manuscript and printed maps of Scotland, cartoons and architectural drawings.

Access funds supported a wide variety of activities and improvements, including extended opening hours, retrospective cataloguing, other enhancements to catalogues, equipment replacement, installation of access control systems, employment of extra staff to improve service in Special Collections and Archives departments, and improvement of physical facilities for researchers.

The Group produced its final report in March 2003 (Research Support Libraries Group, 2003). This analysed the provision of library resources to researchers in the UK and recognized that a considerable proportion of those researchers were based outside academic institutions, for example in industry. It came to the conclusion that solutions to the problems it identified, which included the rapid but uneven development of electronic publication and electronic delivery, would have to be cross-sectoral. In the view of the Group, the biggest problem once this situation was identified was the lack of strategic direction on a national scale. Its key recommendation was that a new body should be created, to be called the Research Libraries Network (now renamed the Research Information Network) to carry out a strategic planning and co-ordination role. Alongside the universities themselves, the British Library and the national libraries of Scotland and Wales would be key players.

After some deliberation by the Funding Councils and the Research Councils in summer 2004 it was announced that the RLN would go ahead with an initial funding of £3 million.

Key points

There are two learning points from these major projects. First of all, the extent of change in the resources available, because of the now pervasive digital access to resource discovery tools and the resources themselves, has had a dramatic impact on the way that we provide research information to users. There has also been a major cultural shift towards the recognition that collaboration and partnership is the only way that we can provide all the resources that researchers need. Nevertheless, there are still significant challenges ahead.

Case studies in collection management

The complexities of managing collections to support research are illustrated in these two fictional case studies.

Case study 4.1   Size matters: collection management at the University of Middleton

Middleton is a small, traditional research-intensive university located in an attractive regional centre. Academics and postgraduate students are recruited internationally, although undergraduates form the majority of the student body.

The main library at Middleton has particularly extensive special collections, combining rare books, archival material and works of art. The management, curation and preservation of these heritage collections is a significant responsibility for library management. National funding was received for retrospective cataloguing of some parts of the special collection and several digitization projects as part of the Research Support Libraries Programme.

Although Middleton was founded in the nineteenth century, one of the challenges facing the library is that compared to other universities with similar reputations, the main library collection is quite small. Yet size, in terms of numbers of volumes and range of stock, is perceived by academics to be a critical indicator of library quality and research capacity. At a university level there is the desire to be excellent in all subject areas, and for library managers it can be a struggle to maintain and sustain print and physical collections when resources are finite and there is a continuing need to preserve the special collections. This is particularly complex as central services are funded directly by departments through a levy on payroll, so the main library is perceived both as an essential resource and a costly overhead. This is made more challenging when many academic departments continue to fund their own libraries from research and commercial income. Departmental libraries are generally reference-only collections in specialist areas, although there are a few lending libraries run by departmental administrators which cater for undergraduates, and the graduate business school has a specialist business information service.

In some areas, especially where the collection dates back to Middleton's foundation and earlier, the quality of the university library's special and general collections helps to attract research students from across the world. A separate library store alleviates the need to make decisions on withdrawing stock, so it is possible to preserve a large amount of currently unused material 'just in case'. In other subjects, particularly the sciences, which have grown significantly quite recently, there is less satisfaction with the resources available. Focus groups with researchers, especially research students, have found a stated reluctance to visit or use other libraries, even though other large research libraries are within easy reach, so promoting use of other physical libraries does not appear to be viable.

The same focus groups and library surveys have revealed that service users are very demanding. Researchers expect that all print materials and relevant journals will be available locally. Document supply services are recognized as necessary, and are valued principally as a way of obtaining material published outside the UK. Taught course students, both undergraduate and postgraduate, also expect that the university library will have all their reading list materials, and want the library to become a more flexible study environment as well.

Budget control

Academic schools and departments are semi-autonomous, with the majority of academic authority devolved to the level of individual departments. This includes responsibility for most library stock selection. In some departments each member of academic staff has a personal library budget and can choose for stock what he or she wants, without any scrutiny or other approval. In other departments 95% of the budget is spent on journals, and in others a single senior academic has control over all purchasing. Issues arise over the provision of expensive resources, such as standards, which are essential for a very small group of users but are too costly for the relevant departmental budget. Similar concerns are raised over large multidisciplinary electronic journal collections, especially maintaining access to services that have restrictions on cancellations when the decision-making is so widely dispersed.

Collection development

A key challenge for the library in this highly devolved structure is in finding ways of establishing a shared institutional view of what should be the collection management priorities for the service and in developing ways to ensure coherence in collection management activities. It is difficult to reach any agreement on more proactive approaches to stock management, in particular weeding, stock relegation and disposal. The institutional repository project is encountering similar difficulties. Subject librarians must establish productive working relationships with their departments, striving to transform their role from an administrative and enquiry-handling function to being perceived as valued, trusted and expert colleagues. This is not easy at Middleton, where academic status is highly prized and librarians have to justify their professional standing. Some subject librarians have been able to establish clear collection development policies and service level agreements, and have facilitated more effective selection and collection management.

There are many instances of service innovation and excellence at Middleton. The library is an active member of CURL, the Consortium of Research Libraries in the British Isles, and senior members of staff are leaders within the research library community, making a substantial contribution to policy-making. There have been interesting international collaborations, establishing partnerships in document supply with other research libraries across the world and international job exchanges. Recently the service has been able to develop its teaching and training activities by targeting research students and drawing down some Roberts funding to finance these developments.

Discussion

Middleton has many strengths as a research library. It has very high-quality heritage collections and research-led collection management. Academics are closely involved in making decisions so there is a strong sense of shared ownership in the service. Its stakeholders have very high expectations and expect the best.

On the other hand, strategic development can be difficult because of the fragmented process of decision-making and resource selection. There is an unspoken tension between provision for teaching and for research, with sometimes limited attention paid to the needs of taught courses. Collection management is highly individualized, and the devolved budget model makes it very difficult to move forward strategically.

Case study 4.2   Access and signposts: supporting researchers at West End University

There can be misconceptions about the strength and quality of research in what in the UK are called modern or post-1992 universities. There are many areas of research excellence across a wide variety of subject areas in these institutions. It is worth remembering that many new universities are at least as old as pre-1992 universities, with many of the former also claiming 19th-century foundations. What was significantly different was the way these institutions evolved in the 20th century, as they focused primarily on vocational and practice-based subjects, teaching courses at degree and sub-degree level.

During this time, it was not uncommon for libraries to build collections. Sometimes these would be heritage collections, built on the history of the parent institution, mergers with other organizations or bequests. Subject librarians and/or departments also developed collections stock to support major areas of the curriculum, and holdings could have a range and depth in stock comparable in some specialist areas to other, more research-intensive institutions. Expansion in higher education during the 1990s led to increased pressure on resources, which was later balanced by greater access to journal literature and other full-text materials with subscriptions to electronic information services. Lack of a library store means that staff have to weed constantly and review the collection in order to meet space constraints.

Budget control

At West End University the stock budget is the responsibility of the library and information service. Some resources are paid for centrally and a small contingency fund is retained, but the majority of the budget is allocated to academic schools. Subject librarians are responsible for managing the school library budgets, identifying in conjunction with library representatives allocations for subject areas. The focus of resource expenditure is normally to support taught provision, especially purchasing items on reading lists. In many areas the whole of the book budget (excluding journal subscriptions and document supply) will be spent servicing reading lists. Where there are large numbers of postgraduates and a lot of overlap between research interests and teaching, researchers are generally satisfied with library collections, supplemented by interlibrary loans.

Collection development

Subject librarians have prepared collection development policies for each school, discussing with library representatives, and senior academic staff, on what basis the library's collections should be built and reviewed. There is an overall collection development strategy, linked to the university and departmental strategic plans. Electronic journals have extended access to full text for students and staff alike and are popular and heavily used. In some disciplines, especially in science and technology, there is a stronger dislocation, with undergraduate and researcher requirements appearing quite separate and different. In these subjects it has been harder to maintain a balance of provision between research activities and student requirements. Although the assumption is that the student experience is the priority, it can be very difficult to deny access to key journals to research teams.

Library services, though not the physical buildings, are used by most researchers, who value document supply and electronic journals services most of all. In areas where the curriculum is informed by teaching and holdings are more extensive, researchers occasionally use print and media resources. Many social science and humanities researchers have also developed alternatives to the library at West End. Some visit other university libraries in the region, others purchase a large proportion of the stock they need or use the British Library and other legal deposit libraries on a regular basis. They see their own university library as one of their information sources, but rarely as the only one they use. There is a general perception that the library collection should focus on taught requirements, as long as appropriate access arrangements are in place.

Discussion

This is a great contrast with Middleton. At West End University the library has control over collection management but research support has a lower priority. Electronic journals have had a significant positive impact on the effectiveness of the service to support research in journal-intensive disciplines like science and technology. The dominant focus on support for taught courses can mean that the needs of researchers may be overlooked by subject librarians, nor are the resources available to develop the collection more systematically.

What is a collection?

Before entering into a discussion about collection management, we need to be clear exactly what we are talking about. Researchers use a wide variety of information sources, ranging from data and artefacts and many other forms of primary sources, to books, journals, conference papers, official publications and more. We must remember always that each discipline and subject area has its own ecology of knowledge, so differing importance may be placed on books, journal articles and conference papers and other information formats.

By extension, what researchers identify as useful collections can vary. If questioned, we probably have some assumptions of what we might use as measures to define a collection. These measures would include:

- range and depth of holdings
- currency and historic value

- sustainability
- level
- lengthy journal runs
- completeness of series
- extensive electronic archives,

all supported by powerful discovery tools and effective document supply services.

Key components of a collection

Books

> The key issue for me is maintaining book stocks.   (Professor of Dance, UK)

Books still make up the core of many research library collections, particularly in arts and humanities subject areas, where monographs continue to dominate not only publishing but also evaluations of academic esteem. The strength of a major research library is the depth and range of its holdings, gathered over many years from many different sources.

Newer universities tend to have more modest collections and rarely have major expansion of print holdings as a strategic objective. This is not to say that collections of value to researchers are absent from smaller libraries – as mentioned in passing above, there are many examples of specialist resources, such as the Booker Prize archive at Oxford Brookes University. Even just the range of stock gathered in institutions where subjects have been studied for many years at a variety of levels can provide a satisfactory basis for research activities.

We must be careful not to overlook the importance of books. We are caught up in the challenges of the ever-present serials crisis and the thrilling promises of the digital age. Certainly subject librarians and collection development staff continue to need to focus on ways of enhancing access to books – for all groups of users.

Journals and electronic journals

> What used to be a major bind in accessing old articles is no longer a problem. I like to be able to print locally rather than have to photocopy. Many titles in my specialist area don't go back far enough electronically, though it is improving.
>
> (Professor of Marine Transport and Management, UK)

Most studies of researcher priorities confirm that journals are the key information resource. The perfect library for the majority of researchers is one which enhances access to extensive journal collections, preferably through robust and reliable electronic delivery of all titles required and supported by extensive online archives. We also need to be aware of the need to support a range of searching behaviours and needs, including browsing, meta searching and proactive alerting services as well as direct searching of the database.

Though the desire for content is quite simple to understand, achieving this is rather more complicated. There are three challenges:

Managing access The management of serials has always been a complicated activity, with titles disappearing, merging or simply not being received. This has not changed with the shift to electronic versions. There are many different subscription arrangements, licence agreements and variations in functionality, which combine to make the management of electronic journals immensely complex.

Selection, collections and holdings Access to journals has increased significantly with the development of electronic journals, which are often made available in packages or 'bundles', from the publisher or via an agent. While this increases the number of titles available often at a very reasonable price per item, in practice it is much less simple. In the first place, not all titles in the package may be relevant to research at the institution and this can lead to difficult conversations: 'Why can't you afford to buy this key journal for me? Can't you cancel some of those ones we don't need?' The purchase of electronic journals collections useful to a large number of people is easier to justify than buying a comprehensive collection for a narrow field.

Librarians also have concerns about access to electronic journals to which they cease to subscribe, or which move from one publisher's collection to another. There have been many examples of publishers taking over the rights to a journal and changing the licence or pricing agreements, sometimes with very little communication with their customer base. In the electronic world we have less control over our journal collection; we may have a very impressive portfolio of titles, but does it truly reflect research interests?

Added to this concern over the stability of electronic archives is a different issue: the need to reduce duplication of print and electronic subscriptions and confirm the replacement of print with electronic. Electronic-only subscriptions are common, as is the removal of print journals from the open shelves.

Cost There are ever-increasing numbers of journal titles, each one of which costs more each year. Most library and information services strive to maintain access, balancing the needs of all user groups, but the costs can be very difficult to manage. Added to this, in the UK, is the addition of 17.5% VAT on all electronic titles, a hidden extra cost of transferring from print to electronic versions.

Advocates of open access will use the case of journals publishing as the obvious exemplar for turning to OA. If research at universities is publicly funded, why should the products of that research be re-sold to the same institutions in the form of academic journals? Surely it would be more rational to make the results of that publicly funded research available to the community of practice without making potential users pay again?

Discovery tools

An important element of collection development activities must be the provision of an appropriate set of discovery tools in the form of full-text and bibliographic databases, including library catalogues. It is particularly important for library and information service staff to be proactive in ident-ifying and promoting specialist services, especially databases, to researchers.

This is also an area where levels and patterns of use must be carefully monitored. As the focus of research shifts within the organization and the range of titles indexed by one source changes, it may be worth considering whether to cancel a less popular secondary title in favour of increasing primary subscriptions. Might it be more cost-effective, for example, to set aside a budget to pay for an external expert (such as the BL) to provide an occasional online search in a very specialized database, rather than maintaining a subscription to the resource locally? Consultation with researchers over this type of decision can often yield surprising results. In our experience there can often be much inertia in managing collections, yet without critical review the collection cannot grow and valuable sources may be excluded.

Data

> In terms of manipulating information – collating statistical data, downloading, analysing is easy and makes data collation much more common. Linked to data analysis you can now do graphics, images etc and it's so easy.
>
> (Professor of Marine Transport and Engineering, UK)

As our professional focus is on managing access to published information, especially scholarly information, librarians are generally less comfortable with working with data. There are exceptions: for example there will usually be at least one specialist in a library who works with financial, census or statistical data. The expansion of e-research (see Chapter 9) and the increase in access to new datasets of, for example, bioinformatics information and gene sets mean that we are brokering access to much more complex information. With our expertise in metadata creation, information retrieval and digital preservation, librarians should play a role in managing access and supporting others in the use of data for research.

Theses

It is very common for a university library to maintain a collection of doctoral theses from its home institution. In terms of managing the collection thought needs to be given to the format in which it is stored (print, digital, microform, etc.) and the security of these unique, often unpublished, documents. Doctoral theses are also deposited with the British Library (see www.theses.com/faqbl.html). Recent developments in e-thesis repositories may allow libraries to decrease their print holdings in favour of electronic archives, but provision will still need to be made for thesis resources that may not be available in digital form, such as paintings, sculptures and other materials.

Special collections

The special collections and archives hidden away in many large research libraries provide a rich source of primary data to scholars both within and without the university sector. This material may be difficult and time-consuming to catalogue and brings with it special considerations of preservation and storage. Precious manuscripts need to be kept in secure areas with suitable ventilation and temperature controls. Collections of papers and letters need to be indexed individually, as do pictures, diaries and other unique documents. This is costly both in buildings and staffing and the benefits of maintaining this kind of collection have to be considered carefully. Is the prestige such a collection brings to the library justified? Are the collections being actively developed to support current research activity and/or local connections, or have they grown up haphazardly, dependent on donation by benefactors? Some collections are of international importance (e.g. the Gertrude Bell collection at Newcastle University, www.ncl.ac.uk/library/specialcollections/collection_details.php?id=49) and attract scholars from across the globe. Others may sit uncatalogued in boxes for years, awaiting their turn for fame.

Collections outside universities

Those of us who work in university libraries often have quite limited knowledge and experience of research collections outside the university sector. Sometimes we are unaware of the range and extent of special collections in local public libraries, for example on John Clare in Northampton central library or the Shakespeare collection at Birmingham central library. Museums, archives and private organizations may all have holdings which are important to individual researchers. There are some listings which can help to identify collections and resources, for example Cornucopia (www.cornucopia.org.uk/html), which is an online database of information about more than 6000 collections in the UK's museums, galleries, archives and libraries.

There have been related regional projects, for example DiadEM (see www.liem.org.uk/results.asp?sortby=d&key=aem12024012151120041528). This was supported by Libraries and Information East Midlands, MLA East Midlands and MLA nationally to identify special collections held in that region's libraries and to create a set of collection-level descriptions using the RSLP schema which were added to the national Cornucopia database. The DiadEM project covered some well-known collections like the D. H. Lawrence Collection at the University of Nottingham and the Tennyson Research Centre in Lincoln, but DiadEM has found other special collections in all corners of the region, such as the material on hunting held at Melton Mowbray Library, colliery disasters at North Nottinghamshire College and the Osborne Robinson collection of posters at the University of Northampton.

Many other libraries and organizations across the East Midlands region also participated in the DiadEM project; these include bodies as diverse as the Chartered Management Institution and the British Horological Institute, and small museum libraries such as the Canal Museum at Stoke Bruerne in Northamptonshire and the Commemorative Collectors Society in Nottinghamshire.

Collection management in practice

1   Collection management policies

Does your library have a clearly articulated collection management policy? How much real detail and guidance does it provide? As our two case studies illustrate, there is a very wide variety of practice in the UK in respect of how library collections are managed and how stock is selected. In some libraries a general statement about providing resources to support research is considered sufficient, whereas others provide a detailed statement of each subject area and the library vision for its future. If possible, we strongly suggest that it is very helpful to try to establish collection management and development principles and priorities at service and subject levels.

Few library collections have developed to a specific plan, most have an element of serendipity and accident in their accumulation of resources. How possible is it to take more proactive control over this process? We suggest that it can be possible to develop your collections, even with limited resources, but close partnership with key stakeholder groups is essential. As a starting point you will need to develop an understanding of research activities and priorities, and what use those researchers already make of your service. You may then be able to give one or two areas some priority in stock development, and the reputation of specialist (and special) collections may even have the potential to attract research groups to the institution and provide opportunities for collaborative project development, thus enhancing status, research output and funding.

It is possible that research funding might also be directed to building up a specific area of the collection alongside a research project, and library staff should investigate these opportunities with their research staff.

These are some key questions in establishing a collection development and management policy:

- What is the purpose of the collection – teaching, research or both?
- Are there any areas of the collection which have regional, national or international importance?
- How is material selected (catalogues, reading lists, recommendations, collection management tools)?
- Who is responsible for selecting material?
- How is collection development activity funded? Are any parts of the budget earmarked for specific purposes?
- Have any areas been identified as requiring specific development or specialist research focus?
- How are digital resources managed?
- How many copies are purchased of print items?
- Will electronic versions of journals duplicate or replace print holdings?
- What is the retention policy for books, journals and other media?

- Are there plans to relegate any material to a store?
- What performance indicators are used to assess the effectiveness of policy and practice?
- What proportion of the budget should be spent on journals, books and other materials?
- What proportion of the budget is allocated to document supply services? How is their cost-effectiveness evaluated and monitored?
- How is your collection management activity evaluated?

At the heart of this discussion is a necessary consideration of whether managed print and electronic collections, rather than access to content, will matter to many library and information services. As a starting point we suggest that it is helpful to understand the strengths and weaknesses of your collections through objective review, data analysis and qualitative evaluation from users.

Let us provide some examples. Imagine you are working in a small specialist institution. The relative emphasis of resource acquisition will depend on the disciplines you are supporting. If creative subjects like dance are major research areas, you will continue to need to purchase print and media items. Although there are good secondary sources to identify relevant material, only a limited amount of material is available full text. Many researchers will also use recorded media, DVDs and formerly video, which are harder to trace and may not be collected systematically elsewhere. To support research in this area, you will need to provide access to your finding tools (including specialist free sources like the New York Public Library Catalog), continue to collect monographs, research studies and print journals, and make available interlibrary loans.

By comparison a similar-sized institution supporting research in science and technology would almost certainly spend a much higher proportion of its budget on electronic journals services. It may be possible to cancel almost all print titles and replace them with discovery tools. Only a small proportion of the budget would be spent on acquiring hard copy, mainly in the form of research monographs and some textbooks.

We should recognize that we are not all starting from the same base and develop our policies accordingly. Research monographs have a much smaller potential readership, so it is logical for many libraries to concentrate the bulk of their book budget on providing texts for undergraduates and taught postgraduates, while encouraging researchers to use interlibrary loans and other document delivery solutions to provide access to specialist materials. Is this an appropriate and sustainable approach in those disciplines where books are still vital? This prompts a response that you will see elsewhere in this book: look at your users and think about your strategy. Is a focus in your collection management activities sustainable within your institution and subject area? What is the impact of national and regional developments in co-operation and resource-sharing?

2   Managing journals and digital resources

We have mentioned earlier in this chapter the difficulties of ensuring that journal collections are suitable for the needs of researchers. Particularly in a digital environment, monitoring and evaluating levels of use and cost-effectiveness are vital. We are not suggesting that you conduct crude evaluations of your collection based only on cost. We should recognize that expensive titles may merit their high prices in terms of the value that immediate access to content provides to researchers.

As in so many other areas, the management of journal subscriptions must be seen as an activity that involves technical and acquisitions staff, subject and research support specialists and academic stakeholders. Command of detail matters in this area. It is easier to negotiate with academics about cancellations or substitution when you have details of use close to hand.

These are some of the key questions in managing journals and digital resources for research:

- How are journal subscriptions selected within your library and information service?
- Who decides what is purchased?
- How quickly can new titles be acquired or cancellations made?
- Who is responsible for monitoring and managing journal subscriptions?
- How are journals and other resources made accessible to users and

what are your protocols for access management?
- What is the scope of your library catalogue or information portal?
- How is the usage of individual journal titles (print and electronic) and electronic subscription bundles monitored? How is that information made available to stakeholders? How does this inform service decision-making?
- Are there any titles where duplicate subscriptions are acceptable?
- What policies exist for binding and preserving print titles?
- Do you have any policies about the priority given to purchasing primary titles or secondary databases?
- What is your strategy for developing an institutional repository?
- Is there any analysis of document supply requests to identify potential subscriptions?
- How proactive are you in seeking to make resources available to researchers in digital form, either through purchase of commercial products or digitization projects?
- What performance indicators are used to review the quality of your journal collection?

3   Outreach and engagement

The previous two points in this section are predicated on the existence of an effective relationship between the library and information service and the academic and research community. This must be a collaborative, co-operative relationship built on trust and respect. This may sound glib, but identifying ways of moving forward for mutual benefit is more productive than adversarial confrontation. This may not always be possible: we know colleagues working in library and information services across the world who find themselves unable to act because a few academics challenge any innovation in collection management policies.

There are some ways to progress your case, and these are themes which we return to throughout this work:

- have a real and defensible reason for the case you make
- understand the subject and disciplinary needs.

For example, disposing of print copies of journals unavailable in digital form might be acceptable if those materials are not used and can be sourced easily from elsewhere. Choosing a crude date for disposing of titles ignores the way that some subjects draw on much older literature – the differences in the 'half-life' of articles can be significant.

Be aware of the strengths and weaknesses of your collections. If a researcher declares that another library is better, find out if that is the case, and if so why, and see if you can learn from it. If you are concerned about the suitability of your collections to support a research project, tell the supervisor. It may not be very pleasant, but it is wiser. After all, you risk finding yourself in the deeply uncomfortable position of trying to explain to a research student why there is nothing relevant available in the library in print or electronic form, and even traceable in the secondary databases. It happens, and not just to people working in small libraries.

Be proactive in identifying material, even if you work in an environ-ment where budgets are devolved to academic schools and departments. This is a way of asserting your knowledge: e-mail a professor if you find a book that might be relevant from a smaller publisher. Do not be afraid of taking risks based on your professional judgement: you do know enough to make a difference and seek out innovative solutions for collection development.

Conclusion

Collection management is not a passive role. In the old days the focus was often on systematic collection building, actively seeking out suitable material. We have a colleague who used to go on buying trips to Russia for a specialist Slavonic collection, and colleagues who used to work through antiquarian catalogues to complete missing series or fill in elements of the collection. This approach is still the case in some countries, where the service focus is still on acquisitions and the quality of a service is measured by the size of the collection.

In the UK, at least, our focus has shifted. We are less anxious about the damage done to research by constraints on collections (following Pocklington and Finch, 1987). We have accepted collaboration – a troublesome area in the post–Anderson report discussions (Pat Wressell and Associates, 1997). We are seeing some national strategic co-ordination through the RIN, leadership from the British Library and shared access through SCONUL Research Extra. Now we have two concerns: staying relevant in the digital age – when scholars turn to Google first; and maintaining access to scholarly knowledge, across all media, when we cannot afford to buy and store everything. We need to shift beyond our traditional working practices and continue our involvement in the hybrid library, which is now a reality – a hybrid library that contains many forms of digital resources, formal and informal forms of knowledge and information.

5 The researcher's toolkit: resources

Introduction

Specific resources, rather than management of the collection, are the focus of this chapter. In earlier parts of the book we have already reviewed some of the drivers that are shaping the ways that researchers are finding and using information and data. In this, the first of two practical chapters on the researcher's toolkit, we aim to:

- revisit the influences on researchers' use of resources
- identify some of the most commonly used types of resource
- provide a listing of some of the most valuable secondary sources.

Influences on resource use

As we have already commented, increasingly interdisciplinary research agendas and changing patterns of scholarly communication are reshaping the ways that researchers find and use information. In addition to these external forces, it is helpful to recognize that individual differences will also shape the way that people search for information. They may be influenced by their learning attitudes and habits or by the stage in their research career, but at a practical level probably the most crucial difference is the discipline in which the research is taking place. Although generalizations are dangerous, we might summarize by saying that arts, humanities and to some extent social sciences researchers need access to a wide range of resources spanning a long time period, whereas science, engineering and medical researchers tend to need newly published research data.

First of all, a point of definition: even the term 'resources' can be interpreted in more than one way. The Roberts Report includes physical resources such as a PC and study space in its consideration of what resources a research student needs, but for the purposes of this work we will discuss information resources.

Learning styles, habits and attitudes

I know my field pretty well. I am aware of the journals and have already read most of the secondary literature. I have a good understanding of information retrieval and I am patient, systematic and organized, as well as being really enthusiastic about my subject.   (Part-time research student, UK)

A person's *learning style* is part of his or her personality. Although we are not suggesting that understanding learning styles is the key to all knowledge, it can be helpful to recognize that people learn in different ways, and that these fundamental traits influence the ways that they process and deal with information. Webb and Powis (2004) provided a summary of some of the most popular theories of learning styles, and we do not wish to repeat what is written elsewhere.

We suggest that *learning habits*, however, can be developed and it is possible for people to change their learning habits through practice or because they have been convinced that another way of learning is better.

Examples of effective learning habits include handing in work on time, less absenteeism, taking harder courses, diligence, paying attention, doing more than is expected, participating in class, and being prepared for class. What we are describing of course is the process of the development of graduate skills: of self-organization and focus. In UK universities there is much emphasis on this, not only for postgraduate students (as we discussed in Chapter 3), but also during undergraduate education.

Attitudes to learning are slightly different again as they are more about how people perceive their learning. As we will mention in Chapter 7, this can provide both challenges and opportunities when developing training and development programmes for researchers.

Understanding that all these variations in learning and hence in research practice occur in the research community can help librarians to ensure that they are providing a range of resources to meet these different needs and also to understand that people will choose to use different resources and to use them in different ways. We cannot provide a 'one size fits all' library and expect it to be successful: effective services rest on knowledge and empathy.

Two different approaches

Research is not a homogeneous activity. In the context of this chapter, it is important to remember that researchers will use resources in different ways at different stages of their research career or even within a short-term project. Let us provide you with two examples of what that might mean: the 'model user' and the 'real user'.

Example 1: a model user

Before the start of a project, at proposal stage, a brief literature review is conducted to ensure that the proposal has value and will contribute to the body of research. Once the project begins in earnest, a more comprehensive literature review is required, covering all expected aspects of the work and situating the research firmly within the discipline. Guidance is sought in using bibliographic databases and other resources which help to identify information sources. Electronic journals, interlibrary loans and requests for purchase are made. Extensive use is made of supporting materials on research methods and practice, as well as practical information about the working of the organization, the academic department and the library. As the research progresses, more specific needs may emerge – access to datasets, maps and images, for example – as well as a requirement for current awareness techniques and updating services. As the project nears completion, a further literature review takes place, confirming and validating research results.

Example 2: a real user

At the proposal stage existing work and resources are consulted, drawing mainly on material available in the researcher's own collection, which is extensive. Given the specialized or applied nature of the topic, only a limited amount has been published, so the researcher depends mainly on materials which are close to hand – often shared within his or her research group and colleague network. Additional resources are purchased with research funding and, rather than using interlibrary loans, the researcher obtains versions of the papers needed from publishers and authors directly – even when the items are available locally. The library and information service is perceived as an undergraduate resource, with limited interest in, support for, or expertise in working with researchers.

All these variations in practice, coupled with individual differences in research habits, mean that we must not assume that once resources have been provided all will be well. You must assert your professional knowledge and expertise in identifying, using and promoting them.

Resources

It is vital to have the kinds of resources that your research community needs, and to be expert in using them. This section considers some of the main types of resources of use to researchers, highlighting issues for consideration and providing links to some key sources for developing collections, as well as some suggestions for further reading.

This is a vast subject, and handled more comprehensively elsewhere. Traditionally *Walford's Guide to Reference Material* would be the starting point for many bibliographical searches and surveys. The latest edition, *The New Walford Guide to Reference Resources, Volume 1: Science, Technology and Medicine*, edited by Ray Lester, continues to provide a comprehensive summary of vital resources. Although other useful tools will be mentioned in this chapter, for almost every category additional ideas will be found in Walford – so use it! Some other general sources are listed in the further reading section at the end of the chapter.

There is real merit in becoming familiar with the resources we are describing and other more specialist sources in the areas you are supporting. Remember that many researchers are very specialized, and may not have thought about exploring some of the more generic tools and resources or services targeted at librarians. In our experience, even the effective enthusiastic library users have learned something new when we have shared our tradecraft and specialist tools. It is your responsibility to ensure that you develop the necessary expertise and knowledge.

1 Books

Will books ever go out of fashion? In spite of increasing reliance on digital media, many researchers told us they like to use and handle books:

> There's something very satisfying about settling down to read a book, it's a feeling you just can't get from reading off your screen or printing off pages. I like to buy books and I like to see lots of books on the shelves in my office and to get to know them, like old friends . . . one of the nice things about coming into the library is being surrounded by all that knowledge . . . it's a physical thing.'
>
> (Chemistry lecturer, UK)

Organizing books

Of course, as we have already discussed, UK academic libraries are struggling to purchase all that is required. But we need to think more widely than just about the size of a collection. Libraries have traditionally collected books and organized them according to an accepted classification scheme. We make assumptions about the impact of this, in particular that scholars are comfortable with using our library and understand how our catalogues work as an aid to locating material. But is this true? Encountering the different subject collocation in a library classified according to Dewey as opposed to Library of Congress can be quite disorienting, let alone what seem like irrational decisions to create different sequences for things that are not nice orderly, regular books, be they oversize books or multimedia items.

We also know that accurate bibliographic description will lead to more precise discovery of relevant resources, but there are significant costs associated with this added value, in particular the cost of cataloguing virtual material and constructing meaningful metadata.

Furthermore, Google-savvy modern researchers, used to using smart search tools and instant responses, may be less conscious of the uncertainties and inaccuracies of our information and organizational systems. Library catalogues may not list all items available, possibly because special locations are listed separately or some material was never added. Nor may all records be rich in the level of metadata needed to facilitate retrieval.

But we can change this if we step back and consider our library and identify ways of repackaging it to make it more user friendly. Can the organization of the physical library reflect the organization of the virtual library? How can we enhance subject collocation and find a way to integrate works on research methods and skills, subject bibliographies and technical dictionaries? Is there any scope to create special areas for researchers, bringing together books which may be scattered throughout the collection? If so the library can send a clear message to researchers that their specific needs have been considered and that the library is attempting to make their life as a researcher as easy as possible. Both research students and staff could take advantage of this section of the collection, containing, as it must, books on how to write research proposals, how to write for publication and writing up a thesis, as well as specific research methodologies such as statistical methods and survey techniques.

Tracing books

The local library catalogue is a key resource for all researchers and it is vital that they understand how to use it efficiently, including whether it is possible to print or download items retrieved from the catalogue. Scholars should also be encouraged to consult other library catalogues as part of their literature search, as these may be the only places that they will identify older, out-of-print materials or specific chapters in edited works. It is still worth providing a health warning about what may not be included, the possible lack of currency and, if necessary, a warning about the limitations of conventions of bibliographic description.

In our experience, many academics may not have used all of these sources as bibliographical tools. One way of engaging interest is by encouraging people to check other library catalogues for their own publications. 'I was fascinated to see how many copies of my books were available in North American libraries. I didn't realize I was so popular in the mid-West. Nor that X [a colleague] was big in Japan . . .' (Research Professor, Humanities, UK).

Resources for finding books

- [ ] COPAC (http://copac.ac.uk) provides access to the merged online catalogues of 24 major university research libraries in the UK and Ireland as well as the British Library, the National Library of Scotland, and the National Library of Wales/Llyfrgell Genedlaethol Cymru (free).
- [ ] The British Library integrated catalogue (http://catalogue.bl.uk) indexes the Reference Collections of the British Library in London, more than 12 million titles in all (free).
- [ ] WorldCat (http://firstsearch.uk.oclc.org) is the OCLC union catalogue, containing records of all the OCLC member libraries around the world (subscription available via FirstSearch).
- [ ] The RLG union catalogue (www.rlg.org) provides access to over 130 million records from a wide variety of libraries in the USA and elsewhere, including research and academic libraries, national libraries, specialized research institutions and archives, museums and special collections (free).
- [ ] The European Library (www.theeuropeanlibrary.org) searches the content of national library catalogues in Europe (free).
- [ ] The HERO website (www.hero.ac.uk/niss/niss_library4008.cfm) links to individual university library catalogues in the UK (free).

Buying books

Checking publishers' catalogues and websites is an obvious first place to look for new books, particularly if the publisher specializes in a particular discipline. Many librarians also scan regular publications which alert you to new books, such as *The Bookseller* and *BNB*, which records all books deposited at the Legal Deposit Office of the British Library. Book reviews in the *Times Higher Education Supplement*, *Times Literary Supplement* and similar publications are also useful.

Large online bookstores such as Amazon (www.amazon.com) and Blackwells (www.blackwells.co.uk) can provide a good starting point for the newest titles and many sites offer added value services such as 'people who bought this also bought . . .', a useful method for building up a collection. Library catalogues can also offer this service as a way of spreading demand for titles ('people who borrowed this also borrowed . . .'). More recently, 'book clouds' have developed on the web. These are sites which allow users to 'vote' for a title; titles which generate the most interest feature more prominently in the cloud (www.bookcloud.co.uk).

Whether you are building your library collection or advising researchers, it is also worth using some of the sites for second-hand books. Remember, just because a book is no longer in print does not mean it loses any of its academic value. The following links provide some useful starting points:

- ☐ LibWeb Global (www.libweb.co.uk) includes in-print ISBNs available in the UK, USA and South Africa. The UK Books Out-of-Print database on LibWeb is a database of all UK ISBNs taken out of print since 1970 and contains approximately 1.5 million titles. Full bibliographic records are provided for each title (subscription required).
- ☐ Books for Academics (www.services.ex.ac.uk/bfa) includes lists of recently published UK academic books as well as links to publishers' websites (free).
- ☐ The HERO gateway (www.hero.ac.uk/uk/reference_and_subject_resources/purchase_and _supply/bookshops_and_publishers3803.cfm) provides links to many bookshops and publishers (free).
- ☐ ACQWEB's Directory of Publishers and Vendors

(http://acqweb.library.vanderbilt.edu) provides over 1000 links by name and by subject (free).

☐ Alibris (www.alibris.com) links to thousands of booksellers (free).

☐ The Clique (www.clique.co.uk) links to sites for buying and selling old or out-of-print books. Includes a list of over 400 UK literary and historic societies and a register of almost 1900 British book dealers with an internet connection (free).

☐ BookWire (USA) (www.bookwire.com) provides links to over 900 publishers' sites, subject guides to booksellers and other book-related resources including features from several American book review publications (free).

☐ JustBooks (Europe) (www.justbooks.co.uk) lists second-hand and antiquarian books offered by over 200 book dealers in Europe, from paperbacks to rare, out-of-print or first editions (free).

☐ Bibliofind (www.bibliofind.com) lists more than 10 million used and rare books, periodicals and ephemera offered for sale by thousands of booksellers around the world (free).

☐ AbeBooks (www.abebooks.co.uk) claims to be the world's largest online second-hand bookstore, listing 80 million titles (free).

2   Reference materials

Collections of printed reference materials are expensive to create and maintain and in many libraries use of this type of material is declining in favour of electronic sources, particularly in science, engineering and medicine. Reference books are useful for researchers to check facts and data, but this information is much more accessible and current online. Popular titles, such as the CRC Handbooks, can be consulted via ENGNetBASE (www.engnetbase.com), and the Knovel collection of science and engineering reference works (www.knovel.com) not only allows researchers to discover and compare facts, but also enables manipulation of the data in spreadsheets and graphical packages.

So can we dispense with reference collections? Probably not just yet – there are still people who prefer to browse through a printed handbook and it is often quicker to check a fact by pulling a book off a shelf then by accessing the online version. We also must remember the wide range of researchers we are dealing with. This is one kind of material whose use, because it is likely to be intermittent and casual rather than consistent and regular, may be directly related to the age, learning habits and discipline of the researcher. Younger researchers are likely to be more familiar with social computing tools and will regularly use sources such as Wikipedia (http://en.wikipedia.org/wiki), the online encyclopaedia which anyone can edit. Rather than dismissing such tools librarians need to be fully aware of their potential and limitations in order to advise readers on their suitability.

Integrating the print reference collection with online resources effectively, so that scholars know which is the most appropriate source for their needs, is challenging, but if it can be achieved it is an area in which librarians can demonstrate particularly focused support for research.

Finding and buying reference books

The sources and techniques described above for books apply equally to reference books, though some electronic reference material will be more easily identified via the e-books sources listed below.

3   E-books

The first ventures by publishers into the academic e-books market in the 1990s were characterized by large reference works (e.g. XRefer, Wiley Encyclopaedias), with purchasing models driven by the print environment. Although, as suggested above, some of these collections offered a replacement for the printed works, they were in general not well used by researchers. The new interactive reference books, such as Knovel, and the added value of sources like the *New Dictionary of National Biography* (www.oxforddnb.com) or the *Oxford English Dictionary* (www.oed.com, are of much more interest to research.

In parallel to the development of reference sources previously mentioned, there were significant developments in the field of scholarly electronic publishing. Probably the best-known example from the 1990s was LION (Literature Online) (http://lion.chadwyck com). Based initially on the English Poetry full-text database first published as CD-ROMs, LION offered enormous potential for anyone interested in English language and literature as it provided a vast well-structured, fully searchable full-text database. It suddenly became possible to search through texts without digitizing them yourself with the benefits of good-quality metadata to facilitate retrieval. Investigations that would have required a month's work could be done in a matter of minutes. More recently, even more sophisticated resources with digital content and images have become available in the form of Early English Books Online (EEBO) at http://eebo.chadwyck.com/home and Eighteenth Century Collections Online (ECCO) at www.gale.com/EighteenthCentury. JISC (the Joint Information Systems Committee) has helped make available both EEBO and ECCO to the UK higher education community. The ACLS History Project (www.historyebook.org/intro.html) is also worth investigating as its aim is to produce a select list of high-quality books in history, recommended and reviewed by historians.

Developments in digital publishing in the humanities aside, the majority of current e-book developments in our sector are focused on textbooks.

Finding e-books

There is no comprehensive source of information on e-books available, as the situation is so fluid, but e-book publishers and aggregators are extending their collections daily and browsing their databases is a good starting place. Below are just a few examples:

☐ EBook Library from Dawsons (www.eblib.com) allows libraries to build a tailored collection from many publishers (subscription required/purchase).

☐ NetLibrary (OCLC) (www.netlibrary.com) boasts more than 100,000 titles (subscription required).

☐ The Academic Library (www.theacademiclibrary.com) concentrates mainly on social sciences topics (subscription required).

☐ Ebrary (www.ebrary.com) offers both subscription and perpetual access models (subscription required/purchase).

☐   Project Gutenberg (www.gutenberg.org) makes 18,000 'classic' e-books available (free).

☐   The Online Books Page (http://onlinebooks.library.upenn.edu) lists over 25,000 free e-books (free).

4   Journals and electronic journals

When asked what they wanted from their library service, nearly all the researchers we spoke to mentioned access to journals, and particularly electronic journals, as key to their research. 'It's nice to have all this stuff available from my office . . . I don't go to the library nearly as often now but I probably use library journals most days through my computer' (Chemistry postgraduate, UK). As already discussed, journals pose specific problems for libraries for three reasons: cost, complexity in managing subscriptions and the importance vested in them particularly by research-active academics. The collection manager needs to find ways of balancing access, cost and need: never easy and sometimes almost impossible.

Identifying key journals

As we have already discussed, the quality of research is judged by outputs and, in the UK, the RAE in particular has driven the publication process. However, even without the RAE, scholars want to publish their work in reputable journals, and have it widely disseminated and read by their peers. Consequently, it is vital that they know which journals in a discipline have the highest impact on their community.

One way to discover this is to use a ranking and citation source such as the Journal Citation Reports (JCR). JCR allows librarians and researchers to identify those journals within a subject area which have been cited the most frequently, the inference being that the more citations a journal receives, the wider the impact it is having. Journals are given an 'impact factor', enabling the comparison of the impact of titles within their group. JCR does have serious limitations, however. It is based on titles indexed in the ISI Citation Indexes, so if a title is not indexed by ISI (and many are not), it will not have an impact factor.

Engineering, newly emerging scientific areas, the humanities and many social sciences are not well covered and the database does still have a North American bias in content.

Note that each discipline uses a mixture of information forms for scholarly communication. In many humanities subjects, scholarly monographs are the dominant form of academic communication. In the humanities and many social sciences there is a less rigid hierarchy of key journals than in medicine and other sciences. 'I am interested in criminology journals, but not all of them – it depends which sort of criminology' (Professor of Criminal Justice, UK). The pattern is shifting across all subjects as research intensity, research selectivity and the continuing development of new disciplines and communities of practice lead to an increase in journal publishing in total.

At a seminar in Southampton in January 2005, Robert Campbell, President of Blackwell Publishing, spoke about the future of learned publishing (Campbell, 2005). At the close of his talk he highlighted as a key trend the widespread increase in R&D funding – for example the UK science budget will increase from £2.4 billion in 2003–4 to £5 billion in 2013–14. It is clear that more funding will mean more papers (he cited forecasts that 1.5 million papers will increase to 3 million papers per annum over the next ten years), and that the impact factor could change. He used some evidence from the Journal Citation Reports (see Table 5.1).

Table 5.1 Journal citation impact factors 1997 and 2003

| Range | Science Citation Index | | | | Social Science Citation Index | | | |
| | 2003 | | 1997 | | 2003 | | 1997 | |
	Number of titles	%	Number of titles	%	Number of titles	%	Number of titles	%
20 and over	24	0.41	11	0.22	0	0.0	0	0.0
10 to 19	62	1.05	39	0.79	2	0.12	1	0.06
5 to 9	178	3.01	114	2.30	14	0.82	9	0.54
1 to 4	2495	42.24	1686	33.97	490	28.59	314	18.78
below 1	3148	53.29	3113	62.72	1208	70.48	1348	80.62
Total	5907		4963		1714		1672	

This demonstrates that as the total number of journals is increasing the impact is shifting. In the sciences, a small number of key journals continue to have very high impact, but the greatest proportion have much lower factors. In the social sciences there is even more scatter with the great majority of titles having an impact factor of below 1.

Some disciplines have developed rankings separately from those available through JCR. For example the so-called Diamond List is a ranking of titles in economics and a topic of continuing academic argument in the subject (see Burton and Phimister, 1995) and there are also listings for management information systems (MIS), business and marketing freely available on the web.

Other sources can be used to analyse journal rankings and impacts, including Scopus (see databases section below), Citeseer (http://citeseer. ist.psu.edu) and Google Scholar. Do not overlook the value of Ulrich's Directory, for it will tell you in which databases a journal is indexed and this is another indication of how widely the information will be disseminated.

It is also worth asking your community of users what they perceive as being important and significant titles. As experts in their own areas, they are likely to understand the relative importance of specific titles, especially if they are involved with RAE panels or refereeing.

Open access journals

As discussed in Chapter 2, the open access movement has resulted in a growing number of journals being made freely available. An open access journal is one which uses a funding model that does not charge readers or their institutions for access. Open Access Now (www.biomedcentral. com/openaccess), campaigning for the freedom of research information, brings together lots of useful OA resources.

The open access debate has become particularly vigorous of late with a high profile interchange of ideas taking place between traditional publishers and advocates of open access.

Finding journal information

- ☐ Ulrich's Periodicals Directory (www.ulrichsweb.com/ulrichsweb) is a bibliographic database providing detailed information on serials published throughout the world. It covers all subjects, and includes publications that are published regularly or irregularly and are circulated free of charge or by paid subscription (subscription required).
- ☐ Cabell's directories (www.cabells.com) cover social sciences subjects and, as well as the publication information on a title, include detailed publication guidelines and editorial policy (subscription required).
- ☐ Current Serials Received (www.bl.uk/serials) holds the titles of over 60,000 serials to which the British Library subscribes (free).
- ☐ The British Union Catalogue of Periodicals (1955–8) is still helpful for tracing old title information (print).
- ☐ Journal Citation Reports (http://portal.isiknowledge.com/portal.cgi) provide journal performance metrics (subscription required).
- ☐ Citeseer (http://citeseer.ist.psu.edu) focuses primarily on the literature in computer and information science, computing citation statistics and showing the context of citations (free).
- ☐ The Directory of Open Access Journals (www.doaj.org) lists freely available journal titles (free).

Examples of electronic journal collections

- ☐ ScienceDirect (www.sciencedirect.com) is a searchable database providing full-text access to over 1750 Elsevier Science titles (subscription required).
- ☐ Metapress (www.metapress.com) is a searchable database from EBSCO Industries providing access to approximately 1900 titles from different publishers (subscription required).
- ☐ SpringerLink (www.springerlink.com/home/main.mpx) is a searchable database providing access to over 2400 Springer titles (subscription required).
- ☐ Swetswise (https://www.swetswise.com/public/login.do) is a searchable site hosting journals from a range of publishers (subscription required).

☐ HighWire Press (http://highwire.stanford.edu) hosts the largest repository of free full-text peer-reviewed content, with 1008 journals and 1,496,010 free full-text articles online (free).

5 E-prints and preprints

E-print and preprint archives are electronic collections of papers that may or may not have been published in traditional journals or conference proceedings but are nearly always made freely available on the web. Preprints allow researchers to read about research before it is formally published, so are an excellent way of remaining at the cutting edge of research and can be a key resource. E-prints may include post-prints, copies of articles after formal publication in a journal (many institutional repositories consist mainly of post-prints) and also electronic articles in their own right, i.e. articles which have only ever been published in this form and have not gone through a formal publishing process. Most e-print and preprint archives rely on authors submitting information and self-archiving. Pre-prints and some e-prints, therefore, may not have been subject to a peer-review process nor scholarly editing and researchers must take this into account when using them.

But it would be misleading to suggest that e-print and preprint archives are invariably of inferior quality. In some disciplines, notably physics, preprint archives have become the accepted means of communication between scholars and are highly regarded, high-quality collections. The first and best-known preprint archive was begun by Paul Ginsparg at the Los Alamos National Physical Laboratory. Now known as arXiv and hosted by Cornell University, it contains over 379,940 e-prints in physics, mathematics, computer science and quantitative biology, has mirror sites all over the world (http://uk.arxiv.org) and remains the leading preprints site.

Many researchers are unaware that these resources exist, so it is up to the library to promote them and to draw attention to their advantages and deficiencies. As they are almost always freely available, the only costs involved for the library are the staff costs in ensuring our awareness and in marketing and promoting them effectively. They can be a valuable additional information resource, particularly in science, and detailed knowledge and understanding of them can add immeasurably to the credibility of the librarian to the research community.

Finding e-prints and preprints

- ☐ Intute (www.intute.ac.uk) indexes preprint sites – just type preprints into the main search box.
- ☐ The British Library Research Archive (http://sherpa.bl.uk) is a database of papers and articles focusing on research by British Library staff. It also contains papers by readers who have used the Library's collections in their research and who do not have any institutional affiliation. Those submitting documents here are usually the author or editor or have the necessary permission to make the documents available via this archive. Some of the material may not have been peer-reviewed.
- ☐ Google Scholar (http://scholar.google.com) will also find many e-print and preprint sites.

Examples of subject specific preprint sites include:

Biology/psychology

Behavioral and Brain Sciences preprints
www.bbsonline.org/Preprints/BBS_Preprint_Links.htm

Chemistry

Chemistry, Mathematics and Computing Science preprint archives (no new submissions since 2004)
www.sciencedirect.com/preprintarchive

Computing

Computing Research Repository
http://arxiv.org/corr/home

Economics

RePEc
http://129.3.20.41/Welcome.html

Energy

E-print Network
www.osti.gov/eprints

Europe

ERPA (European Research Papers Archive)
http://eiop.or.at/erpa

International and area studies

GAIA (Global, Area, and International Archive) eScholarship Repository
http://repositories.cdlib.org/gaia

Mathematics

Global Directory of Mathematics Preprint and e-Print Servers
www.ams.org/global-preprints

Physics

arXiv
http://uk.arXiv.org

Psychology

CogPrints: Cognitive Sciences EPrint Archive
www.iam.ecs.soton.ac.uk/projects/CogPrints.html

6   Institutional repositories

We have already discussed the factors behind the development of institutional repositories. As we have noted previously, many university and research organizations have institutional repositories of their research output, facilitating access to current work and acting as a public archive for older material.

Finding institutional repositories

- ☐ Project Romeo (www.sherpa.ac.uk/romeo.php) lists publishers' copyright policies with regard to self-archiving.
- ☐ OAIster (http://oaister.umdl.umich.edu/o/oaister) searches across institutional repositories.
- ☐ ROAR (http://archives.eprints.org/index.php?action=browse) is a registry of open access repositories.
- ☐ Google Scholar (http://scholar.google.com) also harvests IR material.

7   Conference papers

Like preprints, conference papers provide access to the cutting edge of research. Often the first place that new research results are reported publicly is at a conference, 'testing the water' of peer reaction before a more formal journal publication. The importance of conference papers to research varies tremendously between disciplines and it is vital that as librarians we are aware of which subject areas place the highest importance on this means of communication, so that our collections reflect this. In general terms, we might say that engineering disciplines rely most heavily on conference papers, while researchers in pure sciences and medical areas prefer to wait for journal articles. However, this is a very broad generalization and any librarian seeking to expand library access to conference papers should consult researchers in their specific discipline.

Forthcoming conferences

As well as providing access to published papers, you can consider extending your service to researchers by making them aware of forthcoming conferences, both as a way of publicizing their own research and of learning about current research. In a small organization you can provide a tailored conference alerting service, but in larger libraries you will probably have to limit yourself to highlighting useful sources for conference information.

Finding conferences

☐   The HERO website (www.hero.ac.uk/uk/inside_he/
conferences3888.cfm) is a good source of news on meetings and
conferences planned.

☐   The Intute website (www.intute.ac.uk) also provides useful links to
conference websites by subject.

☐   AllConferences.com (www.allconferences.com) is a directory
focusing on conferences, conventions, trade shows, exhibits,
workshops, events and business meetings.

Finding conference papers

Many bibliographic databases index conference papers along with journal
articles. Coverage is not comprehensive, for example neither ABI/Inform
nor Business Source Premier, leading bibliographic databases in business
and management, index any conferences. In those cases it is important to
use general sources which do include conferences, such as Web of
Knowledge Proceedings and ZETOC, or to seek out more specialized
listings.

8   Theses and dissertations

First of all a point of clarification. In the UK, thesis is the term normally
given to the work written and defended for the award of a doctorate. A
dissertation is usually a piece of work produced for a lower level of award.
The terminology is reversed in North America. Whatever the name, they
are invaluable sources of research information. As they report the work
done to attain a doctorate, they detail original research, often linked to
major research projects being undertaken in universities around the
world. The reputation of the awarding university within the discipline, as
well as the authority of the supervisors, can have a bearing on the quality
of the thesis and researchers must be made aware of quality issues such as
these when consulting this material.

Finding theses

- ☐ Index to Theses (www.theses.com) indexes theses accepted for higher degrees in Great Britain and Ireland from 1716 to date (subscription required).
- ☐ ProQuest Digital Dissertations (wwwlib.umi.com/dissertations) allows users to search the most recent two years of 'Dissertation Abstracts', and is free to members of academic institutions. Coverage is mainly of North American doctoral theses. Subscriptions are available for earlier years.
- ☐ Individual library catalogues usually index their own theses, so it is also possible to use the links detailed in the books section above to search for theses.
- ☐ For historians there is a wonderful resource published in print and online by the Institute of Historical Research (www.history.ac.uk), which lists theses in progress and those recently completed.
- ☐ A comprehensive listing of other sources for theses is available from www.ulrls.lon.ac.uk/resources/theseslistings.asp.

Obtaining theses

British and Irish University PhD theses can usually be borrowed through the British Library Document Supply Service (www.bl.uk/britishthesis). Older theses are usually held on microform, but newer ones may have to be borrowed from the originating institution and digitized before being available for loan. The British Library has a selection of North American doctoral dissertations up to 2001. Other theses can be purchased direct from the ProQuest service mentioned above.

9   Bibliographic databases

Databases are key research resources as they index the literature. Most indexing and abstracting services are available online, often concentrating on broad subject areas or types of resource, but there are still a few specialized abstracts and indexes which are only available in print.

There is a lot of confusion among scholars about the difference between a database and a collection of electronic journals – understandably, as the searching facilities are very similar. Librarians should explain the limitations of e-journal collections (including small scale, often limited by publisher and date, and constrained by the library budget and subscription agreements) to researchers who see only the benefit of instant full-text access.

In theory databases are more comprehensive or specialized, giving the researcher access to the whole world of published information in their discipline. Inevitably, this is not always the case: particularly when researchers are working in multidisciplinary and interdisciplinary fields they may find that no databases cover their area of study very effectively. Federated search tools, such as Metalib® from Ex Libris™ (www. exlibrisgroup.com/metalib.htm), which act as portals to a library's electronic resources, allow cross searching of multiple databases. This may be convenient – and of significant value for our interdisciplinary, multidisciplinary researchers – but there are some notes of caution for these tools rarely enable access to the deep indexing of the native interface so search results are inevitably less comprehensive, nor are all secondary databases compatible. It is important that scholars are made aware of these issues so that they are able to evaluate the results of their investigations.

Technology like SFX®, an open URL linking resolver (www. exlibrisgroup.com/sfx.htm), allows libraries to link directly from the records in a database to their holding information, providing the user with a seamless transition to the full text (and adding to the confusion between databases and electronic journals!).

In the UK, many resources are provided through the Joint Information Systems Committee (JISC) Collections Company, and the JISC Collections Portfolio of Online Resources is a good starting point for identifying key databases, such as the examples listed below. JISC also provides a model licence agreement, guidance for both librarians and publishers, and works with librarians to identify new resources to add to the JISC portfolio. The new JISC UK federated access management infrastructure (www.jisc.ac. uk/whatwedo/themes/access_management/federation.aspx) is based on the latest Shibboleth technology, and will provide the next generation access management facilities to users and institutions across the UK.

Examples of databases

☐ The Web of Knowledge (www.thomsonisi.com) comprises a
multidisciplinary collection of databases including the ISI Citation
Indexes, ISI Proceedings and the Journal Citation Reports
(subscription required).

☐ Scopus (www.scopus.com), a new product from Elsevier, is again
multidisciplinary, though biased towards science, technology and
medicine (subscription required).

☐ FirstSearch from OCLC (www.oclc.com/firstsearch) is a collection
of databases from many subject areas which can be searched
individually or together (subscription required).

☐ Business Source Premier (EBSCO) (http://search.ebscohost.com)
combines a database with some full-text access, mainly in business
and management topics (subscription required).

☐ CSA Illumina (www.csa.com) is a collection of over 40 databases
which can be searched individually and in topic groups (subscription
required). The new CSA Illustrata service provides deep indexing of
data, such as figures and tables, within articles.

☐ PubMed (www.pubmed.gov) is the free version of the Medline
database.

Finding out about databases

☐ The Gale Directory of Databases (Mueckenheim, 2006), at
www.galegroup.com, profiles thousands of databases available
worldwide in a variety of formats (purchase).

☐ JISC Collections Portfolio of Online Resources (www.jisc.ac.uk/
index.cfm?name=coll) (free).

10   Official publications

Official and technical information can be vital to research and is an area of
documentation often overlooked by researchers focused on the journal
literature.

Government documents

Government publications can be a major source of information and data in almost all subject fields and librarians can highlight relevant subject-specific resources for their research groups. As well as legislation, individual departments and laboratories provide a wealth of valuable research reports. This type of material is often voluminous and organized in a complicated way and can be difficult to source, so library staff can be vital in providing clear guidance and in gathering together relevant materials. The Newcastle Library web pages at www.ncl.ac.uk/library/ gov_pubs.php provide a good overview of the range of materials available in the UK (parliamentary papers, green papers, acts, bills, etc.) and are a good example of the kind of support the library can provide to researchers. Long-term access to this material can be a critical issue. 'My major concern is about the archiving of government documents, reports etc. for they are one of my fundamental sources. These are now often published on-line as PDF files. Libraries do not get these. Government departments have no archiving strategy' (Professor of European Housing, UK).

Finding government documents

- ☐ BOPCRIS (www.bopcris.ac.uk) is a useful way into UK documentation.
- ☐ European information can be sourced through the European Union website at http://europa.eu.
- ☐ FirstGov (www.firstgov.gov) is the US government's web portal.

Standards

The use of standards can be seen in all aspects of life. They are used to ensure uniformity and consistency, reliability and safety. Standards reduce unnecessary duplication of effort, and provide a quality benchmark. They can be produced nationally, internationally or by industry. Most standards organizations have their own website, and often provide an online catalogue or index of their standards. Many of these catalogues will give free access to brief bibliographic details of the standard.

☐   WSSN – World Standards Services Network (www.wssn.net) is a
      network of publicly accessible standards organizations from around
      the world. It provides links to many national and international
      standards organizations.

Patents

A patent is a legal and technical document that describes an invention and
grants a property right to the inventor for a limited period. Patents are an
important source of technical and scientific information, as they are often
the first source of published information on a new technology. Over 70%
of patents are never published elsewhere.

☐   The British Library Patents web pages
      (www.bl.uk/collections/patents/polinks.html) give access to a
      comprehensive list of worldwide Patent Offices.
☐   Esp@cenet (www.espacenet.com) gives access to patent information
      from around the world. Coverage depends on country. Full-text
      information for many patents is available.
☐   USPTO (US Patent and Trademark Office) at www.uspto.gov/patft
      covers US patents from 1790 onwards.
☐   International organizations, such as the United Nations
      (www.un.org), the World Bank (www.worldbank.org), OECD
      (www.oecd.org) and professional bodies, are also worth consulting.

11   Grey literature

By grey literature, we mean any written material which has not been
published commercially; it has often been produced 'in house' and
typically includes resources such as technical reports, working papers and
other documents, often written as the outcome of a specific project.

Grey literature is often ignored by researchers and librarians because it
is notoriously difficult to track down. It can be found in any discipline but
is more commonly sought after in science, technology, medicine and
applied policy areas. It is often not well indexed as it has not been written

for a wider audience than the author's immediate workplace and researchers rely on personal contact and word of mouth to track it down. Issues of reliability and quality also need to be considered.

However, grey literature is often the only record of individual research projects and it can be a rich source of data. Small specialized research libraries have in the past built up extensive collections of grey literature, but it is increasingly becoming available on the web, making it much more likely to be indexed by search engines and other web indexing services. Our role as librarians supporting research is to keep researchers up to date with this type of literature, pointing them to sources for identification and helping to exploit them successfully.

Finding grey literature

- [ ] The British Library National Reports Collection (www.bl.uk/services/ document/reportsuk.html) includes reports, papers and technical notes from private and public sector organizations, charities, action groups and research institutions. They currently receive documents from more than 4,000 sources (free).
- [ ] GrayLIT Network (www.osti.gov/graylit) is the US portal into Federal grey literature (free).
- [ ] Greynet (www.greynet.org/greysourceindex.html) provides GreySource, a list of sources of grey literature in all subjects, and also facilitates information sharing about grey literature, so is a useful tool for librarians (free).
- [ ] SCoRe (www.score.ac.uk) is the UK national catalogue of printed company reports (free).

12   Archives and special collections

Archives, rare books and special collections are terms variously given to the valuable primary resources held by many university libraries and other organizations. They can include original manuscripts, collections of letters, early printed books, maps, scientific notebooks and any other rare and often unique materials deemed by virtue of their age or rarity to be deserving of special treatment. Traditionally these collections have been the preserve of arts and humanities researchers, but they can provide essential material to all disciplines. Digitization of rare resources increases access and we can use technology to exploit our collections by making them available on the internet. The Oxford Digital Library (www.odl.ox.ac.uk/collections/index.html) is a good example of this.

Finding archives

☐ The National Archives of England, Wales and the United Kingdom (www.nationalarchives.gov.uk) has one of the largest archival collections in the world, spanning 1000 years of British history. The National Register of Archives contains information on the nature and location of manuscripts and historical records that relate to British history. The Access to Archives (A2A) Project provides descriptions of archives in Record Offices and in other public repositories in England (free).

☐ The Higher Education Archives Hub (www.archiveshub.ac.uk) is a gateway which provides descriptions of archives in UK higher education institutions (free).

☐ The European Archival Network (www.european-archival.net/ean) gives details of archives across Europe (free).

☐ The British Library Manuscript Catalogue allows detailed searching of the manuscript holdings of the British Library (free).

☐ The Research Information Network (www.rin.ac.uk) has a role to lead and co-ordinate new developments in the collaborative provision of research information for the benefit of researchers in the UK.

13   E-science and datasets

Research practice has changed enormously over the last ten years. Terms such as e-science, e-research and e-scholarship have been coined to describe this phenomenon, which, while it initially predominated in the science and technology disciplines, is rapidly gaining ground in social science, arts and humanities. E-science involves the use of large datasets, often by groups of scholars simultaneously around the globe. Improved technology allows collaboration, communication and sharing of information and resources in new ways. Researchers are increasingly using IT for data mining, modelling, simulation, analysis and data collection and are familiar with interactive tools and resources which are often instantly and freely available across the world wide web.

Examples of datasets currently available (these tend to be collections of data from social research) include the following.

☐ The UK Data Archive (www.data-archive.ac.uk), established by the Economic and Social Research Council in 1967, is the largest national resource of computer readable copies of social science and humanities statistics and data in the UK (subscription required).

☐ The National Digital Archive of Datasets (www.ndad.nationalarchives.gov.uk) contains archived digital data from UK departments and agencies. The system has been available since March 1998 and provides open access to the catalogues of all its holdings, and free access to open datasets following a simple registration process.

☐ The Census Registration Service (http://census.data-archive.ac.uk) facilitates access to UK census data (free).

Examples of databanks (these are collections of scientific data) include the following.

☐ GenomNet Japan (www.genome.ad.jp/dbget) (free).

☐ BRENDA (www.brenda.uni-koeln.de) is the main collection of enzyme functional data available to the scientific community (free).

☐ Entrez databases (www.ncbi.nlm.nih.gov/Entrez) include nucleotide sequences, protein sequences, macromolecular structures and whole genomes (free).

☐ The European Bioinformatics Institute (www.ebi.ac.uk) manages databases of biological data including nucleic acid, protein sequences and macromolecular structures (free).

14   Academic information on the internet

Most of the resources discussed above are internet resources, but many are part of the invisible web, areas which a search engine may not find, hidden behind passwords and firewalls. It is our role to promote and encourage their use. We should not ignore the value of the open internet and its role in retrieving so much useful academic information. A good starting point for high-quality internet resources is the Intute service (www.intute.ac.uk), created by a network of UK universities and partners. Subject specialists select and evaluate the websites and write high-quality descriptions of the resources. Nor should we spurn search engines, most especially Google. If we explain how advanced search options work on Google and elsewhere, and discuss the advantages and limitations of Google Scholar and Google Books, we help both to maximize search effectiveness and place general internet resources into an appropriate context alongside what we might define as traditional academic resources. After all, an important part of our role is to enable our users to find the information they need, in the best way.

Finding out about internet resources

- ☐ FreePint (www.freepint.com) is a global network of people who find, use, manage and share work-related information. Members receive a newsletter via email every two weeks (free).
- ☐ The Internet Resources Newsletter (www.hw.ac.uk/libwww/irn/irn.html) is e-mailed to 39,000 recipients each month from Heriot-Watt University Library, to raise awareness of new sources of information on the internet, particularly those which are relevant to research interests at Heriot-Watt, including engineering, science and social science. An RSS feed is available (free).
- ☐ ResourceShelf (www.resourceshelf.com) provides a weekly newsletter on a variety of topics (free).

15   Current awareness services

Researchers need to keep up to date with new research and developments as their own research progresses. There are many automated services which provide current awareness services very effectively.

E-mail alerting services

Alerting services send regular e-mails to update on new publications. Once the alert is set up, it happens automatically, so researchers do not have to engage with the publication regularly unless they wish to.

☐   Current Contents Connect (CCC) (http://wok.mimas.ac.uk) is a current awareness service from ISI, the producers of the Citation Indexes, covering over 7350 journals in all subjects. Alerts by journal title or subject are sent weekly (subscription required).

☐   ZETOC Alert (http://zetoc.mimas.ac.uk) from the British Library sends TOC (table of contents) or subject alerts from 20,000 titles (free to UK HE).

Many databases and electronic journal collections include an alerting service, so scholars can conduct a complex subject search and save the search strategy as an e-mail alert.

☐   Publishers will often send regular e-mail alerts of the tables of contents of their periodical titles.

☐   The website http://newsnow.co.uk is a useful way of keeping up to date with news stories.

RSS feeds

RSS (usually defined as Really Simple Syndication) feeds can also be used to have the journal tables of contents sent to a personal webpage or RSS reader. RSS feeds can be more convenient than e-mail alerts, such as those from ZETOC, as they have direct links to the full text of some articles. The RSS reader will alert users to unread TOCs. Look out for one of these icons: RSS or XML on e-journal sites.

Finding out about current awareness services

☐ The BBC website (http://news.bbc.co.uk/1/hi/help/rss/default.stm) has simple instructions on setting up RSS feeds.

☐ The UKeIG website (http://ukeig.xwiki.com/xwiki/bin/view/Main/RSSFeatures) also provides useful information on RSS feeds and readers.

16   People and networks

Once researchers are established in their field of study, they build up their own network of colleagues around the world and often turn to this network first for information, rather than using any of the more formal systems detailed above: 'I can usually get what I need from people I know. They will e-mail things to me . . . I always try them first because it's quicker than searching in the library' (Biology researcher, UK).

These communities of practice provide very important communication mechanisms, particularly for researchers at the cutting edge of their field where research is moving more rapidly than the conventions of academic publishing allow. Some networks will develop through personal contacts, conference attendance and work relationships, but others can be fostered by directing researchers to relevant e-mail discussion lists and web-based communities.

Finding out about people

☐ JISCmail (www.jiscmail.ac.uk) is a UK-based service whose mission is 'To facilitate knowledge sharing within the UK centred academic community, using e-mail and the web, through the provision, support and development of specialist mailing list based services, enabling the delivery of high quality and relevant content' (free).

☐ ListServe (www.listserve.com) based in America, also facilitates e-mail discussion lists (free).

☐ COS Expertise (www.cos.com) is an international database of 500,000 researchers at over 1600 institutions worldwide. Individuals can register on the Community of Science database to promote their research and expertise to colleagues (subscription required).

Conclusion

This chapter has listed some examples of resources which are valuable for research; it does not attempt to be comprehensive, just to give a flavour of the kinds of materials to which librarians can guide their users. As so many of the resources listed contain links, it is inevitable that some of these will be out of date very quickly. However, by checking other library websites it should be relatively easy to update the links regularly.

Of course, making research resources accessible is only the beginning. To be effective we must also provide a range of other services and foster the development of an information literate research community – which we shall discuss next.

Further reading

Bailey, C.W. (2005) *Open Access Bibliography: liberating scholarly literature with e-prints and open access journals*, Association of Research Libraries. Presents over 1300 selected English-language books, conference papers, e-prints, journal articles, news articles, technical reports and other sources that are useful in understanding the open access movement.

Bloomfield, B. C. (ed.) (1997) *A Directory of Rare Book and Special Collections in the United Kingdom and Republic of Ireland*, 2nd edn, Facet Publishing. Lists many rare and special book collections held in over 1200 libraries with details of their history, contents and access to readers.

Bradley, P. (2004) *The Advanced Internet Searcher's Handbook,* 3rd edn, Facet Publishing.

Burton, M. P. and Phimister, E. (1995) Core Journals: a reappraisal of the diamond list, *Economic Journal*, **105** (429), 361–73.

Campbell, R. (2005) Open Access Institutional Repositories: the views of a learned-society publisher, *Open Access Institutional Repositories*

(OAIRs): Leadership, Direction and Launch, University of Southampton. 25–6 January 2005, www.eprints.org/events/jan2005/programme.html.

Harnad, S. et al. (2004) The Access/Impact Problem and the Green and Gold Roads to Open Access, *Serials Review*, **30** (4), www.ecs.soton.ac.uk/%7Eharnad/Temp/impact.html.

Jellinek, D. (2000) *Official UK: the essential guide to government websites*, HMSO.

Lawrence, S., Lee Giles, C. and Bollacker, K. (1999) Digital Libraries and Autonomous Citation Indexing, *IEEE Computer*, **32** (6), 67–71.

Lester, R. (ed.) (2005) *The New Walford Guide to Reference Resources, Volume 1: Science, Technology and Medicine*, Facet Publishing.

Poulter, A., Hiom, D. and McMenemy, D. (2005) *The Library and Information Professional's Internet Companion*, Facet Publishing.

6

Services to facilitate research

Introduction

In this further practical chapter our attention shifts away from providing appropriate resources to ways of creating distinctive, targeted services.

The chapter aims to:

- identify ways that librarians can act as facilitators rather than supporters of research
- discuss a range of services which the library could offer to researchers.

Researchers will always need information, but will they always need libraries? Traditionally, research libraries have been sure of their position within the research environment but in the digital age such complacency is dangerous. We face challenges to the ways that we develop and deliver our services, as researchers are much less dependent on their own organization's library and information service than in the past. We must evolve and enhance our work to continue to provide vital, essential services.

In Chapter 4 we discussed the challenges of managing and developing collections across media in complex organizations during times of financial constraints. We now turn our attention away from resources to the ways that libraries should develop their role and relationship with the research community.

In Chapter 3 we discussed the diversity of the modern research community, a diversity that brings with it a much more complex pattern of library and information use. Many researchers use a wide range of different libraries and other sources to gather information. Access to catalogues, databases and physical spaces is much easier. Some researchers claim never to use libraries at all: 'The importance of *physical* libraries is minimal: books are less important due to the fast moving pace of my subject' (Professor of Housing, UK).

In our interviews we discovered how many libraries our researchers used: 'I use [my university] library, and New York Public Library Dance Collection (virtual use almost daily, regular visits) . . . the Dansmuseet in Stockholm . . . the Bibliothèque de l'Arsenal.'

Do these changing patterns of use mean that research libraries are now in competition (or collaboration) with each other? What is it about your library which will make researchers choose it over another? Do you have specialist resources, is it the most convenient or cheapest option, do you offer a well known specialist service, or does it simply provide a supportive and pleasant environment?

> I moved to [Russell University] with my research group because I knew that your collection of specialist biology resources is a lot more comprehensive that my old university. My colleagues here had also told me how supportive the Library here is, really seeming to show an interest in what researchers are doing. So far I haven't been disappointed.
>
> (Head of Biology Research Group, UK)

Keeping in touch with the research community

Learning attitudes and habits have changed over recent years in many ways. These changes are often most apparent when working with undergraduates whose informal, gregarious learning habits can seem at odds with traditional forms of library organization – and provide the inspiration for so many building redevelopments. They affect not only the newest entrants to higher education, but very many people. Library staff need to be aware that new researchers may be sceptical about and unfamiliar with traditional approaches to research. Researchers have developed their practice in the digital age and have learned in different ways, so their needs may be different from those of researchers in the past. More mature researchers may return to academic study after a break of some years and find that the information world has changed completely. Well established researchers often confess that they rely on tried and tested techniques and resources and can be wary of moving to newer approaches:

> I'm slightly old fashioned in that I did enjoy browsing journals and looking at things often outside my field of immediate interest – good to see what is going on else-where, other applications, etc. Sadly not very easy with e-copies. Now, when I'm writing papers I focus more attention on the abstract – often that is as far as most people (including me) get with e-journals.
>
> (Senior researcher in government agency, UK)

Inevitably, too, the services and resources themselves have evolved and changed in response to changing research needs and also in response to exter-nal factors such as changes in information technology and higher education in general. This was exemplified in a response from one of our researchers – a Professor of Library and Information Science in Japan: 'And I also check some questions through Google, rather than using reference books.'

It is important not to make assumptions that librarians know best about what researchers need. Of course we *should* have a better overview of which resources are available, but research is a very individual activity. It is important to listen and learn from what the researcher is saying: only through this collaboration can we really connect and support the fundamental information needs. Note as well that each researcher will be at a different stage in terms of their information literacy development, so you might be starting with simple explanations or working very much at the edge of your own knowledge base.

Expectations and demands will also vary depending on the type of library the researcher is using and whether the service is provided free at the point of use or is charged for. Libraries need to move away from a passive, reactive role to a more active role in which they can anticipate as well as respond to demands from researchers. Our role is not merely about supporting research, acting as handmaidens to the process, but more about facilitating research, acting more as midwives. We must change the perceptions of scholars (and some librarians!) that the library (and hence the librarian) is a passive resource waiting to be consulted to one in which we are active, indispensable participants in the research process. To some librarians this is a daunting prospect, as it heralds a shift away from the traditional, comfortable, custodial stance of library staff to a more vibrant, active membership of the research community, but if librarians want to maintain their position within the academic community this shift is inevitable.

What does the research community want from the library?

One of the most basic tenets of a well planned service for research is to ensure that you really know what the research community wants and needs from the library service. The best way to find out is to ask! Research staff and students must be included in library surveys and feedback mechanisms. This is rather easier to declare than to implement effectively in practice. Libraries have learnt to good effect the value of surveys as a way of understanding user needs, wants and expectations and of identifying action and agenda for change. In our institutions we are now overwhelmed by surveys. Some we administer ourselves, including LibQual+™, and more general library satisfaction surveys; others are managed elsewhere, including module feedback, course surveys, staff surveys, the National Student Survey (www.tqi.ac.uk) and others.

Research support is a more substantial element of the work of pre-1992, research-intensive university libraries, where collections have developed to support research over many years, but these libraries may nevertheless have been unable to adopt proactive approaches to service development. There may be many reasons for this, including different cultures of governance, a very dominant focus on collections rather than service, lack of support for any change programmes, and organizational inertia. Newer university libraries may never match research libraries' collections, but, we suggest, through enhancing the quality of service provision and support, they may provide a parallel experience. Now, of course, digital opportunities can make the information gap much narrower, especially when print budgets are so constrained.

However, for a first class service to research, it is not enough to react to comments in more general library surveys, or to respond to the small minority of vociferous (and often highly placed and powerful) researchers who make daily demands on the library service. They do, of course, play a vital role in providing feedback to the library, but it is the silent majority that we need to reach, the 'nice customer' of customer care training who never complains to the organization but does complain to friends and thus undermines the service, or is so dissatisfied with provision that he or she abandons the local library completely. One way to understand what your researchers need is to undertake a focused survey to discover researchers' views. These views can then be incorporated into service and strategic planning for the library.

The CORSALL report, discussed in Chapter 4, is a good example of a survey that illuminates the researcher experience – even if it can be difficult to draw up positive responses to what you find.

Examples of surveys

In 2001, the Research Support project team at Newcastle University asked 123 researchers across the university what their priorities were in terms of the library. Researchers across all faculties were sent paper questionnaires to complete (see Figure 6.1 overleaf) and library staff also ran focus groups and solicited opinions at academic research committee meetings.

Not unexpectedly, the survey found that the most important services were perceived to be access to electronic journals, followed by a comprehensive collection of up-to-date material and a wide range of specialist materials, including access to archives and special collections. Document delivery services were also highlighted as vital to research, so we can see that the traditional view of the library as the custodian of printed knowledge was prevalent. However, specialist help and advice in tracing resources and keeping up to date also featured in the responses. A surprisingly large number of researchers commented on how thrilling they found the atmosphere of a big research library and we must balance this feeling of awe, excitement and reverence with our new virtual presence.

Library support for research at Newcastle University

What can the Library do to support your research?

Library staff are considering the services and resources which we offer to support research. We are keen that the services we offer are appropriate for the needs of all staff involved in research. The outcome of this survey will be a comprehensive and consistent package of services and resources for all Faculties, raising awareness of the contribution the Library can make to planned and active research in the University. Your opinions are very important to us. Please answer the questions below, giving as much detail as you are able:

1.   Do you use the Library services to support your research at the moment?

2.   If yes, which services do you find the most helpful?

3.   If no, what are your reasons for not using the Library?

4.   Can the Library contribute to research proposals/submissions? If yes, in what way?

5.   How can the Library contribute to the RAE?

6.   From the following list of services for research, please tick the six that you would find the most helpful:

   • Advice/training on selecting and searching electronic and print databases
   • Mediated literature/bibliographical searches
   • Advice on general information/research skills
   • Advice on finding information on the Internet
   • Literature on putting a research proposal together
   • Literature about how to do research
   • How to find out about current research around the world
   • Help on finding impact factors for journals
   • Information on access to other libraries and resources
   • Advice on how to keep up to date in a research area
   • Document delivery/ILL services
   • A comprehensive collection of up to date materials
   • A wide range of in depth specialist materials
   • Improved access to Special Collections
   • More information about Special Collections
   • Advice on finding Government Publications
   • Longer opening hours for the Library
   • A regular Library Newsletter keeping you up to date with developments
   • Easy access to electronic journals
   • A database of Departmental publications
   • A central collection of Newcastle University/departmental publications.

Do you have any other comments in relation to how the Library can help with your research? (don't be restricted by space allowed here!)

Name/email (optional):

Department/Research group/Area of Research:

Figure 6.1 Library support for research questionnaire

The Bodleian was very different [from other libraries] . . . but what was fantastic was the ability to get anything and the great atmosphere made you feel like you are a real scholar – who else has been sitting in this seat . . .

(Professor of Marine Transport and Management, UK).

I still love going [to the library] and browsing books. In the library you can pick up things you never thought of. It's exciting! . . . I can't believe they are getting rid of the old lovely shelving. I have always liked libraries. It was the library which inspired me to do what I'm doing now . . . I went to the library and I was struggling and then I saw the link – it changed my whole life and was the making of me. I owe a lot to libraries.

(Dean of Research, UK)

A similar survey undertaken at Queensland University of Technology (QUT) in 2003 (Robertson and Young, 2003) mirrored the Newcastle findings, and also highlighted researchers' concerns that libraries would maintain printed resources while at the same time increasing access to e-resources. An interesting outcome of the QUT survey was a recognition that during a project researchers like to create a 'nest', surrounding themselves with all the resources they need. This can be at odds with library policies to centralize resources and manage loan periods but QUT Library has resolved to facilitate this temporary assembly of resources in research offices as part of their commitment to involvement in the research process.

Research undertaken into information sources preferred by scholars in Australia (Houghton, Steele and Henty, 2004) found that researchers rated refereed journals, books and conference papers as important resources, but it also noted a shift towards electronic resources for current information, with print viewed 'more as a historical record than a current dialogue'. (This of course has parallels with the usage and purpose of institutional repositories, as we will discuss briefly elsewhere.) Houghton et al. found that two-thirds of their respondents viewed Google as an essential source, peer-reviewed electronic journals scoring 60%. Highlighting disciplinary differences, they point out that researchers in social science, humanities and arts place less reliance on electronic sources and desktop access than do scientists and medics. 'I use online databases and catalogues but in my own area – dance – there is much less available online than in other areas, somehow we are not so well developed' (Research Professor in Dance History, UK).

While it is vital to listen to researchers and ensure that the library responds to their needs, we must do more than listen and react. Many researchers are unaware of the potential services and resources available to them and will only ask for what they already know about. This ignorance could easily compromise the quality of the research output. How much better might their research have been if they had been better informed? This is an area where librarians can demonstrate their value to the community as information professionals. Ensuring that the research community is as well informed as possible is the responsibility of the library and its staff and we have to find as many ways as we can to achieve this.

The ResIN case study, detailed below, is an example of an attempt to provide a comprehensive and consistent package of library services and resources for research alongside an improved dialogue between the Library and research staff and students in the university.

Case study 6.1   The Research Support Project at Newcastle University Library, UK

The Newcastle Research Support Project, which began in 2001, gave library staff the opportunity to step back and review the support provided by the library to both planned and active research across the university. There were three main strands to the project. To begin with, a clear picture was needed of the services and resources which were already provided in support of research at Newcastle. After this, an overview of services and activities at other university libraries around the world helped to inform and develop new service models. Most important was a clear understanding of the needs of researchers at Newcastle, so that existing services could be integrated with new developments.

The project group noted that many other university libraries in the UK had recently set up similar working parties to review library support for research, indicating the growing interest in developing services. A survey of other libraries' web pages was undertaken to ascertain how easy it was for researchers to find help from their library web pages. It appeared that although many provided a wide range of support (for example, Leeds University provided a lot of support for the RAE and did some early work on document delivery services and Kingston ran a project to investigate the needs of their researchers, appointing a research support librarian as a result), few had transparent sections of their web pages devoted solely to research support. The best examples of this tended to be at subject-specific level (e.g. engineering at Southampton). By 2006 the situation had not changed markedly.

The main thrust of the project was to develop new services as appropriate and to integrate them with existing services in an easily accessible way. The project deliverable of a 'package of services' began with the creation of the ResIN web pages (www.ncl.ac.uk/library/resin), which drew together the services and resources already provided, best practice ideas from elsewhere and some new ideas from the project team. These pages have expanded as new services are developed. Although the ResIN website is fully embedded in the Library web presence, it also retains its own specific, recognizable identity, with a logo which is used on publications, posters and PowerPoint presentations as well as on the website (see Figures 6.2 and 6.3 overleaf).

The project team also developed stronger links with other groups within the university involved in support for research. The link with the Business Development Directorate was particularly effective since it gave library staff access to the University Research Beehive. This £2.2m facility opened in June 2004, providing a dedicated space where research staff and postgraduates can meet to generate ideas, foster networks, develop new projects and socialize. A new adjacent dining and bar area help to make the Beehive a very attractive venue. ResIN was invited to establish a presence there by running seminars in the Beehive for researchers and holding its own working group meetings there. Staff from the Business Development Directorate provide the information on funding which appears in the ResIN web pages.

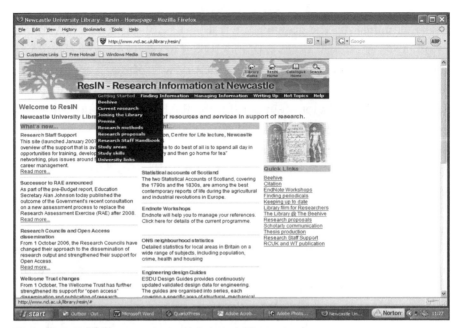

Figure 6.2 ResIN homepage, www.ncl.ac.uk/library/resin
Reproduced with permission of Newcastle University Library with thanks.

Figure 6.3 ResIN web page on scholarly communication,
www.ncl.ac.uk?library/resin/scholarly.php
Reproduced with permission of Newcastle University Library with thanks.

An important benefit of the project was the development and strengthening of the links between the Special Collections staff and resources and the liaison librarians and current stock. The project highlighted the need to raise the profile of Special Collections and Archives, so that current and potential researchers are aware of the rich resource of primary material which is available to them. An exhibition, Agriculture in the North, demonstrated how archive material is still relevant today, even in less traditional research areas. Posters on specific themes (e.g. bridges, nature) were designed to hang in the stairwells, bringing together images from Special Collections with modern images of research activity in the university. The posters were created in collaboration with active researchers, creating a community of interest which was also beneficial in strengthening links between the Library and research staff.

It is important to remember that the ResIN website is only part of ResIN. ResIN also encompasses a wide range of other services and resources, such as a handbook for research staff, a series of seminars and much more. Some of ResIN's activities are discussed in more detail later in this chapter, and the seminar series is described in Chapter 7. Five years after the start of the project, ResIN is an accepted, recognized brand at Newcastle (in fact, they have recently successfully resisted a takeover of the brand by the Graduate Schools – another opportunity for positive liaison!). There are links to the web pages from the Graduate Schools and from many other sections of the University website.

The ResIN approach has since been adopted by other university libraries in the UK, including Warwick, Portsmouth and Liverpool.

Services and support: some specific considerations

In order to provide a comprehensive service to researchers in the 21st century, libraries need to take stock of where they are now, list the services and resources they currently provide, ask users what they want from the library and combine the results of these investigations with new ideas and developments. The SCONUL vision 2010 (SCONUL, 2005) envisages that 'LIS will develop enhanced support for research groups who operate across traditional boundaries' – this seems inevitable as advances in technology and e-science proliferate. For research libraries to survive in this new era we must be flexible and constantly seek new ways to position ourselves within the research community. This section considers some specific services which a research library might provide and suggests practical ways in which the services might be developed. It can be used as the basis of a checklist for development and should be applicable to all types of library to some degree.

1   Space

Although more and more researchers access library resources from their desktop, many also tell us that they value the scholarly atmosphere of a research library: 'It makes me feel special, as if I'm a real, grown up, proper researcher now' (Research assistant, UK). Senior staff like the opportunity afforded to them of getting away from the administrative pressures of their job, especially the telephone, although at the same time confessing that they cannot afford to do this very often. 'I really value the times when I can come to the library and just sit and think without any interruptions, the phone is the worst of all, I never seem to have any thinking space in my office' (Dean of Research, UK). This need for 'thinking space' highlights a possible area of conflict in the modern use of library space. Current teaching and learning approaches for undergraduates favour independent learning in groups, where students use the library and resources in a collaborative way in order to progress in their learning. In order to accommodate this, library and information services have been developing information commons, spaces where group work is encouraged, there is easy access to technology and often integrated learning and study support services. These have been immensely popular with learners. However, many of our interviewees made it clear that this trend is actually disenfranchizing those researchers who value the library as a haven for scholarship and research. They feel crowded out by these developments and left with no suitable alternatives.

We would suggest therefore that libraries need to consider whether they can allocate space in such a way as to protect some traditional solitary work spaces while at the same time developing modern, buzzing, shared working areas.

Issues to consider related to space include:

- Do researchers need separate carrels?
- Can you provide small study rooms?
- Should you provide lockable or secure storage areas so researchers can create research 'nests'?
- Is a large silent study area more effective?
- Should you have a separate research-only library? If so, where do you draw the line in terms of resources?
- Do you have stock which can be designated 'research only'?
- Do you want undergraduates to have the opportunity to mix with researchers?
- Do researchers want to mix with undergraduates?
- How important is the noise policy?
- How important is a refreshment facility?
- Do you want to create a research study and learning centre in the library?

2   Involvement in research activity

Is there a true partnership between library and research staff at your institution? It is clear when talking to researchers that although they value the resources provided by the library and often recognize the value that specialist librarians can add in terms of information literacy, they do not often picture the librarian as part of the research team. But should this be the case? Probably our professional perception – and the experience in many private sector research-intensive organizations – is that librarian involvement will enhance research effectiveness.

At the most basic level, knowing what research activity is taking place means that library staff can alert researchers to other resources of which they may be unaware outside the immediate organization. This might mean directing people to specialist or unusual collections, like a special collection in a local museum, or sending on details of new publications or conferences. Of course, this may be difficult in a large university with hundreds of researchers and very few liaison staff, but it is still possible to develop personal networks of information and help. Remember, even within a single organization researchers may be unaware of other local research projects and the librarian, working across departments and schools, can be a facilitator in bringing groups together.

The development of institutional repositories creates very different opportunities for proactive involvement in research activity. In the context of this chapter, the shift from facilitating access to published material to building a digital open access resource means that library staff can potentially become much more closely integrated into research activity and management within the university. Much is written elsewhere on institutional repositories, and we are reluctant to repeat what others have written with more authority elsewhere. Our experience has been that being involved with repositories can create new territories for service development, as librarians become much more closely involved with the production and management of research information rather than dealing mainly with the finished artefacts.

One of the driving forces behind senior staff support for institutional repositories has been the Research Assessment Exercise; publishing in an IR can increase visibility and hence potential inpact fact, as well as providing a convenient central store of the institution's research output. Although the economic cost of the RAE is disputed (the Government suggests £45 million in the recent White Paper (DfES, 2006), but given the impact on the whole labour process in higher education more impartial sources suggest a higher figure), there are substantial administrative burdens. For example, universities need to provide detailed, absolutely accurate lists of publications under each unit of assessment. The need for accurate reference lists provides an opportunity for the library and information service. Your organization could offer a checking service for publication details, training in the use of impact factors, a hosting service for submitted papers and a co-ordinating role in the whole process.

There is scope to go beyond this administrative supporting role. For example, Warwick University Library staff investigated publishing opportunities for academic staff and ran a project to see to what extent it was viable for librarians to identify specific journals in which academics could publish, hoping to produce a hierarchy of publishing opportunities in specific subject areas (Bradford, 2005). They concluded that the adoption of a publishing strategy, targeting articles at journals with high impact factors, was essential for academics in preparation for the RAE and felt that their intervention within the School of Education had been welcomed.

A growing number of library staff are involved in the development of research proposals. At this stage in the research process, librarians can offer valuable advice about the strengths and weaknesses of the library collections in support of the proposed research. Costs of obtaining new resources to support the research can be factored into the proposal, allowing the library to develop the collection alongside the research activity and demonstrating a true partnership between the library and research staff. This is also a good way of managing expectations. If the library is able to highlight deficiencies in resources before the research begins, researchers are less likely to become frustrated later on.

Library staff can also offer literature searching support and advice at the start of a new research project, sometimes actively becoming part of the research team for this vital part of the project. If the project has factored the cost of the literature search into the proposal, as it should have done, this can also be a means of generating income for the library. As well as aiding the research process, this collaboration allows library staff to track current research and thus ensure that collection development mirrors research development in the institution.

Issues to consider related to involvement in research include:

- Can you develop a brief profile of research activity within the institution?
- Do you have an institutional repository?
- Is there an institutional database of research publications? Or is this the responsibility of faculties, departments or schools? Who maintains it?
- How can you get involved with the RAE or other research monitoring activities?
- Could you draw up guidelines for library staff to help them integrate into research groups?

- Do library staff have the skills to undertake specialist literature reviews (or in undertaking systematic reviews)?
- Can you identify collection strengths and target research groups?
- Could you organize exhibitions of library materials and local publications as part of local conferences?

3   Distance research

Distance learning is now an established mode of study in higher education, as increasing numbers of students learn from home or spend time on placement, usually as part of a recognized study programme, but we may not often consider the numbers of researchers who are working at a distance. Yet this may be the case for many students, registered for a degree many miles from their main location.

Across our own institutional and colleague networks, we can provide several examples:

- the part-time research student, working while undertaking an advanced course of study
- the full-time researcher based at a distant location (for example a research centre linked to your own institution)
- limited attendance students (i.e. where students are only required to be on campus for a few weeks a year)
- people writing up research who may have already moved on to a new phase of their lives and work
- researchers on fieldwork away from the university
- staff who spend much of their time working from home.

Very few libraries offer a formalized distance research support service. True, some needs, such as straightforward postal loans and digital document delivery, can be met by the distance learning or document supply. There are of course many arrangements for reciprocal access, exemplified in the SCONUL Research Extra (SRX) scheme (www.sconul.ac.uk/using_other_libraries/srx), which permits reciprocal borrowing for researchers whose home library is a member of the scheme. But is this the limit of what the service can and should provide or facilitate?

We suggest that there should be scope for other activities. Remember that many distance researchers will be working in isolation, physically distant from the social networks of campus life, and hence do not gain the benefits of some of the physical community of practice that develops around face-to-face contact. Access to information can sometimes be problematic if researchers are based in remote areas without immediate access to facilities, or in countries which have a different approach to research support. We suggest that this means it is ever more important to establish proactive contact with your distant researchers, so that they too are able to make full use of the service. Your contact may be in the form of enquiry support, virtual presence in online environments or even just personal contact as a source of information.

There is another dimension: when students are studying a topic which is very specific to another country. In these cases, the problems are not of the distance of the researcher from the library, but the distinct possibility that the library stock will not be comprehensive enough to provide the range of international material which may be needed. Library staff need to work with academic supervisors to alert them to the limitations of library provision before students are accepted for research degrees for which local material is inadequate.

Issues to consider related to distance research include:

- How far away is 'distant'?
- Can researchers based in other countries expect the same level of service as distance researchers in their base country?
- Do distance researchers need different treatment from distance learners? (e.g. loan periods and support)
- How will time differences affect the quality of service?
- Are there language issues which need to be taken into account?
- Can you offer information literacy support?
- Is a virtual research environment being used? Can the library contribute to this?
- Have you built up links with postgraduate supervisors?

4   Special collections and archives

Although digitization increases the possibility of accessing rare resources without travelling long distances, many researchers in arts and humanities have no substitute for seeing and handling primary and secondary source material. Stewardship of collections and enabling access to resources is the central mission of a library, and one that we neglect or undervalue at our peril.

As we have discussed elsewhere, there are very different patterns of information need and use, with science, technology and medical researchers often using journals and preprints as their primary information sources. It is feasible to imagine that research libraries of the future will host print collections supporting the social sciences, arts and humanities, while the majority of scientists' research needs will be satisfied in the electronic environment.

This does not diminish the importance of maintaining these collections. Many libraries, especially well established, traditional research libraries have hidden treasures, donations which may never have been catalogued or promoted to their full potential, or unique titles getting dusty in the stacks. Services like COPAC, enhanced reciprocal access and national support through the RIN mean that we have opportunities to unlock access to these treasures. The quality of the service counts. In the words of our Research Professor of Dance, what he hates are 'claustrophobic, airless special collection rooms where the librarians and security guards treat you like irresponsible children'.

Issues to consider related to special collections and archives include:

- Do you have a space reserved for consultation of rare books?
- Does this space help create the ambience which many scholars enjoy in their library?
- Do you provide specialist equipment to enable the resources to be consulted adequately?
- Would provision of specialist book rests and magnification equipment enhance the use of your rare documents?
- Can you offer in-house scanning/copying services for valuable material?

- Could your archivists offer a specialist advice service on preserving and dealing with old documents?
- Can you publicize the collection through 'treasures' events, posters, bookmarks, etc.?
- Could you hold open days for the general public to view the collections?
- Do you mount regular exhibitions of the materials?
- Can you digitize archive material? It may be possible to obtain funding to digitize nationally recognized archival resources.

5   Subject and specialist support

Our interview sample was of course biased, as all the participants were interested in the topic of the book. Yet to us one of the most surprising elements was the value placed on the contribution of members of library staff, especially subject librarians.

> An efficient librarian/s makes the experience memorable – especially if they go out of their way to source relevant material on one's current research.
>
> (Professor of Tourism and Hospitality, South Africa)

> There is a subject specialist who gives exceptional support.
>
> (Professor of Biology, UK)

We are aware that there has been considerable discussion over the last few years about the role and purpose of subject librarians. Some libraries have moved away from a subject liaison staffing model and introduced staff with a functional focus on learning and teaching or research support. As two of your authors come from a subject librarian background, what we have written is obviously coloured by our own experience and opinions. In this section, we are focusing on library staff – be they subject librarians or research support specialists.

When we started to tease out what was valued by our researchers, it became clear that there were in fact a number of different roles which some library staff fulfilled. These included:

1 *Gatekeeper*   The librarian is someone who filters through key information, highlighting topics and new resources which are of specific value. In order to achieve this role successfully, you must have a reasonable knowledge of the interests of your research community, combined with a commitment to proactive communication.

   To act as an effective gatekeeper, start by getting to know your researchers. If you are new to a post, take some time at the beginning to go out and meet with key people and listen to what they want to say about your library and information service. Ask how they keep up to date with what is happening, and think about whether there are ways you might be able to assist them. Proactive contact and regular, focused communication can be of great value. You will soon learn who values your communication – and will act as a gatekeeper within his or her community of practice, thus giving you access to informal networks.

   Many libraries are using blogs to record new information and developments. This can be a useful approach, but do remember to think about who you are targeting, and whether you are guilty of one of the librarian's cardinal sins: prioritizing the existence of the resource ahead of its value to the user.

2 *Translator*   'I get to know librarians who explain things so that I understand more about the systems they use and have a clearer idea about what is possible and what I can't expect' (Professor of Dance History, UK). Just because the people you are working with spend large amounts of time reading and researching does not mean that they are librarians. Our conventions of bibliographic description and classification may not be immediately logical to others, nor our rules for lending, photocopying and many of our other services. Remember always the principle enshrined in Mooer's Law: 'An information retrieval system will tend not to be used whenever it is more painful and troublesome for a customer to have information than for him not to have it.' We have a professional obligation to try to make our systems easy to use and, failing that, to support people in their use.

3   *Information specialist*   Returning to a discussion of what we see to be our key professional responsibilities, we must remember that the librarian should be an expert at finding information, resources and data. If we deserve to be described as specialist librarians, we should as a minimum be confident users of resources in our specialist areas. We would probably go further to suggest that we must be *expert* users of those resources. Surely unless we have command of our own subject we do not deserve our professional status? Our understanding of the content, scope, structure and idiosyncrasies of the material is a core professional competence. It is also one of the most effective ways of demonstrating our specialist skill set to researchers: 'To find x, use y, but remember that the data is collected in this kind of way . . .' or 'To find x, start here, it's the most effective starting point because. . . .' And of course, this isn't a fixed set of knowledge: you must commit yourself to continuing professional development in this area of your work.

4   *Subject expert*   We are differentiating this from the information specialist role described above, as we suggest it has a rather different focus. The subject expert is someone who may also be an active researcher, and has an academic research background at least equivalent to the people with whom she or he works. The influence of the scholar librarian, in the UK at least, is much diminished, and such librarians are most often found in special collections or the largest research libraries, or working as information scientists in research and development. In many ways our professional focus has shifted from being specialists to more managerial and co-ordinating roles, but we should not neglect some of the valuable elements of this role. At a minimum, we suggest you should try to develop an empathy with your subject and build up your role as an authority on library provision to support it.

5   *'Safe harbour'*   Research lives can be intensely competitive, and the atmosphere in departments is not always comfortable or harmonious. Many of our researchers valued libraries as a haven for study and research and appreciated the impartial friendliness of library staff. Remember to make your researchers feel welcome when they visit or contact you.

6 *'The fount of all knowledge'* This is analogous to the gatekeeper, but rather than being a provider of focused information, the librarian becomes the main interface between researchers and the library service. The information required can of course range from answering questions on how much photocopying costs to advising on the best starting points, special collections and literature searching strategies. Remember that the organizational divisions and role specialization in our workplaces are often invisible to people outside, and that being able to help with what may seem quite mundane queries can be much more valuable than we realize. We have found that being effective and efficient in dealing with what may seem like quite small matters has often been a gateway to getting involved in more significant things.

7 *'A counsel, colleague and critical friend'* We would suggest if you are really effective in your professional practice in supporting research and researchers, you will find that the way you are perceived will shift from being seen as a support assistant to a valued and trusted colleague. For example, if you have proved that you understand journal impact factors and have supported academics in getting material published, you are more likely to be drawn into publishing and research projects yourself.

We are not claiming that these roles are unique to those supporting research: the same principles apply if you are supporting mainly taught provision as well.

Issues to consider related to subject and research support include:

- Are librarians regular members of university/faculty/department research committees?
- Do you offer specific support to university research centres and projects?
- Can you run subject-specific or specialist workshops on resources for research groups?

- Can you organize Personal Library Update sessions (PLUS). These can be popular with older researchers embarrassed about admitting they are falling behind in information skills.
- Is the library embedded in any postgraduate training programmes?
- What approaches do you take in upgrading your professional skills and knowledge?

6   Document delivery and supply

Studies on the information needs of researchers have always emphasized the importance of document supply services, especially to researchers in science, technology and medicine, for whom only a small proportion of the most relevant material may be available in the institution's library.

Document supply services in the UK nationally have reached a steady level after some years of dramatic increase and then decline. The 1990s and the early part of this decade demonstrated the impact of easy access first of all to bibliographic databases and then to electronic journals. LISU statistics illustrate the changed pattern – in 1995–6 5.3% of total HE library budgets were spent on interlibrary loans. This had declined to 2.5% of the budget in 2004–5. This is a 49% decline over ten years (Creaser, Maynard and White, 2006). It seems as if most library and information services have now achieved a balance between what they can provide locally and what can be provided through interlibrary loans.

Additionally, the development of online services like Google Scholar and many electronic journals databases means that individuals have the option to order the full text themselves without recourse to the library's document supply service. This can be particularly appealing if the researcher is able and prepared to pay for immediate access, especially if the institutional document supply service seems unnecessarily obstructive or inefficient. We should also be aware that faster, easier access to a wider range of resources, plus increased pressure on individual productivity, can mean that the researcher has higher expectations and more intense needs, and so he or she is less prepared to wait patiently for a significant article or paper.

Recent developments like Secure Electronic Delivery from the British Library have enabled library services to increase the speed of delivery, with 1–2 day digital delivery of material. However, the PDF version of documents ordered through this route cannot be retained permanently as this would not comply with copyright legislation.

To a researcher this seems illogical: why is it that if you access a journal from one route you can save the full text of the article, yet if you request an article from a similar journal, even from the same publisher, through your document supply service, you are not able to keep an electronic archive? As service providers we understand the network of copyright and licensing agreements that create such a complex environment, but this can be hard to explain to researchers.

This raises another issue: how well does the organization of your document supply services support the needs of researchers? There are several related issues. As a starting point, for librarians and budget holders, unrestricted access to interloans can threaten the capacity to acquire any other material. For the individual researcher, restrictions like quotas appear to be both bureaucratic and arbitrary. Second, how is the quality of your service assured? How responsive is the document supply section in addressing delays and difficulties, and identifying ways of resolving access supply problems by service enhancement or alternative suppliers? Third, how do you monitor what is requested through document supply services: are you sure that you are making cost-effective use of your services?

This last point is important: research interests and needs should be represented in your own collections, and there should be opportunities for researchers to request items for purchase.

Issues to consider related to document delivery include:

- Interlibrary loan services – what do they cost? Who pays?
- Are they limited in any way for researchers? (e.g. 50 requests per year)
- Can users track their requests online?
- Can you offer a direct document delivery service?
- Can postgraduate researchers and contract research staff recommend books for purchase?
- Is there any specialist photocopying provision for researchers in the library?
- Can the library offer scanning services?

7 Access

One of the unexpected findings from our interviews was the number of libraries most of our researchers used regularly. Very few of our interviewees used only one library and information service, and a number used at least two on a regular basis. Several of the humanities researchers talked fondly of 'The Library' meaning the British Library in London, and they were irregular and sometimes reluctant users of their smaller local university libraries.

The libraries they visited were very diverse, and included national libraries, services at their own and other universities, museum and specialist libraries and even public library services. The arts and humanities researchers in particular had travelled widely to use special collections, as did some of the social scientists.

Yet access to libraries beyond your own institution, especially for research students, is perceived to be a matter of concern for policy makers. Is it appropriate that researchers and learners from one institution make extensive use of the resources elsewhere, when budgets are under pressure and institutions are in competition? Surely it is the responsibility of the home institution to make adequate provision for their users, rather than expecting what is in effect a subsidy from other organizations? Our researchers saw the matter differently: they were funded to research and had a right to use other library and information services which also received support from central and local government. There is of course truth on both sides of the argument.

The focus of the discussion has now moved on. As discussed in Chapter 4, the Research Support Libraries Programme had led to a recognition of these issues at a national level, and special funding to support enhanced access. At the time of writing, the Research Information Network (www.rin.ac.uk) was sponsoring a number of programmes to enhance access, which include:

- support for SCONUL (Society of College, National and University Libraries) Research Extra, the largest borrowing scheme for Higher Education researchers in the UK and Ireland

■   a Challenge Fund in conjunction with the Consortium of Research Libraries (CURL), aimed at significantly extending the range of the research material covered by the COPAC union catalogue

■   a study to identify priorities for researchers in cataloguing library holdings that are as yet uncatalogued, and in converting manual catalogues to digital form accessible over the internet (retroconversion)

■   an investigation of researchers' use of academic libraries and their services in order to develop a better understanding of how academic library services are used.

Although physical access and identification of resources have been made easier, those visiting other university libraries can still find the experience frustrating, as more and more material is available only in electronic form to registered users. Of course, with document supply services and the extensive range of secondary sources, this should not be problematic, but it can still be frustrating.

Access to the British Library has also been made more permissive, so that anyone may register to use the reading rooms, although this has caused some dissatisfaction (Hunt, 2006).

Issues to consider related to access include:

■   Who is allowed access to your collection?
■   Do you charge external users?
■   Do you promote it to the local community?
■   What about licence agreements for electronic resources?
■   Are there any local/national access agreements from which researchers can benefit (e.g. SRX) and do you promote them?
■   Can external users access e-resources?

8   General research support

In addition to the subject specialist support we have discussed above, there are other forms of specialist advice. At Newcastle, one of the aims of the ResIN project was to bring together best practice in research support from other libraries with the current practice locally. The result was a list of possible services in support of research.

The area of greatest potential was the provision of support in use of reference management programs like ProCite, EndNote and RefWorks. These databases enable researchers to construct databases of references with the full text, images and data, and to incorporate references, correctly cited, into documents. The database of references – or library – can be constructed by the researcher inputting the references individually or by importing references from bibliographic databases.

As this brief description suggests, these are complex programs, and users require training, support and advice, often provided by university library and information services via workshops, individual appointments, e-mail and phone help. In some organizations this is the responsibility of a designated post, in others, all liaison staff incorporate it into their work. Library staff tend to focus on the software features of most interest to them – how to populate the libraries with the results of searches from library-purchased databases. Researchers may be interested in other aspects, in particular, using the programs in conjunction with word-processing software for the production of articles and constructing different output formats for specific journals or publishers. In our experience, library and information services staff are often less comfortable with this stage of the research process: construction rather than production is our comfort zone. It may be helpful, therefore, to find ways of facilitating the establishment of a community of practice, so researchers can share their experience of using these programs in a variety of ways.

The second area of general research support is the provision of regular newsletters or bulletins for research staff, perhaps including announcements of new journal subscriptions, free resources, spotlight on existing resources, tips for using resources and more. Harrison and Hughes (2001) reported that at Manchester Metropolitan University (MMU) this activity was well received by the research staff. Library staff at MMU also alerted researchers to calls for journal articles and conference papers, a very proactive approach which has interesting parallels with the mediated current awareness services and online searches of previous decades. The communication may not necessarily be in the form of a newsletter, for many libraries are using wikis and blogs to make know-how and new information available to researchers. The critical issue though is whether these are sufficiently proactive forms of communication: it might be helpful for instance to ensure that you have enabled RSS feeds to push out new content.

Issues to consider related to general research support include:

- How do you evaluate the quality of your services in support of research?
- Have you established dedicated services and/or roles in support of research and researchers?
- Do you support reference management software?
- Do you publish a newsletter, wiki or blog with content relevant for researchers?
- Is research integrated into your departmental mission?

9   The service as a whole

Finally it is important to remember that researchers are users of our library service: they borrow books, access electronic resources, study in our buildings and use our photocopying and printing services. As we have discussed before, although we may focus on researchers when we make our collection management decisions, do we sometimes forget that they are active users of many other aspects of the service? And do we really want to find out that their strongest impressions of libraries are what some of our researchers said:

> I'm a bit uncomfortable in libraries – I was told my pencil case was too noisy and later got caught eating a sweet and was asked for my card (same bloke but two years later!)   (Marketing lecturer, UK)

> The thing I really dislike about libraries is other users, especially noisy ones. I also hate the lack of flexibility you find in services – when staff refuse to do something even though it's entirely possible. That kind of petty-minded adherence to rules

for no other sake than 'rules is rules' is really frustrating.

(Part-time research student, UK)

When I was a PhD student . . . I had problems finding a book and said to one of the librarians, 'If you had your way you lot would not let any books go out' and she said, 'Yes, exactly!' (Professor of Biology, UK)

Achieving an appropriate balance between the needs of different groups of users may not be easy, but it is an obligation.

Conclusion

Although researchers can – and do – use a full range of services that the library provides for the benefit of all its users, it is valuable to identify and promote those activities that are of particular use to the research community. It is the responsibility of librarians to facilitate research activity by ensuring that researchers can access efficient and effective library services. One of the best ways to do this is to become an accepted part of your local research community, an active participant in the research process. Perhaps an unfamiliar skill for librarians is that of marketing, but, in essence, this is what we need to do: to be able to 'sell' the concept of the 21st-century library to the researchers of the 21st century.

7

The information-literate researcher

Introduction

In the first part of this book we explored the diversity of scholars' information-seeking behaviours and academic cultures, concluding that effective library services for researchers must be based on the principle of understanding the multiplicity and complexity of user needs. And, following on from the previous chapter, it is important for libraries and librarians to provide an array of support activities so that researchers develop their information fluency. We will now move away from the range of informal 'library' services already discussed to a more detailed account of the ways that libraries and information services can create training and staff development opportunities for researchers at every career stage.

Starting to teach

However advanced your audience, remember that you are designing learning and teaching opportunities, and you need to approach the design, delivery and evaluation of these activities professionally. If you are new to this role, we strongly suggest that before starting out you find some time for personal learning and development. This may in the form of attending courses on how to teach, mentoring from a colleague, or guided reading. Our starting point for the development of learning and teaching activities are the principles discussed in Webb and Powis (2004), summarized very briefly below:

1   Audit the needs of your learners and be clear about the context in which you will place your learning and teaching.
2   Be conscious of the learning and teaching preferences of your students. It may be helpful to consider any cross-cultural issues raised by working with international staff and researchers.
3   Plan your learning and teaching activities based on what you have found out about the needs and wants of your learners, combined with your own understanding of the information environment.
4   Choose appropriate delivery techniques suited for the needs of your learners, resources available (time, information, technology) and your preferences as a teacher and designer of learning opportunities.
5   Use formative and/or summative assessment to ensure that the learning outcomes have been met.[1]
6   Evaluate the effectiveness of what you have done and modify and enhance your practice for the future.

We do not claim to offer sure-fire recipes for success, but instead a mixture of theory, discussion, experience and a few suggestions which might help to illuminate your own situation. Remember that your circumstances and resources will be different, and you should decide for yourselves what will be the best approach.

Researchers' training needs

In preparing this book we asked researchers for their views on the value of formal training:

> You're not going to be very good if you're not curious and patient. Those are attributes that you are unlikely to learn in any class.
>
> (Professor of Mass Communication, USA)

We have a research methodology course but the danger is that students having taken it think they can now do research. The only way to ride a bicycle is to do it not by theoretical workshops.

> (Health Sciences researcher, South Africa)

I don't think I was a good researcher for my PhD. You need to have a mentor – to show you the ropes and pitfalls. You can train for some things but best is to work alongside someone successful and learn from them.

> (Dean of Research, UK)

Yes, training would be useful though I don't have to attend any of it.

> (Part-time PhD student, UK)

I have always felt a content management approach for my research would be a really useful personal resource, but the technologies have not enabled easy development, and I've not had the time to devote to it. . . . Given the developments in online resources I think keeping up to date with what's available and how to get to it is particularly useful, but again, I've not dedicated much personal time to development in this area.

> (Marketing lecturer, UK)

The research techniques that I employ I arrived at deductively – I had no formal training, but later in my career I did find that my technical skills were falling behind – my coalface skills were being diminished and I didn't like that. I like to do my own stuff so I did a lot of training – some was good and some was bad and I still sign up for training. I may not benefit immediately but I will usually pick up something useful.

> (Professor of Marine Transport and Economics, UK)

So, what were we able to conclude from the interviews? Generally, there was measured support from researchers themselves for the provision of training and development opportunities, coupled with the enthusiasm for using libraries and information services which we have already discussed. And of course, they may have no option, as increasing amounts of mandatory training have been introduced as noted in Chapter 3. So there is evidence that library-based training is wanted, needed and even welcomed. Therefore, in principle, it should be easy to develop training opportunities for researchers. In practice it is not always so easy, especially in terms of getting the timing right.

Information literacy: key areas of knowledge

The literature search we undertook established what is already known about researchers' information-seeking behaviour. Our findings indicate that the training we provide must be designed around the needs of individuals and framed by an understanding of the structure of knowledge in their discipline(s), and the impact this has on their use of published information.

The best overview of training doctoral research students (and by extension their supervisors) appears in Barry (1997). Her principal argument was that the internet had changed the previously finite process of searching a clearly defined collection (and series of secondary sources) into the almost infinite task of sifting through the ever-changing resources available on the internet; and that in order to ensure effective literature searching and information use librarians should work with users – academics who can pass on these skills in a subject context – and develop self-help tools. She concluded that supervisors had the most important role in influencing student searching behaviour but found in the Information Access project at King's College London working with maths and educational studies supervisors that they had quite limited search skills. Her research subjects used only single keywords and did not display flexibility or tenacity in the interrogation of databases.

She also produced a detailed taxonomy of 'information skills required in an electronic information world' (Barry, 1997, 226), which translated a pre-existing taxonomy (from Marland, 1981) into terms more appropriate for using electronic information sources. Table 7.1 provides a summary of some her points.

The context in which Barry's work was written – that of the early days of internet use – means that some of the issues and difficulties identified have now been superseded. There are several very interesting points of continuing value:

- establishing links with supervisors – training the trainers
- browsing and searching – and how to achieve a balance between them
- information literacy across different forms of media.

Table 7.1   Basic and electronic information skills

Basic information skills	Electronic world information skills
Formulate and analyse need	Define information need to fit information retrieval requirements Focus questions to enhance precision
Identify likely sources	Understand range of IT systems Use browsing alongside traditional retrieval techniques
Local individual resource	Knowledge of how to access
Examine, select and reject sources	Need to apply range of information science techniques – broadening and narrowing, Boolean logic, etc.
Interrogate sources	Internet navigation skills Reading hypertext
Record and store information	Translation of information across interfaces from search system to personal bibliography
Interpret, analyse, synthesize and evaluate information collected	Awareness of how to make quality assessments for material outside the peer review process
Present and communicate resulting work	Web page development skills Use of electronic communication for dissemination
Evaluate what has been achieved.	Use of discussion lists

Adapted from Barry, 1997, 226

One of the strongest themes that emerged from our discussions with real-life researchers was that the ways they find and use information change during their career – but not in the same way for everyone.

> I hardly ever use databases, probably because I'm not usually starting from a position of knowing nothing. At my stage of life, you always tend to know a bit about the subject already. I tend to start with a few key papers from people I know are the eminent writers and then follow up their references. I suppose I

might use that database that lets you see who has cited a paper and follow the
research up to date that way too.   (Senior Lecturer in Biology, UK)

I used to be quite focused in my approach to finding mainstream resources, now
I'm less so, more explorative, I guess looking for inspiration to my more
mainstream ideas. I talk to a lot of people about things they are doing, so know
what to look out for in my areas also. Possibly because I work more with
colleagues now, I tend to engage in a conversation with someone to find
something out before I go into a library – I share and borrow books from other
people and exchange articles more as a result.

(Senior Research Fellow in Creative Technologies, UK)

I have not been able to browse serendipitously in libraries since I left Oxford and
Berkeley, both of which had comprehensive national collections. I have therefore
always used e-sources for my physico-chemical and materials science work. Initially
I used some of the Chemical Abstracts spin offs (and indeed was a member and
later chair of the RSC Users Group for secondary services), using CA Selects and
also ISI individual profiles – my industrial research grants used to pay for these.
These days, my articles are all invited plenaries and similar tertiary reviews so I go
into Athens and then ISI Web of Science under its new name and then search by
topic and then by cited author.   (Dean of Research, retired, UK)

Motivation

In our experience research students and staff can be some of the most
challenging – but also the most rewarding – individuals to work with in a
learning and teaching context. We suggest that these may be some of the
reasons:

1 *'Know it already'*   Some of the people you will work with have been
   highly successful learners, so why do they need any training from
   some librarian? If you have just graduated with a very good
   qualification, be it a first degree, master's or doctorate, surely you
   already know everything there is to know . . .? (And sometimes they
   have a point.)

2 *'Tell me more, and more . . .'* The opposite of the previous group: sometimes people want to know everything in great detail. In a group situation this can be disruptive, because you can risk going beyond the interests or understanding of other participants.

3 *'My hidden agenda'* Researchers are often confident, articulate and passionate about their work. This can translate into very strong special interests. Examples from within our own experience include the whole of a workshop series being hijacked by someone who had problems obtaining materials as none of it was accessible via inter-library loan (mainly unpublished or commercially sensitive reports not in the public domain); individuals with a very strong personal identification to their research area and who get very emotional about their work; and people who are bringing other baggage to the class (problems with research topic or supervisor for example).

So how can you address these three challenging areas? We have already indicated that developing your practice in learning and teaching is a good starting point. More specifically if you are working with researchers you might wish to think about what the concept of andragogy means to the way that you will design your learning activities and the way you will relate to the group.

Andragogy: a brief introduction

Andragogy is a term that defines a separate science of teaching adults (using the Greek word *andros*, meaning a man) as opposed to pedagogy (the art, occupation or practice of teaching – which has the Greek for child *pais/paid* in its word stem). In his work Malcolm Knowles developed andragogy into a theory of adult education (see Knowles, 1978, for an introduction).

Andragogy, according to Knowles, is based on a number of assumptions:

1 The need to know – adult learners need to know why they need to learn something before undertaking to learn it.

2   Learner self-concept – adults need to be responsible for their own decisions and to be treated as capable of self-direction.

3   Role of learners' experience – adult learners have a variety of experiences of life which represent the richest resource for learning. These experiences are however imbued with bias and presupposition.

4   Readiness to learn – adults are ready to learn those things they need to know in order to cope effectively with life situations.

5   Orientation to learning – adults are motivated to learn to the extent that they perceive that it will help them perform tasks they confront in their life situations.

Taken from Atherton (2005) and based on Knowles (1990, 57).

Knowles' theory of andragogy is an attempt to develop a theory specifically for adult learning. Knowles emphasizes that adults are self-directed and expect to take responsibility for decisions. Therefore if you are working with adults you need to recognize their experience and motivation. In practical terms, it is suggested that instruction for adults needs to focus more on the process and less on the content being taught. Strategies such as case studies, role playing, simulations and self-evaluation are most useful. Instructors adopt a role of facilitator or resource rather than lecturer.

There are many critiques of the value of Knowles' theories – discussed very effectively on James Atherton's excellent website – but nevertheless we suggest that the key principles are of great value when working with researchers. If you acknowledge what your learners are bringing to the session, make your content relevant to their problems and act as a facilitator rather than distant teacher, you are likely to create effective learning and teaching opportunities, engaging in that essential dialogue with the research community.

Training and development opportunities

One of the most interesting strands to emerge from our interviews was that many of the most experienced researchers were also most aware of their continuing need to learn and develop: 'I now recognize and boast about how little I know as opposed to claiming how much I think I know' (Mid-career researcher, Business School, UK).

We have identified the following opportunities to provide training and development:

Induction (or orientation)

Introductions to the library and information services for new staff or students are invaluable for individual researchers and for the library service, research unit and more widely within the institution. First impressions count! In earlier chapters we have provided you with anecdotal accounts of the importance placed by researchers on effective links with libraries and librarians, and equally we have gained great professional satisfaction from establishing cordial and rewarding relationships with staff and students.

Remember that researchers and research students are an international labour force, and many of those joining your institution may not have studied or worked at a UK institution before. They may therefore be unfamiliar with UK protocols for obtaining interlibrary loans, reciprocal access arrangements and password management.

Wherever they have worked or lived before, there are other areas which may be different. These include:

1   The change in status (from being a taught student) and the consequent impact on entitlements and loan periods.
2   The availability of special collections and resources from or via the local library.
3   Different arrangements for access. This can be an important issue for contract researchers, clinical researchers and those working at a distance from the institution.
4   The extent of support (both in terms of help and resources). This can range from procedures for photocopying and printing (and whether research students are subsidized) to software assistance and literature searching advice.

It is worth asking a few questions to find out whether any of the people you are meeting have used your library before. In our experience many library and information services fail to check whether the new researchers and research students are new to the organization. In a group you are likely to encounter people who have progressed from previous study and research at your institution, others who have moved from another institution and yet another group for whom much will be very unfamiliar, perhaps because they are returning to study or in a different country. We suggest it can be helpful to encourage students to share experiences with each other, as discussed earlier.

There are often formal induction events arranged for new MPhil/PhD students, perhaps just at the beginning of the year, sometimes more often. Try to ensure that an LIS element is incorporated in the programme. New members of staff (either contract research or academic) may have structured inductions, which include an introduction to the library and information service, but this is often a much more haphazard process, with the introduction to the library including little more than registering for a library card and passwords.

Library and information services should take a proactive approach in identifying opportunities for getting involved in orientation and induction. It may be helpful to contact the university (or faculty or school) research office to see if there are introductory sessions for new students (and then get involved with them), or if details of new student registrations can be sent on to a suitable library contact. At De Montfort University, for example, details of all new research degree students are sent to a named person in the library, who passes the information on to the subject librarian who then gets in touch with them. This personal introduction complements the mandatory formal induction session which may not be at the very beginning of their studies. (For further explanation see the case study on page 164.)

Finding out about new members of staff also requires use of formal and informal systems. Formal systems may include information from the University's Human Resources department (which will run the institution's HR database of all employees). How widely this information is made accessible will vary, but most new staff will want to obtain library cards, so perhaps one of the keys is to find ways of linking the issue of library cards to personal introductions to subject or research support library staff.

Being involved in informal academic networks can often be the most efficient way of finding out about new people. If the induction provided is deemed to be valuable, a session with the library contact will become a fixture in an organized induction, or you will be able to get in touch with the new person and arrange a meeting.

Research training courses for students

The intensity of literature searching requirements for postgraduate research students is generally very different from the kind of academic study they have previously encountered. This requirement – to search and read intensively and extensively – is a key part of the initiation into research culture and practice. The challenge for library and information services is therefore to create experiences and opportunities which enable students to build and extend their knowledge and skills.

This shift in understanding occurs to a large extent through practical experience at every stage of the research process, although the need is most pressing at the beginning of the research degree.

> I reckon I spent nearly all my first year reading journal articles. I would search Science Direct, print one out, read it, make notes and move on to the next one. I averaged about ten articles a day. I didn't realize my first year would be mainly reading.
>
> (Final year PhD student in Computing Sciences, UK)

Training and instruction courses for research students have been provided for very many years, as discussed previously. As suggested by Barry (1997) the focus of many of these courses has been on the development of a generic set of literature searching skills. This is illustrated by the results of an informal survey of LIS training for research students across the UK in 2006, which identified these common elements in their training:

- using interlibrary loans
- access to other libraries
- password management
- searching electronic journals and databases
- tracing conference papers
- support for bibliographic software.

Although many of the elements are common there is strong variation in how the training is delivered. Library input can vary from a single lecture or workshop to a series of short sessions or courses delivered online. The courses may be organized centrally, at a faculty or school level, or by specific research groups.

Case study 7.1   The Research Training Programme at De Montfort University

A central university research student training programme (RTP) was established at De Montfort University in 1997, in conjunction with an increased role for the central university research office. At this stage the training was a mixture of compulsory and optional elements, with an assessed element. Library input appeared in four stages: a talk during the residential induction, a session on literature searching, another on referencing and a third on using the internet. Attendance at the library workshops was mandatory for all students, irrespective of how many years the students had been registered. As there were over 800 research students at that time, classes could be large and levels of student engagement could be fairly unpredictable.

Over the years the RTP has been evaluated and revised. Rather than a residential induction, there is now a half-day session with informal opportunities to meet with other research students. Faculties have developed their own subject–based research training, so students complete some mandatory, centrally provided courses and some faculty-based training in conjunction with some optional courses, for example on creating large and complex documents using Word.

Since 2001, the library input has standardized into a one-day course,

'Literature searching and reference management', which is run about five times a year for a maximum of 12 students. There are in fact two versions of the course: one for computing, engineering and science students and the other for research students from art and design, humanities and social sciences. The reason for the division is quite simple: as we have discussed elsewhere, disciplines have differing requirements from library and information services. Although student numbers outside computing sciences and engineering are not sufficiently high to run a course for students in single research groups, dividing the arts, humanities and social scientists from the scientific, technical and medical (STM) researchers is at least a starting point. From experience the principal difference is that for social science, humanities and arts researchers one of the key issues in developing their literature search is scoping the topic and its boundaries, refining their research questions and defining the nature of their research. By comparison, STM researchers tend to have more clearly identified topics, so some of the soul-searching that the former group discuss in their session is alien to the latter. This is not an exclusive distinction, especially for some computing students who draw much social science theory into their work.

The course is divided into two parts: a morning session on literature searching followed after lunch by an introduction to using the EndNote reference management program. Within this general framework, content is dynamic, changing in response to student feedback, the needs of specific groups and tutor evaluation.

The learning outcomes are that by the end of the day participants should have:

- reviewed and reflected on any practical issues relating to the process of literature searching
- identified how to search and access databases and other key sources in their subject area(s)
- used and evaluated general sources for research (including theses databases)
- registered for at least one current awareness service
- been introduced to some of the basic functions of EndNote

- explored the use of import filters and connection files
- found out how to get further help in using endnote
- received details of how to obtain their own copy of EndNote.

Teaching and learning methods are a mixture of lecture, group work and individual work on the computers. At least one librarian is available throughout the class, and sometimes the course is team-taught with more than one subject librarian contributing to the day. There are handouts of the slides and an EndNote workbook.

Following university guidelines for inclusive practice in learning and teaching, all handouts are printed on cream paper using a 12 point minimum sans serif font. It has also been helpful to offer the PowerPoint handouts in a choice of formats – usually either three up (small images with space for notes by the side) or two up (larger slides which are often easier for people to use for mind mapping).

The structure tends to follow a standard pattern:

10.00	Introduction
10.15	Literature searching
10.45	Literature searching practical
11.30	Tracing conference papers and theses
12.00	Google Scholar and Open Access
12.30	Current awareness
1.00	Lunch
1.45	EndNote
4.00	Close

Timings at the beginning of the day are fairly relaxed to allow for later arrivals. Many research students are part-time and can encounter problems in reaching Leicester for 10 a.m., and often full-time students have other commitments. When most of the attendees have arrived, the first exercise begins: a group discussion activity (and latecomers can just slot in).

Participants are asked to work in groups of three to five people, and share their responses to the following queries:

- who they are
- what is their research topic/question
- what stage they are at with their research
- what progress they have made with their literature review
- whether they have any specific questions or queries to cover during the course.

After ten minutes' discussion, there is then a brief feedback session to the session leader.

Immediately after this activity, it is clear how the class dynamics have changed. Participants are much more forthcoming about their research, offering suggestions to other learners and posing questions (and challenges) about library and information use. The exercise also serves to shift the day from being a tutor-led programme into a much more conversational event, enabling collaborative working and a constructive dialogue to emerge.

The morning part of the course follows a fairly standard format: there are discussions about the nature of literature searching (usually developing issues already raised in the introductory exercise), brief mention of key housekeeping issues (including how to use interlibrary loans, access to other libraries, sorting out passwords) and then hands-on use of a range of information resources and services. The range of resources is predictable (and we have already discussed many of these in Chapter 5): tools to find books, journals, theses, conference papers and semi-published information, including how to search subject and institutional repositories. From experience 'generic' resources are usually the novel ones. Research students are often familiar with the key databases and gateways in their subject areas, but they may not have encountered some of the more general services, like COPAC, ZETOC, sources for theses or multidisciplinary bibliographic and full-text databases outside their immediate disciplinary domain.

The training course does not aim to be merely an opportunity for social interaction and a chance to use some different resources. To have value, the day must be educational, i.e. it should help to develop knowledge and understanding, and to achieve this in a way that provides more benefit for the learner than a (possibly shorter and focused) one-to-one session with a subject librarian. The structure of the morning, which is designed around the logical development of a literature search, also provides opportunities for reflection and review of both content and process in literature searching. So by the end of the morning participants should have developed a clearer understanding of the structure of academic knowledge within their area, had opportunities to think about how they prefer to find and use information (and be conscious of an array of different techniques for searching and retrieving) and more actively engaged with issues relating to how scholarly knowledge is disseminated and communicated. They will also have had opportunities to put what they have learnt into practice through plenty of hands-on access and individual support if required.

The second part of the course, after lunch, is an introduction to using EndNote for reference management, with emphasis on building an EndNote library by searching databases and downloading references.

Student evaluation is in general very positive:

I would like to thank [the trainer] for the useful and informative talk. I just came to tick the box, but found out it was a very good and useful training course.

Very interesting and practical.

Really well put together . . . a must for research students.

Participants described the key benefits as increased knowledge, confidence and skills. Many of them found that the mixture of theory and practice was well balanced, providing opportunities for active learning and reflection.

As always when discussing research and research support, it is important not to oversimplify either the complexity of the relationships which researchers have with finding and using information, nor to misunderstand the expertise of these groups. For example, just because research students have had prior (and one would assume, successful) experience of higher education, it is not guaranteed that they will have done extensive library-based research previously, certainly not to the extent required for formal academic research, so you need to plan any training or development activities very sensitively, conscious that you may need to advise people at one moment on advanced information retrieval and at the next to explain what an interlibrary loan is.

The course could always be better. There are always questions about whether or not the timing is appropriate as students may register for their course at different times of the year. Attendance is often part of the required training for MPhil students before transfer to PhD but people may not book on to it early enough, so as a training opportunity it is often too late to support people who have already completed the main part of their literature review. Not all students will use EndNote, with many computing and engineering researchers preferring to use BibTeX (the reference management software associated with the LaTeX document preparation system). Sometimes it is clear that participants are already very sophisticated library and information users, so the day brings little added value to them. On the other hand, unlike other elements of research training, its full-day mode means it is easier for part-time students to attend than a series of two-hour workshops, and its concentrated nature means it can be easier to shape the day around the needs and interests of the students present.

There are plans for short-term developments, based around developing a supporting site on Blackboard, aimed at 'six-week rule' students (who only attend the university in person for six weeks a year), making available more resources for supporting the use of reference management software and a course on use of Web 2.0 applications.

The model of a one-day course is very intensive for students and teacher alike, and it is not a cheap way of delivering training, as the tutors tend to be senior librarians. All the evaluations of the programme by the Research Office and Library Service have concluded that the course is both popular and effective. And for the trainer?

Speaking personally, this course is the one which I enjoy teaching most of all. I love the opportunity to work closely with a small group of enthusiastic learners, and I find the course a genuinely developmental opportunity for me: helping people actively research, finding out about sources and services and really getting into a dialogue about the value of libraries and our services has influenced my working life and philosophy profoundly.'

As we stated in the introduction, we are not providing simple recipes for you to follow. The next case study illustrates a similar, yet very different, programme.

Case study 7.2   The SAgE PG research programme at Newcastle University

At Newcastle University, a more research-intensive university than De Montfort, there are higher numbers of research students. At this university, rather than having programmes organized centrally, content is determined by individual faculties. In practice, the library-based courses follow a very similar format although the arts and humanities course has assessed coursework which is marked by library staff.

Before 2005 attendance was voluntary and there was limited promotion of the course by the faculty, with the consequent negative impact on attendance. More recently the programme is listed in detail in the postgraduate handbook and clear instructions are provided about which sessions are compulsory and how to register for them.

The postgraduates get credit for attending sessions, which has led to much higher attendance. Feedback has been very positive, with requests to rerun sessions from students who had enrolled late and been told about them. As part of a continuing review of course effectiveness, sessions have been subdivided into specific subjects to make the content as relevant as possible.

The programme consists of:

- three compulsory sessions repeated over the course of three weeks; participants can choose which day they attend
- four optional sessions (sessions 4–7), each of which is run once.

Each class lasts between two and three hours. Content is as follows:

Session 1 So now you're a researcher? How can the library help? (2 hours)

This introductory session provides an introduction to literature searching and literature reviews, how to find other theses, how to identify where your research fits into the bigger picture, plus an excursion into ways of avoiding plagiarism and maintaining your academic integrity. This is followed by an optional tour of the library and an introduction to library facilities, aimed at students new to the University.

Session 2 Finding and managing information (3 hours)

This is the most subject-specific session, with three different variations: engineering, computing and natural sciences. The focus of the workshop is how to use library resources to find information on a topic and includes e-journals, databases, conference papers, standards and other material as relevant depending on the subject. It also incorporates using EndNote for reference management.

Session 3 The academic internet and keeping up to date (3 hours)

The final compulsory session looks at going beyond Google and using the internet for academic research. It includes ways of using technology for current awareness, including RSS, blogs, etc.

The mandatory elements in the programme are complemented by optional sessions led by expert speakers on specialist topics including:

Sessions 4–7

4   Using SciFinder (for chemistry and chemistry-related subjects). SciFinder Scholar is a chemistry database, based on Chemical Abstracts. It allows structure and reaction searching as well as bibliographic searching. This is an essential resource in chemistry and related areas.

5   Statistical and Data Sources. This session looks at the wide range of statistical and data sources that are available, including government resources, the UK Data Archive, economic time series data, population data.

6   Government Publications and Digimap. This session covers how to find and use printed Parliamentary Papers and statistical sources; using electronic resources to find government publications; databases; how to access full-text government publications, including Parliamentary Publications on the web; and an introduction to Digimap, a service providing online Ordnance Survey Map Data to UK Higher Education.

7   Patents Information, including intellectual property.

The library runs a very similar series of sessions for contract research staff but attendance at these is voluntary. The programme for CRS is again organized centrally by faculty staff via dedicated web pages for contract researchers so publicity is effective. Because of the range of interests these have been run as multidisciplinary training events with librarians from all faculties in attendance to pick up specific queries, and they have proved similarly successful.

Training in using specific resources and programs

Another established form of training and development activity is the provision of topical and relevant courses aimed at staff and research students. In some institutions where there is less centralized control over the research training, open courses offered by the library are the main form of information skills training. As attendance is not a requirement of a training programme it can be harder to target users and to market the events. Many institutions have been most successful in providing this training when it is linked into new developments for which there is a general need for more information and training, for example the provision of reference management software like Procite, EndNote or Reference Manager. Other successful topics have included using Google Scholar, current awareness using ZETOC and the launch of the SCOPUS service.

If you are thinking about developing this kind of training programme, consider carefully the kinds of training activities you are going to develop. These are some of the issues you might wish to consider first of all:

1   Who will the training be aimed at? Are you targeting a specific group of researchers?
2   What benefits will the training bring? Remember you are not training librarians; participants will want some tangible benefit to take away that is usually more substantial than knowing how to use another bibliographic database. You have to demonstrate that this new resource has a special value.
3   Is this a one-off event, part of a series (for which prior knowledge will be assumed) or something that you will repeat several times?
4   How does this fit into the overall design of the library service? It can be a risk to promote resources and tools which are unavailable or where insufficient support is available.
5   Is it the right time to do this? Timing is crucial, not just in the sense of running courses when people are able to attend but also because you can derive maximum benefit from offering training when something is new, and refreshing what you offer when people are more familiar with the resource.
6   Can you extend access to part-time students and distant researchers? Remember that researchers are busy, often with many other commitments, and you may need to think creatively about outreach to more isolated groups.

E-learning

E-learning (or e-teaching) is not a single technologically mediated experience. There are different kinds of e-learning opportunities, ranging from a standalone tutorial on how to use reference management software, content delivery via a virtual learning environment or the interactive experience of online teaching and conferencing. Salmon (2000) defines a five-part model of e-learning, which describes the stages which a learner may go through:

■   access and motivation
■   online socialization
■   information exchange

■ knowledge construction
■ development.

This is a helpful description of the experiences on a rich, interactive e-learning course, and we suggest that you use it as a simple checklist in the development of any significant e-learning projects.

Think carefully about the context in which you are planning to deliver the e-learning. Will it be:

■ campus-based blended learning, i.e. developed to be run in conjunction with other training and development work?
■ campus-based e-only, so it is a standalone e-learning programme?
■ off-campus blended learning – not all the learning and teaching happens online – possibly in the form of traditional postal distance learning materials?
■ off-campus e-only, where all materials, learning and linked assessment are delivered online?

E-learning offers many opportunities not offered by conventional course delivery, which include:

1 *Time*   Learning opportunities can be synchronous, where the learning event happens in real time, like an online chat or videoconferencing session, or they can be asynchronous, when communication is not intended to be 'live' and people can participate irrespective of physical location or time zone. This time-shifted contact can be offered in many forms, from discussion-board postings to podcasts.
2 *Building groups and reaching individuals*   One of the most significant reasons for non-completion of postgraduate study is isolation (Rudd, 1985). You can enhance the development of communities and networks and reduce the isolation through technology: e-mail and online discussion fora are obvious examples.
3 *Delivery of content*   One of the challenges when working with researchers is knowing how much detail to provide, especially when

people have very specific needs. If you develop web pages that contain that detail – lists of current awareness services or how to trace theses for example – you have supporting materials for your teaching and useful resources for independent learning. There are also opportunities to create collaborative resources, for example using wikis or blogs to support a research project.

Training and support for academic staff and contract researchers

Established researchers are a much more complicated group to work with than students at the beginning of their academic careers. Most staff researchers have been appointed after successfully completing at least one major piece of original scholarship, normally in the form of a doctoral thesis, but sometimes a substantial amount of other work too. It could be assumed, therefore, that they are people who have already achieved mastery of their subject and are conversant with the range of resources and tools necessary to operate at the leading edge of their field.

Sweeping generalizations, as we have stated elsewhere, are rather dangerous. This is another instance where it can be helpful to unpick the truth from your assumptions. You might need to find out about what use your researchers make of libraries and information services. This can be very illuminating, for you will probably discover a huge diversity of experience. Some academics will be expert and proactive library users, travelling to visit libraries and special collections, with exact and accurate understanding of how to find and trace information in their specific field and in other areas as well. Others, by no means inferior scholars, may not do this to the same extent. Often researchers use a variety of ways to search for information, relying extensively on colleagues, their research teams and academic networks to identify new material in their fields.

> If I couldn't find it myself on the internet, then I'd ask my students first, my RAs [research assistants], then I'd come to the library. The RAs live and die finding info.
>
> (Dean of Research, UK)

Yet, it is possible and probable that both academic staff and researchers may still welcome the chance to extend their knowledge in a number of ways. Opportunities for training include:

1   *Tracing information in other disciplines*   Some subjects – cultural studies for example – are interdisciplinary and multidisciplinary. Many academics move into cultural studies from another field and may not be immediately conscious of the range of secondary sources that might be relevant. Whether this is an appropriate topic for a course rather than a one-to-one session depends to some extent on the nature of the need – if a research group is moving into a new field it might just be possible to arrange a course. Otherwise this should be an informal training or coaching activity.

2   *Impact factors, citation counts, metrics and other measures of esteem*   As we will discuss in the next chapter, it is crucial that library and information professionals are aware of the structure of knowledge in the disciplines they are supporting. One of our key contributions to supporting the research process should be expertise in identifying key indicators of how scholarly knowledge is communicated. A session on this topic could cover a range of different topics, ranging from comparisons of citation counts on Scopus and Web of Knowledge, the free Citeseer service, how to trace journal rankings and even an introduction to some of the principles of bibliometrics.

3   *Support with reference management software*   The introduction of reference management software or software upgrades offers a valuable opportunity to run structured training and development events for groups of academic staff and researchers. Most LIS professionals focus on how to use the software programs to construct bibliographies, focusing on how to link the reference management package to preferred databases. There are opportunities to go further than this, offering advanced sessions on academic writing and reference management software and advanced applications of the programs.

4   *Advanced searching and retrieval*   Many academics and researchers are confident searchers, although many will not have received formal training. If you have opportunities to work with research groups or

departments, it might be valuable to see whether there is any scope in running a session on advanced internet searching, covering advanced features of Google, plus other search engines (and perhaps a bit about 'library' sources thrown in). For this kind of training, perhaps more than any other, do try and find out about the knowledge levels of your participants and set the level appropriately. Remember as well that researchers will probably be interested in ways of enhancing the quality of their own metadata. Incorporating some content about precision and recall in information systems, information-seeking behaviours and ways of improving your indexing are likely to be of interest.

5   *Online archives and repositories*   If you are running an institutional repository, try to find opportunities to train people in how to find material available in open access archives and repositories – and then how to self-archive their own materials.

6   *Web 2.0 and personal information management*   Library and information professionals tend to focus their training on the use of published academic sources. Yet if we reflect on the ways in which we ourselves find and use information, other sources – e-mails, websites, blogs, RSS feeds, aggregators and so on – are often at least as important in our information universe. We suggest that there are really significant opportunities to offer introductory courses on using social software and other applications for managing research information. Content could range from an overview of the range of tools available to more targeted accounts of how to enhance your effectiveness at tagging and archiving your research on the web.

7   *Training the supervisors*   Try to get involved with any training for research supervisors. As well as being active researchers in their own right, they are the most important source of information to students.

Case Study 7.3   Working with supervisors in Northampton

For a number of years the academic librarians at the University of Northampton have run a half day course for research supervisors which is similar to the training course offered to new research students.

The rationale for the workshop is that supervisors have the most important relationship with research students, and so are the main source of information, advice and support for all aspects of doctoral research including the development of information skills (see also Barry, 1997, 234). It is important therefore that the supervisors are aware of what sources their students need to use – which are often what they themselves use (as mentioned previously).

The session covers the following:

- introduction to the session (with introductions, aims, objectives and learning outcomes)
- a review of generic search tools (including ZETOC, Web of Knowledge, the British Library catalogue and COPAC)
- access arrangements (including use of the British Library, SCONUL Research Extra, identifying special collection and interlibrary loan procedures)
- academic material on the web, particularly Intute (formerly known as the RDN)
- using Google and Google Scholar
- general questions and answers.

So supervisors have the same briefing as their students, plus the opportunity to explore any specific issues and concerns either for themselves or others.

8 *Training support staff*   PAs and administrative staff are crucial members of many research teams. They support senior researchers and are often responsible for managing research contracts and database administration, and act as information and knowledge gatekeepers. Not only are they useful access points for sometimes difficult-to-contact researchers, but they have complex information needs themselves. Recognize their importance and support their skills development.

9 *Advocacy and outreach*   The library can act as a hub for professional development activities and conferences, linked to current hot topics.

Newcastle University has held a series called 'The library@the Beehive' since 2005 (see the previous chapter for background to the Beehive). Advertised on the library web pages and linked into the university message of the day, the meetings have been well attended. Topics have included scholarly communication, open access and its impact on academic publishing. In 2006 De Montfort University started a smaller-scale though similar series as part of advocacy activities for its institutional repository; the opening event was a talk on the RAE and metrics, given by Professor John Feather of Loughborough University.

The examples given above are possible courses and training opportunities at the time of writing this chapter, and the content and needs are likely to change over time.

There are some key principles which should remain constant:

1   *Don't dumb down*   You are working with people who are very sophisticated users of information, and are often producers of the academic information for which you are searching. Be aware of this when you are developing and delivering any training, and don't pitch your content at too low a level. At the same time, remember that your course participants have not received the same academic training in library and information science as you have, so explain any jargon. Or to put it more simply: use simple language but cover complicated concepts. As an aside, think about how you label your courses: humanities researchers might not want to be taught how to be 'literate', for example.

2   *Share your knowledge*   One of the most effective ways of providing training for researchers is to recognize them as people who are probably at least as enthusiastic about finding and using information as any information professional. Sharing what you might consider to be tricks of your trade can be a useful focus for any training or support activities, for not only do you impart new knowledge to people, enabling them to work in smarter ways, but it actually reinforces your professional expertise.

3   *First impressions count*   Show that you can make a difference and

emphasize the value of your input early on. You might want to share a winning practical tip – how to set up current awareness alerts or the inside track on Google.

4   *Think about your contribution*   What exactly are your learners going to get from the teaching that you have developed? In our experience there have often been three key learning outcomes from our sessions: clarity about how to structure a literature search, insight into the organization of knowledge in given disciplines, and software training.

5   *Put the learner first*   Ask your participants what they are interested in, let them tell you their issues and concerns and if you are demonstrating resources, see if you can build examples from their own field. This may not always be appropriate but do listen to your colleagues. Not only will you make the training more relevant and meaningful for them, but you will also learn about your users' needs.

6   *Make it short and sweet*   Many of your intended participants are under a lot of time pressure. Try to focus on the key and core messages in your training, and don't stretch out the session unnecessarily.

7   *Provide back-up*   Don't fall into the well-meaning mistake of providing reams of handouts that would take hours to read and work through. By all means provide something for people to take away, but if you want to supply a lot of detail, try linking your content to supporting materials on your web pages, intranet or some other online solution. If you are talking about open access, make your handouts available online through a Creative Commons licence, for example.

8   *Learn from feedback*   By this we don't just mean how to improve your delivery, but find opportunities to reflect on whether the content was right, and whether there are any other potential opportunities for further outreach and development work. If you are using evaluation forms, remember to add in scope for qualitative feedback: this will usually be very helpful to your own reflections on the effectiveness and value of the sessions.

Formal courses are not the only way of reaching out to staff and researchers. Most of the time you will find that you are working one to one with individual researchers. The nature of your contact will vary considerably. It may be face to face in the library, with researchers coming to the enquiry desk or calling in to see you. It may be virtual – through e-mail exchanges or telephone calls. It may be an arranged appointment, going to visit someone in his or her office. Or it might just be an informal meeting in the staff restaurant, at the close of a meeting, en route to the staff car park, and so on.

Never underestimate the value of this kind of interaction. These informal encounters can help people to resolve problems which are stopping them from progressing with other things or to broach something they have been mulling over for a while. For your part, these are prime learning opportunities. You can develop your enquiry skills and find out more about your community of researchers, as well as making personal contact with individuals. Although you should be conscious that you are representing your service, you are also personalizing it, and thus making it just that bit more accessible to people. If you are effective in these informal encounters, you will often find that you generate more enquiries and contacts from personal recommendation. This does not necessarily mean that you will be overwhelmed, but it is a sure way of generating respect and getting the level of access and consideration that will enable you to achieve your research support goals. Often the people who are proactive in contacting you are key gatekeepers within their work area, so by helping them you are communicating indirectly with many others.

Communities of practice

So far we have mainly explored fairly traditional ways of developing and enhancing information skills, but there are other ways of supporting and promoting information literacy among the research community, not all of which require direct intervention by a librarian throughout their course. We suggest that one of the ways you might wish to do this is through establishing communities of practice (CoPs). The organizational development concept of a community of practice refers to the process of social learning that occurs when people who have a common interest in some subject or problem collaborate to share ideas, find solutions and build innovations.

This has been defined in several different ways in the literature. Stewart sees it as an affinity group or informal network where tips are exchanged and ideas generated (Stewart, 1996), while Cox (2005) describes it as informal and situated social interaction leading to authenticated, motivated learning of what needs to be known about real practice. In essence, a community of practice is about mutual participation or, as Wenger (1998) puts it, 'coherence through mutual engagement'. There is an obvious affinity between theories of communities of practice and the culture of research teams, and also that of the 'invisible college' of researcher networks.

Communities of practice can develop on bases other than subject discipline or physical location. A group of research students learning about research methods and information literacy concepts can develop into a community of practice by means of open discussion, group working and a common goal – one of the obvious developmental outcomes of formal research training programmes. Some faculty research training programmes will include seminars or reading groups where the research team meet weekly to review and critique current papers or work in progress.

In the wider institutional arena researchers may be bound together by the need to find answers to similar questions, sharing information openly. There are opportunities to foster virtual communities of practice using online discussion, collaborative blogs, wikis, chat and mailing lists. At Newcastle University an EndNote CoP has been established which includes an internal mailing list for discussion of EndNote-related problems and solutions. Library and information services can facilitate the establishment of such communities of practice built around information literacy concepts, but these activities no longer need to be library led and imply that groups of researchers have taken ownership of their information literacy development.

Conclusion

In this chapter we have reviewed a wide range of training and development opportunities in support of researchers. It may seem difficult to approach acknowledged experts in their own field and propose that certain training may be helpful for them. Many established researchers, as we have discussed, can be reluctant to attend training courses, but this does not mean that we cannot work with those colleagues to develop their knowledge and skills. As a starting point, we suggest that it can be helpful to conceptualize researchers as learners, with different kinds of needs and requirements. If we develop a learner-centred practice, we can find ways of building learning and development opportunities around the needs of our communities.

There are rich, varied and challenging opportunities for building the information literacy of those in the research community. We might wish to target different groups and use a range of approaches, some directive, others developmental. Library and information services – and individual librarians – create opportunities for constructive dialogue and collaboration with our research community through these encounters, facilitating the development of truly user-centred services, and creating essential learning opportunities for academic communities.

We must not forget that for the end-user access is key, especially in the information-intensive world of researchers. We cannot rely on being intermediaries: we need to shift the focus to empower, enthuse and engage the user!

Note

1   Formative assessment is developmental and usually used for feedback only; summative assessment counts towards a final mark, although this is not always the case.

8

Facing the future: key challenges

Introduction

This more speculative and reflective chapter explores issues and key challenges for the future. We should not fix our gaze only on what is to come, but nor should we exist only in the present nor again nostalgically yearn for the past. By developing some sense of what may happen in the future, and what we would like that future to be, we can shape both the present and our direction in the years to come.

At the time of writing this chapter, the Research Information Network and the Consortium of Research Libraries (CURL) were conducting a survey designed to provide a clearer understanding of UK researchers' current use of library services and their thoughts on the future of research libraries. In parallel, they developed a similar survey to ascertain the views of library and information professionals and the differences between those two groups. Unfortunately, we do not have the benefits of these research findings for our discussion of key issues for the future, so the contents of this chapter are based principally on themes already discussed within the literature, interviews with researchers and our own opinions.

Some theories of strategic management suggest that the key to effective planning is for organizations to draw together their internal resources to meet the challenges of the external environment. Through maximizing internal capabilities to meet the challenges of the external environment, such organizations thrive. This is the rationale behind the structuring of this chapter. We will consider three key areas where the research environment is changing:

- the research information environment (from e-science to physical spaces)
- competition and collaboration in universities
- future trends in scholarly communication.

This discussion will then move on to our analysis of what the research library of the near future should comprise, and therefore what the key capabilities should be. This will include the need to develop a distinctive identity within our institutions, what skills we need, who among our staff should work with the researchers and some key issues ranging from Library 2.0 to research spaces.

We need always to be conscious of our past when thinking about the present and the future. In 1964 Verner Clapp's *The Future of the Research Library* divided his discussion into chapters entitled: Gateways to the world's treasury of recorded knowledge, Extension of local self-sufficiency, Extension of the sharing principle, and Data-processing – information storage and retrieval. These headings will not be unfamiliar to current librarians, although one of the proposed solutions – the extensive use of microphotography – may be less compelling than it was over 40 years ago! Some other concerns, in particular universal bibliographic control and consistency in cataloguing, are, if no less important, possibly closer to realization.

The research information environment of the future

The Grid and more recently 'the Cloud' (*Economist*, 2006) mean that data can be distributed and manipulated much more easily than ever before, creating hybrid research environments where immensely powerful networks create shared data resources with powerful analysis tools. This tends to change the nature and potential of research in all disciplines and creates new opportunities for collaboration.

As we have discussed elsewhere, much research is international and collaborative, and we have already witnessed global information-sharing through the development of subject-based repositories like ArXiv, which mirror the internationalism of the research community in those disciplines. E-science (also called e-research) has been described as a set of technologies to enable people to collaborate: to share computing, data, and the use of remote instruments, etc.

An article in *Library & Information Update* by Tony Hey (2004) offers some very clear examples of what this means in practice. He uses the example of a UK research group which creates simulations of the electrical activity of heart cells. To convert the results of these cell-level simulations to measurable results like electrocardiagrams, the group must couple its models to mechanical models of the beating heart. These models and the data they generate are the research output of a research group in Auckland, New Zealand. In order to complete the chain from gene malfunction to measurable electrocardiagrams indicating heart irregularities, the two groups collaborate, sharing models and data and accessing each other's computing resource as well as national supercomputing facilities.

In order for this collaboration to work effectively, 'middleware' – the software that enables different programs and protocols to work together – must be in place to link together distributed computers, also described as grid computing. Access to data must be straightforward, secure and reliable. At the time of writing, JISC is funding a variety of activities to support the work of research and researchers, which includes supporting infrastructure development through the UK e-science GRID, training and awareness programmes to encourage adoption of e-research and support for data curation and data mining.

Effective digital curation requires a metadata catalogue to manage the attributes of the digital objects in a collection. It is important to recognize that there are several different types of metadata. The *Update* article previously mentioned (Hey, 2004) describes one scheme for metadata from the San Diego Supercomputer Center. The metadata is classified into four different types:

- system metadata – for storage and access operations

- provenance metadata (based on Dublin Core) – the basic descriptive information analogous to a catalogue record
- resource metadata – specifying user access arrangements
- 'discipline' metadata – defined by the particular user community.

The latter area of discipline metadata is particularly important if the data is to be shared across different subject areas as ways of creating definitions which are valid across disciplines. This requires the development of ontologies. An ontology is a development from controlled vocabularies and thesauri, with applications that define the relationships between terms. Ontologies underpin the development of the semantic web, enabling the creation of intelligent retrieval systems.

The e-research environment of the future will comprise vast quantities of scientific data, held in distributed data repositories, together with computational resources for analysis. More than ever before, we will witness the development of academic information repositories, accessible possibly without any mediation or involvement from a library and information service. It may be that – in common with many of the institutional repository developments – those library and information services that are centres of expertise in the development and management of information systems also become responsible for managing and developing virtual research environments.

Competition and collaboration: research in universities

We also predict changes to the level of competition and collaboration in research. At one level it is likely that a small number of research-intensive universities (in the UK the so-called 'golden triangle' of Oxford, Cambridge and London plus Manchester) will continue to draw in very significant funds and build their international standing. It is not clear how many other universities will maintain global recognition for their excellence outside specific subject areas and disciplines.

We are not in a position to predict the outcomes of the 2008 Research Assessment Exercise in the UK, but we do think that the higher education landscape will continue to broaden and diversify, especially if the market for taught courses changes with increased diversity (including international students) and different expectations from fee-paying students. Some of the most research-intensive institutions will build up their postgraduate recruitment and reduce their undergraduate numbers. Although there will not be many postgraduate-only institutions, the balance between undergraduate and postgraduate students will shift in many universities. This will necessarily have an impact on the nature of library services.

It is likely that distinctions between and within universities – for example in treatment of different kinds of staff, including contract research, research-active and teaching – will continue, although there will be strong policy pressure to integrate teaching and research and ensure equality of treatment for all working within the universities. Pay modernization will also lead to the development of local reward policies, and significant salary differentials between organizations will influence the development of the labour market for researchers, possibly counteracting the strength of measures of academic esteem that have often determined the desirability of posts.

Research will continue to be essential to the meaning of the university and very few institutions will neglect it completely. This will continue to be a key distinction between universities and other organizations offering higher education, in particular colleges of further education that deliver foundation degrees. The key difference will be in terms of the volume of the research and the disciplines; sciences in particular are costly to support without major income streams.

Scholarly communication, open access and intellectual property

Publishing in scholarly journals has been the traditional way for researchers to disseminate their work, but this model is starting to break down for a wide variety of reasons such as journals pricing (and VAT on electronic journals in the UK), digital preservation and archiving, cultural changes in the use of resources, awareness of IPR issues and the potential of new technologies.

One of the forces to extend collaboration will be increased information-sharing and faster dissemination of research. We are not sure whether we will see the wholescale transformation and revolution in scholarly communication forecast by some of the prophets of the open access movement, but more research papers will become available, more easily and more promptly than ever before. Local information and knowledge management will be increasingly important, and this must be an emergent role for librarians.

The research library of the future: some themes

1   Marketing

The first of our themes for the research library of the future is marketing. By this we do not mean merely promoting services, but a more fundamental definition of marketing as a way of aligning your organization to the needs of its clients and stakeholders, offering the best range of services and resources in the most appropriate way. If you are working in a research library you will share responsibility for large and prestigious collections that will inevitably attract researchers. Do not forget that many libraries have resources which should be marketed to potential users. We must find ways of unlocking these hidden treasures.

Librarians should no longer take pride in the expense of storing unused and possibly even uncatalogued archives 'just in case' some lucky researcher stumbles across them. We have a professional responsibility and ethical duty to maximize access to our resources. Even more fundamentally, libraries have to be very clear about the services and resources they can provide for researchers and then market them proactively and professionally. Instead of expecting researchers to come to us, we have to be perceived as an integral part of the research community. In universities which do not have a long tradition of research, there may also be less expectation among researchers of the range of resources and services they can rightfully demand from their library.

Promotion of resources and collections also means that research activity can be based on existing collection strengths and research proposals can be underpinned by good quality, realistic information about resources available.

Marketing ideas

Below is a selection of ideas drawn from existing library research support services around the world.

Research portals   Dedicated web pages for research can draw together all the services and resources the library and information service provides, maintaining a specific, recognizable identity for research support. For the service to be relevant to researchers these pages must be up to date and responsive to changing needs and interests.

Publication   A handbook for research staff can summarize all the services and resources and package them appropriately. This content may be replicated on your researchers' portal, but a handbook can be particularly useful for staff and researchers new to the institution or based some distance away. You could even provide multimedia content by including a DVD in the handbook, and do remember to provide some straightforward information about whatever passwords are required in order to make the best use of services.

Communication   A newsletter for researchers or inclusion in discipline-specific research newsletters can ensure that the library or information service is perceived as an organization keen to support and enhance research activities. Remember though that you should consider what you want to communicate or promote. Too often you see librarians promoting services or resources without any indication of their purpose or benefits. There should be scope not only to promote new library-purchased resources, but also provide information and advice on using other libraries, internet searching tips – in short, using the full range of your knowledge and expertise as library and information professionals.

A blog   for researchers can provide updates on topics of interest, forth-coming conferences and encourage academic debate about scholarly communication. Remember that a blog is intrinsically different from a newsletter, and should be treated as such. Develop systems for adding interesting and topical content, and allowing others to contribute and comment.

e-mails Regular, targeted e-mails from designated staff in your department about new resources and services for research remind researchers that library and information professionals are ready and able to provide specialist support and advice.

Publicity Leaflets and posters should not be dismissed as effective awareness-raising tools. Images from manuscripts, special collections, attractive physical spaces within your buildings and so on will all appeal to researchers. As we have stated before, most researchers like libraries, and library-related materials will be popular. Use them within your building, but also make them available – free or for sale to others. Noticeboards and posters can be placed at strategic points within the current collection, highlighting relevant special collections and archival material.

E-learning and multimedia Audiovisual presentations like a library video or DVD should not be dismissed as tools suitable only for undergraduates. If you are working with large numbers of international researchers, a filmed introduction to the library and information service, available through your researchers' portal, might be a useful introduction. It can also be helpful to produce short podcasts on topics of interest. These could be recorded versions of printed guides, excerpts from talks or teaching tools such as the information literacy podcasts at Curtin University of Technology (http://library.curtin.edu.au/podcast/index.html), which provide additional information for researchers.

Events Find opportunities for the library and information services buildings to be the hub for scholarly activities. If you have suitable spaces, find opportunities to host book launches, invite speakers and hold seminars. Make the library into a destination, not a place of last resort.

Think of the whole service Today's students are the researchers of the future. However popular and populist you may wish to make your services, remember not to forget that the advancement of learning and scholarship is at the heart of your work.

2   Research spaces

We expect more flexible and probably more comfortable working spaces than previously. Twenty years ago when you visited a university library there were fewer kinds of working spaces. There would be individual study carrels, possibly bookable and enclosed, discrete spaces to use technology, often in the form of catalogue terminals, and a few computers in addition to open reading room spaces. Some libraries also provided common rooms and cafés outside the study area.

During the 1990s, more university libraries incorporated information technology, usually in dedicated IT zones, and more of their activities, ranging from library management to information resources, became focused on information and communications technology. The provision of spaces for group study also became the norm. Noisier activities started to centre on the library as a physical space. Service convergence with computing and also student learning support became common in the UK.

In the first decade of the current century, there has been a fresh focus on learning spaces to accommodate blended learning and working patterns. The first wave of these developments has centred on creating effective environments for mainly undergraduate students, but it is clear that accommodation for researchers must also evolve.

The information commons developments of integrated learning, study and ICT support spaces have been immensely successful. Libraries now need to turn (or possibly return) to creating spaces for researchers. It is less necessary for many researchers to spend the hours in libraries that they once did – digital delivery of material, combined with the provision of well-equipped spaces for research students, has changed this. But although many researchers visit the library less often, it does not mean that those visits are less important, especially to researchers in the social sciences and humanities who still depend on access to monographs and printed collections. Any time spent in the humanities reading rooms of the British Library will attest to the continuing need for library space!

Are we returning to a model of separate undergraduate and research libraries, seen in the UK in the 1960s, albeit with radically transformed notions of what the 'library' comprises? Whether you choose to do this of course depends on the resources and opportunities that you have available as well as on whether you think this is the right approach to follow. Remember though that one of the fundamental principles of marketing is about understanding and meeting the needs, wants and expectations of your different user groups. The utilitarianism that governs many of our judgements (i.e. that researchers are a minority group in terms of physical use of space) is not so easy to justify when research excellence is a key competitive advantage for institutions.

We have already discussed space planning in Chapter 6 but here are some additional suggestions:

Researchers and their library use   Find out what use your research community already makes of your library and other libraries. A survey is probably the most straightforward way of doing this, but focus groups and interviews would be equally valid approaches. Of course, as we caution elsewhere, there may be inevitable survey fatigue, so choose your time. You should aim to find out the level and nature of use that your researchers already make of your own and other libraries. Our interviews indicated that many researchers visited the library to consult specific texts, make photocopies and borrow or return books. Those who studied in libraries often made specific arrangements to use particular texts or collections. Many of our researchers commented how uncomfortable they found 'modern' spaces, which were too noisy for the level of concentration they required. This may not be a particularly easy process: often we have found that users will state what they need and then not use it when it is made available to them. Triangulate your findings from your discussions with these groups with reference to the literature and visits to other institutions.

Create silent study spaces   There is always a demand for silent study spaces but maintaining silence can be problematic. Try to find ways of designing comfortable, silent working spaces which have IT access.

Provide good levels of access to technology   Researchers will often be deeply attached to their laptops and other portable technologies that contain their current work. If you are developing dedicated work spaces, ensure that there is enough space to work with books and computers, a good power supply, high quality lighting (possibly even desk lighting – very popular in libraries that have it) and wireless access.

Think about a research information commons   Is there any scope to provide a researchers' equivalent of the student learning spaces? By this we mean spaces for meetings, good levels of access to a mixture of technology for presentations, information creation and publishing, a mixture of study environments, including soft seating and food-tolerant zones, as well as individual, reservable formal study and working spaces, with some storage. After all, one of the problems that many researcher students and contract research staff may encounter is a sense of isolation; we can create spaces and services to reduce this.

Collections   Are there any materials which might be located in a specific researchers' space? Although we are reluctant to suggest wholescale segregation, collections of research methods texts, academic staff development materials and some reference works might help to reinforce the sense that you are creating a working space for scholarship and research.

3   E-research and Library 2.0

The phrase Web 2.0 was first used by Dale Dougherty of O'Reilly in 2004 and is viewed as the first step towards the Semantic Web. It refers to innovative web applications and services, including the rise of social networking tools such as weblogs, wikis and instant messaging. Enthusiasts recognize that data is as valuable as functionality and look for ways to exploit their unique data and share it with others. Web 2.0, the Grid and the Cloud, as we have previously discussed, have much to offer researchers both in practice and in their underpinning principles of collaboration and co-operation.

Basically, Library 2.0 = Web 2.0 + Library. The concept of Library 2.0 is about user-centric developments in library services, harnessing the power of social networking tools to make real differences to the ways in which users interact with their library. With so many complex and different technologies, what scope is there for a Research Library 2.0? Current examples include the University of Huddersfield's development of the library catalogue to include borrowing suggestions and serendipity, and in the use of wikis including Ohio University's Biz Wiki (www.library.ohiou.edu/ subjects/bizwiki/index.php/Main_Page). Many libraries are developing RSS feeds and SMS messaging as ways of connecting with users.

Operationally the challenge is to establish seamless access to quite different technologies, and to integrate the paid-for and free scholarly information resources with other material and services. It can be difficult to establish a median point between focusing on managing the complex array of information resources you already have and developing novel, interesting and innovative services. Yet we must always remember that libraries often make themselves difficult to use because of the arcane rules and procedures that we establish. Social technologies offer user-centred forms of information management which could complement our own more rational and scientific forms of knowledge organization.

Semantic applications offer us more intelligent information retrieval, reducing uncertainty in selecting the most effective keywords and search strategies. Data mining would enable the extraction of meaningful patterns from data. Visualization software would enable easy analysis of patterns of authorship, co-authorship and citation, enabling the easy tracing of the impacts of theories, ideas and individual authors. Full-text searching provides the potential to extract key sections not just from journal articles but from monographs whose contents would have otherwise been overlooked. We will have opportunities to build truly user-centred library and information services.

Key websites

☐ CURL: the Consortium of Research Libraries in the British Isles (www.curl.ac.uk) currently has a joint working group with SCONUL, looking at the role of libraries and e-research.

4 Users of the future

Research is an international activity with a global reach and power that is likely to increase. Higher education and research activity is expanding rapidly in China, in particular, and it is likely that research activity and collaboration will continue to internationalize. However, we continue to be aware of major national cultural differences in libraries and educational systems. Although the outcomes and outputs may be similar, our languages and values can be very different. We need to be prepared for an increasingly international, if not globalized, research information environment and to look beyond our own national library systems for innovation, collaboration and development.

It is suggested that our users will be different as well. New researchers will come from the so-called 'millennial generation'. These millennials, also referred to as Generation Y, digital natives or more descriptively 'screenagers' (Candy, 2006), are defined as those born after 1982. It is suggested that this generation has particular characteristics which need to be taken into account when considering the future of library services for research. In general terms, millennials tend to be better at processing visual information and are comfortable with multitasking and with new developments in social software. Byrnko (2006) describes them as 'optimistic, adaptive, flexible, collaborative, format agnostic and forever entrepreneurial'. This does not mean that they are necessarily more expert users than older people, but they have grown up immersed in interactive technology from gaming and mobile phones to instant messaging, and are used to switching between a wider range of digital formats, implicitly understanding their differences. Their approaches have been described by some as 'transliterate', able to switch between and across media, but perhaps with less regard for the canon and traditional academic practice than has hitherto been taken for granted (see www.transliteracy.com for further details).

Researchers of the future, therefore, may approach research from a different perspective. They have grown up used to collaboration and teamwork and studied in educational systems that foster the develop of such important transferable skills. They also expect to be connected 24/7 and have no tolerance for delays. Many are confident in the Web 2.0 environment, which can also be seen as the 'age of the amateur', where everyone is able to publish. In terms of how this might affect libraries, Brindley (2006) suggested that millennials think analogue is static and dull, have gaps in critical thinking and research skills, can be poorly versed in technology tools or web resources needed for academic work, and are ill-acquainted with concepts of intellectual property and plagiarism.

In our view, it is as important as ever to reflect on the knowledge and skills of your user community and never to base your practice on assumptions without evidence.

5 Collaboration

The rhetoric of collaboration is easy to espouse, but rather more difficult to implement. Yet, as we have discussed above, there are likely to be more significant cross-organizational collaborations particularly in the realm of e-science and the related development of research information environments. It may be helpful to identify ways of sharing access to key electronic information resources across the collaborators.

It is also clear to us that library and information services will not return to the imagined golden age when local budgets could support the majority of teaching, learning and research needs. Most library and information services buy what they can afford. This may be principally selected by library staff or by academics. However managed, in practical terms we rarely have scope to buy for the future or to develop policies and practices which complement holdings at other institutions, or even at other sites within our own organization.

Yet this is hugely inefficient: we carry duplicate subscriptions, we haphazardly select or fail to buy material, and it can still be difficult to trace an elusive monograph, save at the legal deposit libraries. Access to electronic journals can be equally infuriating for researchers who have found abstracts but cannot access the full text because of some problem with authentication or cancellation in the renewals processes.

We suggest that there will need to be three main forms of collaboration between libraries in the future:

Collaboration in collection management

This will take two different forms. There will continue to be attempts to develop a National Research Reserve (NRR), as suggested in the Anderson Report, previously discussed in Chapter 4. At present there is the potential that unique holdings may be withdrawn from collections because they are never used at that institution. The threat of this – that no issues of some print journals are left in the UK or that monographs disappear from public access – is real though subject to hyperbole. Yet large research libraries do not have the recurrent resources to manage their heritage collections. Something different must develop, although most proposals are wildly expensive and administratively unwieldy. Local collaborative collection management arrangements seem logical in principle, but are unsatisfying in practice as one library may collect material that seems less essential as priorities change.

The second form of collaborative collection management will be in increased centralization of purchasing. The benefits of national access to services like EEBO (see Chapter 5) will surely be replicated by the JISC in other areas, especially so-called 'big deals' in purchasing journals. For libraries and individuals this makes a great deal of sense: it is much easier for a small institution to pay a modest access fee to use a resource of interest to a small number of active researchers. Operationally, for libraries with highly devolved budgeting, it will require much advocacy, but the justifications are compelling. Publishers may need to be convinced of the value of this approach, but national agreements will often guarantee higher total sales.

Collaboration across sectors

Although there is more staff mobility between different types of library than perhaps in the 1990s, our professional perspectives are very much dominated by the sector in which we work. We have reached more mutual accommodation and understanding with the health sector, although some tensions continue, but we will need to think of ways of building partnerships with libraries and archives supporting research outside higher education. As individuals we may not be aware of the range of different services that many of our researchers use, ranging from collections, archives managed by local government, national government and other organizations. Yet if we wish to uncover and make accessible the treasures of our national collections, we will need to work beyond our institutions and the HE sector.

Collaboration with other stakeholders

The third form of collaboration which we envisage is in establishing alliances outside our own profession. We are already familiar with converged service models, and close partnership and collaboration in infrastructure development will continue. Many of the technical and delivery dimensions fall into the grey areas of metadata and standards development claimed by both library and computing professionals. Over the years we have worked with publishers and aggregators in the development of electronic journals collections, and in other publishing initiatives. Open access publishing and other developments in scholarly communication have meant the development of different forms of relationships with academics, where library and information services assume responsibility for publishing. Although university libraries may have been involved in university presses, the nature and extent of our involvement in repository seems to be different in scale. A final form of collaboration will be with commercial organizations through continued third strand research funding and knowledge transfer partnerships.

6   Research support and the role of the librarian

We have already discussed this in some detail in Chapter 6. As two of your authors have backgrounds as subject librarians, it is not surprising that we are strong advocates of the effectiveness of this approach in providing or brokering individual support to research and researchers.

The focus of the role will shift. A recent study commissioned by the Research Information Network found that 84% of researchers use general search engines, 66% use specialist databases and only 15% use the advice and expertise of librarians. Unsurprisingly the future role of library and information professionals was one of the questions asked in the CURL/RIN survey previously mentioned. At the e-mail stage of the survey (Research Information Network and Consortium of Research Libraries, 2006) researchers and librarians were asked separately how important they envisaged the following roles to be for library and information professionals in the future:

- teacher of information literacy and related skills
- subject-based information expert (based in library building)
- subject-based information expert (embedded in department or research group)
- administrator dealing with the purchasing and delivery of information services
- custodian of print-based and digitized archives and special collections
- manager of institutional repositories of digital information
- manager of the vast datasets generated by e-science and grid-based projects
- facilitator for e-learning, supporting virtual learning environments
- technology specialist, creating and managing virtual research environments (to support virtual research communities)
- technology specialist facilitating electronic access to information resources
- manager of (non technical) metadata issues, developing and applying ontologies
- information technology expert supporting the technical aspects of information provision (e.g. networks, authentication)
- specialist adviser in copyright and intellectual property rights issues.

A number of these roles describe existing and embedded practice in supporting learning and teaching as well as traditional roles in information support, purchasing and collection management. Others are more recently established roles, notably the management and development of institutional repositories.

Some other suggested roles are not particularly novel – for example the proposal to be a departmentally based subject information expert is an established role in health information and in other domains drawing from a strong information science tradition. It is less common in universities, where qualified staff have blended subject work with functional or supervisory roles which are tied to the library.

Key to success is the need to learn from areas where we have already been successful – particularly in the achievements of library and information services staff in supporting the taught student experience, and to apply that expertise and other areas of our professional knowledge to more proactive engagement with research and infrastructure development. We will continue to build on our experience of converged service delivery and multi-professional partnership working.

None of these potential roles is beyond the existing skills and knowledge of people working within library and information services. What may be necessary, however, is for us to reorient our professional training and development on a more fundamental level to rethink how we develop our leadership and strategic planning. There are also challenges in areas, mentioned in previous chapters, in relation to intellectual property and the management of digital assets, which will be particularly valuable in supporting e-science.

Our key professional values and knowledge must be sustained: we lose our specialisms at our peril, but they must evolve. We need to provide access to information in a wide range of forms and expert advice on finding, accessing, using and sourcing information through developing user-centred services.

7 Managing resources

What does the future hold in this area, which many perceive to be at the heart of librarianship? We have an obligation to ensure continuity of access to the record of knowledge. As suggested above, we will continue to need to find ways of doing more things with the same resources. Technology will make much of this potentially easier, with the reality of having immediate access to resources, easy and cheap archiving, electronic data storage, and the creation of a new kind of canon created by ease and frequency of access.

Of course we will continue to give priority to delivery to the desktop, aware that the richness of the traditional library must be replicated in virtual environment. This will not be easy. We sometimes forget the value in retrospect of 'just-in-case' collection development policies where material that would have been neglected becomes valuable. We will continue to manage print resources in the form of monographs, and our role in digital curation will become increasingly important. We do not think that there are any immediate solutions to the complexities of managing e-resources and journal subscriptions.

Academic journals developed and evolved as academic disciplines themselves started to professionalize. Although the first British academic journal started in 1665 (the *Philosophical Transactions* of the Royal Society), the great majority of titles are of relatively recent origin and act as markers for the development of a clearly defined discipline or community of practice. As academic knowledge becomes increasingly interdisciplinary and multidisciplinary, so there will be more demand for titles that reflect new and emerging areas of specialist interest. The recommendations of quality that come from peer review will not disappear, although it may be transformed by open access.

So we will still need to manage our journals – and find ways of reconciling their increasing cost with our limited budgets. Let us just illustrate the scale of the problem. Journals purchased by UK academic libraries have gone up in price by an average of 11% per annum since 1991–2, while the consumer price index has increased by only 2.7% per annum. This means that in 1999–2000 academic libraries in the UK spent 19% more per FTE student to purchase 18% fewer journal titles per FTE student than in 1991–2. Though it is impossible to predict future developments in scholarly communication, straight-line projections suggest that reductions in journal collections in libraries could range from 20% to 50% by the year 2012. While electronic journals have improved accessibility, the model by which publishers bundle together high demand titles with less popular journals means that library collections are constrained by supply rather than demand. At the same time, the total number of scholarly titles being published is continuing to increase.

We have mentioned already the pilot of the National Research Reserve to hold rarely used serials provided through a comprehensive national service, thereby reducing space – but how feasible is this? The forthcoming pilot will provide proof of concept, but it will be difficult to persuade academics to change, especially to surrender local resources for the national good. This is an area full of contrasts for in other areas researchers will travel to find the materials they need.

The challenge for librarians is that in parallel with the challenges facing our management of traditional academic resources, scientific digital libraries are being created now by global collaborative e-science experiments. These too will need the same sort of facilities as conventional digital libraries (those that store text, audio and video data), that is, a set of services for manipulation, management, discovery and presentation of the data. In addition, they will require new types of tool for data transformation, visualization and data mining. The tools, of course, are the domain of the computing community, but management and organization is probably our domain.

Key websites

☐ ALPSP: Association of Learned and Professional Society Publishers (www.alpsp.org/default.htm) is the international trade association for not-for-profit publishers and those who work with them.
☐ SPARC: Scholarly Publishing and Academic Resources Coalition (www.arl.org/sparc) is an alliance of universities, research libraries and organizations. As well as campaigning to raise awareness of scholarly communication issues, SPARC actively develops alternatives to high cost existing journals.

Conclusion

How radical are our aspirations for the future role of libraries in support of research? Our goals are perhaps not so different from those of our predecessors, which we could summarize as:

■ *Universal and seamless access to academic knowledge and information*, ranging from metadata to the curation of printed archives and special collections, including repository development
■ *User-centred services* that consider the needs of all stakeholder groups in their diversity and do their best to create exceptional library and information services.

■ *Cost-effective and efficient use of resources to maximize value and impact.* Value and impact are not purely economic and utilitarian measures: we must consider the academic, educational and cultural dimensions.

The shift is in context and environment, especially technology, so although the definitions of problems and difficulties may recall previous discussions, the focus is different. The democratization of access to information – seamless access brokered through search engines most especially, together with the opportunities created by current developments in computing and networks – means that we must reconsider how we can achieve our research support goals. The challenge applies to us all – leaders in the profession, senior library and information service managers, practising librarians at every level and those planning to join the profession. We need to develop our vision, but we will also need to ensure that the vision is delivered. It may not be easy, but it should be exciting!

9 Key principles for supporting research

Every piece of research that I do or assess needs a solid base of a review of the literature to make it good research. The best repository of that kind of info is the library. . . . You can use Google and you might find something but that's not good enough for academic research.   (Economics Professor, UK)

Introduction

Much of our professional discourse is based around quests for absolutes: how to manage e-resources, be the best teacher, win resources, evaluate our impact, develop or create peerless metadata and so on. The basis for many of our services is the operation of restrictions, in the form of loan entitlements, borrowing periods, limitations on access based on where you work and what licence agreements specify. We order and categorize our collections and services. We are bound by rules and regulations – both a professional strength and a weakness. Rules give us clarity and working definitions, but they can also serve to limit our flexibility and provide a refuge for a lack of innovation and creativity.

Yet when it comes to managing, developing and delivering services, there are so many variables depending on our organizations, resources and culture that we do not think it is appropriate to specify to an exact degree what you should do. Instead, this final chapter consolidates the preceding chapters into ten key principles for the provision of effective library services for research.

Laws, values and principles

There are other, much nobler antecedents to our principles. S. R. Ranganathan's Five Laws of Library Science (Ranganathan, 1931) offer fundamental guidance on our practice. They are:

1 Books are for use.
2 Every person his or her book.
3 Every book its reader.
4 Save the time of the reader.
5 The library is a growing organism.

The laws can be applied to our current environment quite easily. We recognize that information resources must be used to have value. We also acknowledge that individuals, especially researchers, have specific information needs. It is also established that our collections, both print and physical, must be aligned to the needs of our users and that we must reduce barriers to accessing our collections. Indeed, time-saving becomes ever more essential as the capacity for speedier delivery becomes ever more possible. The final law, that the library is a growing organism, is also vital. We cannot let our services and resources ossify.

Michael Gorman's polemic *Our Enduring Values* (Gorman, 2000) identified eight core or central values, as follows:

1 Stewardship

In Gorman's terms this encompasses preservation of the human record, nurturing professional education and 'do[ing] good work and earn[ing] the trust and respect of the communities we serve' (Gorman, 2000, 72). This value is clearly essential to research support.

2 Service

This must inspire and inform every aspect of librarianship, for libraries exist to serve their communities and society as a whole. The service ethic should inform relations with users and every aspect of how library policies and procedures are designed and evaluated. This commitment to users is evident also in our principles though expressed in much simpler terms.

3 Intellectual freedom

According to Gorman libraries must maintain a commitment to intellectual freedom through access policies, support for minorities and opposition to censorship. We have discussed this to some extent in Chapter 2.

4 Rationalism

'First, all the practical aspects of librarianship . . . benefit from the application of reason. Second, there is no better antidote to the forces of unreason than a well-stocked, well-organized library' (Gorman, 2000, 103). Who could challenge these statements?

5 Literacy and learning

Libraries of all kinds must support literacy and learning, encouraging reading and making the library a focus of literacy teaching. It is self-evident that our role in supporting research is focused on the discovery and communication of knowledge – the leading edge of education.

6 Equity of access to recorded knowledge and information

Equity of access appears in two forms: ensuring the accessibility of resources and activities, and overcoming technological and monetary barriers to access. This value is clearly applicable.

7 Privacy

This is also discussed in Chapter 2. Libraries must protect the confidentiality of their users.

8   Democracy

This is a concept that is discussed less openly in European libraries. Gorman argues that libraries must uphold democracy by applying it in library management, participating in the educational process and upholding the values of democratic society.

Our principles are rather more prosaic than the laws and values specified above, but we hope they will provide you with some opportunities for further reflection.

Principles of library support for researchers

Key Principle 1: Know your users

A service based on assumptions and supposition, rather than real understanding, can only be mediocre. To deliver first class library support it is vital that you know your users. How well do you understand the nature of the academic work undertaken by staff and researchers at your institution? What do you know about them as individual researchers, rather than as a collective group?

Here are some suggestions:

Develop personal contacts with research units and researcher   From our analysis of the literature, research findings and experience, the most effective means of building user-centred services is by understanding the needs, wants and expectations of the community. Many benefits result from adopting a proactive and user-centred approach. Instead of being seen as 'just the librarian', you will be perceived as a key collaborator and ally. Remember that researchers are passionate about their subject, and about access to knowledge and communication. They can be great supporters and are key consumers of library and information services. Only by engaging in a dialogue with the research community and actually listening to what they say can you understand how the library and information service meets, or could meet, their requirements. This knowledge may range from understanding more about people's training needs and recognizing the difficulties faced by international students and faculty to being able to identify material of interest to research groups and individuals.

Use formal surveys and feedback mechanisms   Personal contacts and judgement based on anecdotes and networks do not necessarily facilitate the establishment of service and resourcing priorities, so we suggest that 'knowing your users' also requires more systematic and strategic approaches. Representation and integration within the university management structure is addressed in more detail under the next point, but getting involved in formal discussion and dialogue with key stakeholders should be an important element in service enhancement. At an organizational level, it is vital to consider the needs of researchers when planning for change, and to find ways of incorporating their views into any surveys or feedback mechanisms. The ResIN case study (page 130) is an excellent example of the positive impact this can have on individuals and the service.

It may not be easy to achieve this. Many colleagues will suggest that it can be very difficult to get a clear view of what researchers perceive to be important and feedback is often contradictory or unrealistic. Nevertheless, even exploring this ambiguity can be of value.

Key Principle 2: Understand the research environment and demonstrate where the library fits into it

The services you offer will necessarily be constrained by the resources available. This is the case wherever you work – there is always more that you could do if your resources were increased. In this context it is important to establish priorities to maximize the impact and effectiveness of your services. This will work at a number of levels, but start by ensuring that your work is aligned to institutional and national priorities.

Emphasizing synergies between your activities and the organizational vision can be a powerful tool in gaining institutional recognition and this is not only the responsibility of the most senior managers in the library. Staff at all levels need to have an understanding of the goals of their service and institution and how their work contributes to the whole. If you are particularly involved in research support, your role may be as much about encouraging your colleagues to understand the research environment as it is about helping researchers to understand the library environment.

You should be able to map your local priorities onto a wider picture and demonstrate the value of your service in this wider arena. Just because you have a good idea does not necessarily mean that it will be adopted and supported by all. You need to understand how to get things done. How to do this will of course vary depending on where you work – the key is finding the right time, place and person (or people). As a starting point, find opportunities to put forward your proposals to those who have a positive influence on their acceptance, support and development. Get involved in university, faculty, school and departmental research committees. Spend some time listening in meetings and talking one to one with key staff. Remember you can always follow up your ideas and leads outside formal meetings. Then, when you have positive developmental proposals that support the achievement of organizational objectives, make your case. Current examples of such proposals include development of systems to support data management for the RAE, input into research student skills development, support for publishing and development plans for library collections.

Understanding the research environment implicitly requires that you devote some of your work time to finding out about the 'bigger picture' within your organization and nationally. You should read the professional press, go to conferences and develop networks. By developing an understanding of how your organizational and external environment is changing, you will find it easier to identify with clarity how best to develop priorities for your own work. We are not suggesting that all solutions can be developed by mimicking what is happening elsewhere, rather that you can gain perspective from stepping back and giving yourself opportunities for some critical analysis.

You also need to find out about the research micro-environment – what are the daily frustrations and top concerns for a researcher? For example, from our interviews, it was clear that many of our researchers, especially contract researchers, needed to be aware of current developments in rapidly changing areas. This suggests that it would be a good idea to promote ways that researchers can keep up to date, using table of contents and other current awareness services, and identify opportunities for other tailored services, targeted perhaps at contract researchers.

We cannot guarantee that by doing this you will always get increased funding, but our experience suggests that if you do a good job and make a demonstrable difference to improved performance, this serves to support your budget case, which in turn enables you to develop your work.

Key Principle 3: Provide a transparent research portal – collections matter, but access is key

Two constants arose from our interviews with researchers: predictably, the need to have rapid access to relevant information and, more surprisingly, an ongoing demand for a scholarly study environment. It is important not to allow the exciting developments in electronic access and technology obscure the abiding need for physical spaces in libraries.

A third frequent comment from our researchers related to the lack of understanding about exactly what services and resources were available and how they could be accessed. A transparent research portal may be mainly a marketing tool; it may not involve making huge changes and investments but will ensure that your collection and support will be visible to your users. If you fail to do this, you face the risk that researchers will substitute sources that they can access directly: 'The internet is usually my first choice for research. . . . You have to wade through the fluff, but it's easy to do' (Professor of Mass Communications, US).

It is also important to review your collection management policies and practices. Of course, it is not easy for librarians in the UK to build collections – the financial resources are simply not available – but that does not mean we should neglect our responsibility for stewardship and effective collection development. 'At the moment, I am furious that the library is so slow to collect the materials. This does not meet our needs' (Professor of Library and Information Science, Japan).

We are aware that access to finding tools and digital delivery is ever more important, and that information behaviours are fast changing:

'Now, when I'm writing papers I focus more attention on the abstract' (Government scientist). 'In an ideal world there would be a digital access to all books and journals published (not only in the West but also elsewhere)' (Professor of Theology, Netherlands).

Nor should we forget that researchers depend on more than published information: we can facilitate access to academic networks, the 'invisible college' and communities of practice. Our research portal can be more than a gateway to our own resources, we can find ways of adding value and applying our professional skills to building expertise directories, supporting knowledge management, moving beyond our management of formal academic information to other forms of knowledge.

Key Principle 4: Develop your professional practice and expertise

In order to be perceived on a basis of equality when dealing with researchers, you need to have confidence in yourself as a professional. This is not about broadcasting our professional qualifications to defend our status, but more about our attitude and approach to our work. Researchers are totally committed to their work, often making little distinction between work and leisure; they may expect colleagues to show the same kind of interest and dedication to their own profession. We are not suggesting that you dedicate your whole life to librarianship at the expense of every other aspect of your life, but think about the value you place on your work and the enhancement of your professional practice. If you enjoy your work, and are interested in it beyond the bounds of the day-to-day job, this will be self-evident to the people you deal with. Researchers are more likely to be convinced of the value of our contribution if we demonstrate our competence, professionalism and expertise. Our knowledge and skills should be self-evident to all of those with whom we work. In our opinion, those key skills are:

Understanding the structure of knowledge and information within disciplines
    Librarians must be information specialists, understanding how knowledge is communicated in the disciplines with which they work. Not only will you gain the confidence of experts in those fields by

recognizing the relative importance of different publication forms, key journals and significant publishers, but you will also provide effective support to people who are new to the field or moving between or across subject areas. You can also use this knowledge to develop library collections, both print and virtual, and to create learning resources and teaching materials.

Such detailed knowledge can be developed through practice – especially from working with and learning from researchers – but understanding the structure of knowledge should already form part of your professional skill set.

Information retrieval skills The second key professional skill is in information retrieval – both in theory and practice. You must be competent, flexible and effective at searching and browsing information retrieval systems, in whatever form they appear. You should be able to use an array of retrieval techniques and communicate their effective use to others. This means knowing search engines inside out, as well as bibliographic databases.

An understanding of user behaviour Awareness of how end-users search for information is also essential. Remember that people often fail to find the information they need, not because it does not exist, but because they fail to search in the most effective way. Linked to your expertise in information retrieval should be an understanding of how people search and how they learn. This will help you to identify why researchers are encountering difficulties in finding the information required and to give advice on how to improve their effectiveness. You should understand the reality of searching: of how information-enthusiastic (or otherwise) end-users may be, the value of browsing and the whole range of human factors that influence the use of information systems.

Information management skills This is another of the mainstays of our profession. In order to support research effectively, either you or your colleagues should be skilled at helping others to compile bibliographies and advising on referencing conventions, the use of reference management software and the creation of metadata. As discussed elsewhere, we will also have a role in leading and ensuring the development and management of institutional repositories and open access publishing. This expertise should also extend to understanding the importance of ethical approaches in information management, promotion of academic integrity, knowledge of plagiarism and plagiarism detection software and services, compliance (data protection, freedom of information, intellectual property) and records management (including advice on version control).

Continuing your professional development   We have already touched on this point under Principle 2, but in order to support research and researchers effectively we must be prepared to learn and develop. The research and information environments are changing so rapidly that we need to challenge our existing conceptions and assumptions, and to commit ourselves to learning and enhancing our practice. There are many ways of achieving this. We strongly support the model of the reflective practitioner, taking time to reflect on work not only after completion but also while it is in progress. Combine this with reading and professional engagement and you will enrich your work. You may also consider taking additional qualifications, including teaching qualifications, accreditation of CPD activities or additional postgraduate qualifications. Taking advantage of opportunities to study within your own institution can also mean that you work alongside academics, shifting your relationship from service provider to colleague.

Continuing professional development is not a burden, nor a distraction from your main occupation: it expands your horizons and gives you time, space and experience to develop your knowledge and skills for your own benefit, and that of your organization and our profession.

Key Principle 5: Monitor and evaluate what you do

As a reflective practitioner you will already be viewing your work in a wider context. This should inevitably lead on to a constant questioning of current practice, always looking for ways to build and improve and learn. One of the most difficult things to accept is not to be defensive but rather to listen to any feedback or comments and to accept criticism in a positive way. We have to be brave enough to invite negative comments – it really is much better for people to tell us directly rather than leave dissatisfaction unexpressed except among themselves. However, we also have to be sensible enough to celebrate when we provide excellent service and not be too modest (there is some truth in our shy and retiring stereotype).

With this in mind, it is important that you give some thought to devising mechanisms for regular evaluation and review, both of your personal performance and of the service you provide.

On a personal level, it may be that your library has formal mechanisms in place, such as personal performance development reviews or appraisal, which you can use to evaluate your own development. Even if there are no formal systems within your organization, remember that CILIP has a useful CPD framework to help structure your reflection, and the Chartership process is very effective at helping to structure your thinking if you are in the early stages of your career, followed by revalidation and Fellowship.

On a broader level, you can seek opportunities to elicit feedback in both informal situations and formal meetings, as well as adding questions to library or university surveys as the opportunity arises. Ask questions regularly at meetings – just because there were no comments last time does not mean there will never be any response.

The most important way of monitoring regularly is to remember to listen! Listen to what people are really saying to you – if they cannot work out how to do something could you find a way to make it clearer for them next time? Why do so many people ask the same questions over and over again at the enquiry point – what can we do to assist? What are the library staff saying – are there frequently asked questions which perhaps suggest some action or changes are needed? Use what you learn to take action, and to influence your organization. Remember, we do not work for omniscient management: as a professional your views should matter!

Key Principle 6: The whole service counts

Do we really see our service through the eyes of our users? Or is our understanding distorted by too much emphasis on what is problematic or challenging to us, and not enough on our users' needs?

Users do not necessarily understand the reasons for separate sections in libraries – many of them may think all librarians do the same job and should be able to help them with any aspect of the service. Of course, in practice, we know this is not the case and we cannot expect every member of staff to understand everything, but we have an obligation to provide a joined-up service. A simple enquiry about a password should not lead to an enquirer being sent to three different helpdesks: we need to identify how our services are designed and interact with each other, and ensure there are no gaps or duplication.

We are also mistaken if we assume that every researcher wants mediated services. 'In my library heaven, all stacks are open to visit and there are photocopier machines nearby. In fact it is called the Harvard Medical History Library; can I live there?' (Microbiologist, UK). We should strive to create library and information services which provide straightforward and seamless access to what matters to the whole range of our users.

Academic liaison librarians must engage with library operational management and vice versa. Liaison librarians should have very good access to library users, and can inform them of issues and obtain feedback to inform service development. But you need to understand all the different ways in which researchers use your service: you may be as proactive and expert as you wish, but if researchers are dependent on interlibrary loans and this service is unsatisfactory, you can never provide an effective library service to support research.

The researchers we interviewed used libraries extensively and they were enthusiastic and observant users. After all, libraries and information services were central to their lives. Sadly, from many we heard tales of unhelpful attitudes: 'I used the Special Collections at X, the people there weren't interested in what I was looking at. When I spoke to them about one of my discoveries, they looked at me as if I was faintly mad. They just sat around gossiping and drinking herbal tea all day' (Professor of English, UK). We may not share our researchers' enthusiasms, but it would probably support our case for increased funding if we did not give the impression of being tea-drinking chatterboxes in our working hours.

Researchers sometimes knew more about libraries than we would assume. Several of them talked about which classification scheme they preferred, demonstrating a grasp of Dewey that would warm the hearts of

many professional cataloguers, and they would spot mistakes in cataloguing and classification: 'Sue Brimmacombe' (see Chapter 3) was not unusual in her comment 'I liked the stock at X library [a private organization] but the standard of classification was terrible; some books were in completely the wrong place' [she then listed and reclassified them].

We also need to remember that library spaces are important. Although digital resources mean that researchers access library resources from their desktops and may use the physical library much less often, we should still consider the needs of researchers when planning or redesigning our library spaces, especially in subjects where there is a continuing requirement to use printed materials and special collections.

Key Principle 7: Support the development of information literacy

Supporting the development of effective skills in finding, using and managing information among our research community is fundamental. This development may come in many different forms, depending on circumstances and opportunity, but should at least include:

- involvement in research training programmes for postgraduates
- proactive support for academics, research assistants, contract research staff, supervisors and postgraduates in identifying and using information sources and reference management tools.

Researchers are not necessarily librarians: their focus is on the information and knowledge, not on its management and access arrangements. This means that you can help to develop their knowledge and understanding of the best ways of finding and managing information. In particular we have found that researchers do not know about some generic tools and sources – like COPAC or ZETOC, for example – and really value hints and tips as well as friendly support and guidance. But be diplomatic and do not, ever, patronize! You must audit the learning needs of your researchers, finding out what they know already and what they want to know about.

Remember that you are working with people who, for the most part, are information-intensive. Many of them have spent a large proportion of their time using libraries and academic information services. Most experienced academics are also producers of the information that you manage: they write journal articles and books, and act as editors and reviewers. By supporting their work, you are contributing to the whole cycle of scholarly knowledge.

Key Principle 8: Embrace change – for yourself and your research community

The steady state organization no longer exists. The information and publishing environments are uncertain, as is higher education. We need to understand the nature of change, how best to manage it, and what is changing in our own professional environment.

We sometimes start with misconceptions of change. Change is not a clean and clear event; it is messy and confusing. We often think that a change is a simple process of identifying a problem, making a change and resolving the problem. This model is rarely true. We have to work through changes, uncertain where the final point will be.

Without wishing to turn to this section into a discussion of change management and library strategy, the following suggestions may be helpful:

- Clarity of purpose – a vision – is important. If you articulate the benefits of change, others are going to be more able to accept it.
- Involve colleagues in the change process – often being open helps to create shared ownership and build trust.
- Recognize that the conclusions reached in a change process are not always the outcomes initially planned

As always we are not suggesting that this is a recipe for success. In our experience, when initiatives do not meet expectations it is more often because the change is misunderstood or mistrusted than because the initiative itself is flawed. We need to think and promote the benefits of change at least among our library colleagues: this may slow down the process, but by sharing and getting buy-in we encourage a shift in values.

Let us provide an example. Academic staff and researchers can be intransigent about change, especially when we are proposing alterations to study environments, establishing institutional repositories or replacing print journal collections with digital ones. Our first principle is important: know your users. Think whether you can promote the benefits of remote access as opposed to the value of browsing. How often, in practice, do your researchers really come and browse your library shelves? Yet browsing and serendipity are still viewed (rightly) as a key activity by many researchers, so how can we deal with this mismatch? We need to convince users that the benefits outweigh the perceived disadvantages. This means being well prepared to counter negative arguments and ensuring that you can enumerate all the advantages of the new situation for your researchers ('Yes, you're losing browsing, but you can use contents alerting in this way, which, as well as actually making sure you see a wider range of material, will also save you lots of time . . .').

But embracing change is not merely about selling decisions to library users; it is also about being open to change yourself. Here is another example. Remote access and e-resources mean that there is less and less face-to-face contact with researchers and anyway, as we have already suggested, many researchers are very comfortable with using information resources. What role should you have? Well, as a starting point, go out to your researchers: visit them in their offices, laboratories, research centres. Think about what they need: find ways of supporting and working with them. Do not be complacent about information resources – find out what researchers are using, and how they are doing this. We need to keep up to date with developments in humanities computing and e-science and ensure our services evolve to support the changing needs of our users.

Key Principle 9: Become an advocate, especially for scholarly communication

We are connected people, working for central services with good access to staff at all levels in our organizations and across organizations, nationally and internationally. We are perceived in a positive way by most university staff, and our service focus tends to mean that we understand the concerns of our users. This level of both access and trust means that we are in a strong position to advise researchers in matters where we have professional knowledge and expertise. Key areas are academic integrity, copyright, freedom of information (all discussed in Chapter 2), as well as scholarly communication, open access publishing and the value of libraries.

Through making suggestions you can start to shape opinion. You may not always be in a position to decide whether publishing in your institutional repository will be mandated, but you can chip away at the monolithic opposition. You can cover scholarly communication and open access in your research training sessions, and open up the debate about the cost of journals and different access and pricing models. Do not forget to practise what you advocate: if you write or publish, put a copy of your publication in the repository, license it under Creative Commons, demonstrate professionalism in all aspects of your work.

Remember, you are always the voice of the profession to those with whom you work.

Key Principle 10: Become a researcher

We are not suggesting that you rush out and register for a doctorate, but by doing research yourself you will become more attuned to the needs of researchers. There are many levels of research and scholarly activity, ranging from small-scale internal evaluation projects to free-standing, major funded projects.

Examples of smaller-scale, practice-based research range from using focus groups within your organization to pedagogic research projects and producing literature reviews and service evaluations. Within our professional sphere we should try to contribute to the literature, broadening and strengthening knowledge and practice within our disciplines. Research and evaluation skills are very valuable: we need to evidence the value and impact of our services always, and a critical awareness of research methodology and its application in practice is very valuable. Other related (and very employable) skills include experience in bid-writing and project management, which can be gained from research work.

You do not have to do this on your own. Your department may have a culture of research and evaluation, especially if there is a tradition of evidence-based practice or quality enhancement. You can also look outside your department. We have all been surprised at how enthusiastic academic colleagues can be in agreeing to co-author papers and research projects: remember the support we got for the 'Researchers' learning lives' idea at the learning and teaching conference.

In our experience, involvement in research and other scholarly activity has not only shaped our development as researchers, but has enhanced our work as library and information professionals. We have all developed a much more grounded understanding of the nature of research and publication, which has in turn improved our information retrieval, management and enquiry skills. We have also increased in confidence in talking both to researchers and about the research process; drawing on personal experiences in research and publishing will make a session on literature searching much more personal, memorable and meaningful. At a very practical level you start to find out different things from the sources with which you work – errors in indexing, common frustrations, things that you always like, and little hints and tips.

Conclusion

So, finally, these are our suggestions for how you should provide effective library services for research: understand the fundamentals of your professional practice, champion it and be prepared to learn and change. Are you ready to do that?

Bibliography

Agrawal, S. P. and Lal, M. (1987) Information Needs of Social
  Scientists, *International Library Review*, **19**, 287–99.

Agriculture Network Information Center, www.agnic.org.

Ahlback, T. (1992) *Information Needs of Humanities Scholars*, British
  Library. Research and Development Department, BLRD Report,
  6075, 109–16.

Aims, A. (1965) Survey of Information Needs of Physicists and
  Chemists, *Journal of Documentation*, **21** (2), 88.

Aked, M. J. et al. (1998) Faculty Use of an Academic Library Reference
  Collection, *Collection Building*, **17** (2), 56–64.

Allen, B. (1990) Effects of Academic Background on Statements of
  Information Need, *Library Quarterly*, **60** (2), 120–38.

Allen, N. S. (1988) The Art and Architecture Program of the Research
  Libraries Group, *Art Libraries Journal*, **13** (4), 5–10.

Alston, R. C. (1996) The Changing Face of Research Libraries. In
  Mullins, C., Deegan, M. R. S. and Kenna, S. (eds), *New Technologies
  for the Humanities*, Bowker-Saur.

Aluri, R. (1996) Electronic Publishing: the unfolding revolution,
  DESIDOC Bulletin of Information Technology, **16** (1), 3–8.

Anderson, D. et al. (2004) *Towards a Canadian Research Strategy: Report of
  the Consensus Panel*, Canadian Association of Research Libraries,
  www.carlabrc.ca/projects/kdstudy/public_html/2005/chapter5.pdf.

Anderson, T. D. (2000) Doing Relevance Research: an ethnographic exploration of relevance assessment, *New Review of Information Behaviour Research*, **1**, 201–18.

Andrew, T. (2004) Theses Alive!: an e-theses management system for the UK, *Assignation*, **21** (3), 33–6.

Andrews, J. E. et al. (2005) Information-seeking Behaviors of Practitioners in a Primary Care Practice-based Research Network (PBRN), *Journal of the Medical Library Association*, **93** (2), 206–12.

Antelman, K. (2004) Do Open Access Articles have a Greater Research Impact?, *College & Research Libraries News*, **65** (5), 372–82, http://eprints.rclis.org/archive/00002309/01/do_open_access_CRL.pdf.

Archambault, E. V. and Gagné, E. (2004) *The Use of Bibliometrics in the Social Sciences and Humanities: final report*, Science-Metrix, www.science-metrix.com/pdf/, Science-Metrix_Use_Bibliometrics_SSH.pdf.

Arrigona, D. and Mathews, E. (1988) A Use Study of an Academic Library Reference Collection, *RQ*, **28** (1), 71–81.

Ashling, J. (2005) The Web and After: the future of scholarly e-publishing, *Information Today*, **22** (6), 33–4.

Ashoor, M. S. and Kanamugire, A. B. (1996) Responding to Researchers' and Faculty Use Patterns and Perceptions of CD-ROM Services, *Online & CD-ROM Review*, **20** (4), 171–80.

Ashworth, S. and Joint, N. (2003) A Model for Inter-institutional Collaboration: the GAELS Project document delivery trials, *Library Review*, **52** (4), 150–8.

Asimov, I. (1959) *Words of Science and the History Behind Them*, Houghton Mifflin.

Association of Universities and Colleges of Canada (2005) *Momentum: the 2005 Report on University Research and Knowledge Transfer*, AUCC, www.aucc.ca/momentum/en/_pdf/momentum_report.pdf.

Atherton, J. S. (2005) Learning and Teaching: Knowles' Andragogy: an angle on adult learning, www.learningandteaching.info/learning/knowlesa.htm.

Atkinson, R. (1995) Humanities Scholarship and the Research Library, *Library Resources & Technical Services*, **39**, 79–84.

Austen, G. (1996) *Libraries and Faculties in Partnership: delivering information*

resources to science faculties, IATUL,
www.iatul.org/conference/proceedings/vol06/papers/full/austen.html.

Awre, C. (2004) JISC FAIR Programme: opening up access to
institutional assets, *Assignation*, **21** (3), 7–10.

Ayers, E. (2004) Academic Culture and the IT Culture: their effect on
teaching and scholarship, *Educause Review*, (Nov/Dec), 48–62.

Ayers, E. (2005) Scholarship in the Digital Age. In *Publication, the Public
University and the Public Interest: conference held on 19 April 2005*,
University of Minnesota Libraries.

Bailey, C. W. (2005) *Open Access Bibliography: liberating scholarly literature
with e-prints and open access journals*, Association of College and
Research Libraries.

Bajwa, V. and Salisbury, L. (2003) Faculty Publications as a Source of
Information for Identifying and Satisfying Users' Needs: a case study
at the University of Arkansas, Fayetteville, *Journal of Agricultural & Food
Information*, **5** (3), 11–25.

Baker, D. (1978) Characteristics of the Literature Used by English
Musicologists, *Journal of Librarianship*, **10**, 183–200.

Banks, M. (2005) The Excitement of Google Scholar, the Worry of
Google Print, *Biomedical Digital Libraries*, **2** (2),
www.bio-diglib.com/content/2/1/2.

Barjak, F. (2006) Role of the Internet in Informal Scholarly
Communication, *Journal of the American Society for Information Science
and Technology*, **57** (10), 1350–67.

Barry, C. (1995) Critical Issues in Evaluating the Impact of IT on
Information Activity in Academic Research: developing a qualitative
research solution, *Library & Information Science Research*, **17** (2), 107–34.

Barry, C. (1997) Information Skills for an Electronic World: training
doctoral research students, *Journal of Information Science*, **23** (3), 225–38.

Barua, P. and Tripathi, T. (1988) An Analysis of Information-Seeking
Behaviour of Research Scholars vis-à-vis Existing Information
Sources and Services of Burdwan University Library: a case study,
IASLIC Bulletin, **33** (2/3), 93–8.

Basker, J. (1984) Philosophers' Information Habits, *Library and
Information Research News*, **7**, 2–10.

Bates, M. J. (1994) The Design of Databases and Other Information Resources for Humanities Scholars: the Getty Online Searching Project Report No. 4, *Online & CD-ROM Review*, **18** (6), 331–4.

Bates, M. J. (1995) Research Practices of Humanities Scholars in an Online Environment: the Getty Online Searching Project Report No. 3, *Library & Information Science Research*, **17**, 5–40.

Bates, M. J. (1996a) The Getty End-User Online Searching Project in the Humanities: the Getty Online Searching Project Report No 6, overview and conclusions, *College & Research Libraries*, **57** (6), 514–23.

Bates, M. J. (1996b) Learning About the Information Seeking of Interdisciplinary Scholars and Students, *Library Trends*, **45** (2), 155–64.

Bates, M. J. (2001) *Information Needs and Seeking of Scholars and Artists in Relation to Multimedia Materials*, UCLA, www.gseis.ucla.edu/faculty/bates/scholars.html.

Bates, M. J. et al. (1993) An Analysis of Search Terminology used by Humanities Scholars: the Getty Online Searching Project Report No. 1, *Library Quarterly*, **63** (1), 1–39.

Bauer, K. (2004) Trends in Electronic Content at the Crushing/Whitney Medical Library: 1999–2003, *Journal of Electronic Resources in Medical Libraries*, **1** (4), 31–43.

Bell, A. (1997) The Impact of Electronic Information on the Academic Research Community, *New Review of Academic Librarianship*, **3**, 1–24.

Berlin Declaration on Open Access to Knowledge in the Sciences and Humanities, (2003), www.zim.mpg.de/openaccess-berlin/berlin_declaration.pdf.

Bevan, S. J. (2005) Electronic Thesis Development at Cranfield University, *Program*, **39** (2), 100–11.

Bichteler, J. and Ward, D. (1989) Information-Seeking Behavior of Geoscientists, *Special Libraries*, **80**, 169–78.

Biggs, M. (1990) Discovering How Information Seekers Seek: methods of measuring reference collection use, *Reference Librarian*, **29**, 103–17.

Blagden, P. (1987) Patterns of Library Use among Researchers in the Field of Women's Studies with Special Reference to the Fawcett Library, *Women's Studies International Forum*, **10** (3), 317–29.

Blagden, P. (2005) The LIRG/SCONUL Measuring Impact Initiative:

overview of phase 1 impact projects, *Library and Information Research News*, **29** (91), 20–2.

Bloomfield, B. C. (ed.) (1997) *A Directory of Rare Book and Special Collections in the United Kingdom and Republic of Ireland*, 2nd edn, Facet Publishing.

Bloor, I. (2001) CORSALL: collaboration in research support by academic libraries in Leicestershire: final report, http://hdl.handle.net/2086/52.

Borgman, C. L. (1989) Bibliometrics and Scholarly Communication, *Communication Research*, **16** (5), 583–99.

Borgman, C. L. et al. (1989) The Design and Evaluation of a Front-End User Interface for Energy Researchers, *Journal of the American Society for Information Science*, **40** (2), 99–109.

Borgman, C. L. et al. (2005) Comparing Faculty Information Seeking in Teaching and Research: implications for the design of digital libraries, *Journal of the American Society for Information Science and Technology*, **56** (6), 636–57.

Bradford, C. (2005) University of Warwick: impact of the library on the research process, *Library & Information Research*, **29** (1), 52–4.

Bradford, K. D. et al. (2004) Bioinformatics Opportunities for Health Sciences Librarians and Information Professionals, *Journal of the Medical Library Association*, **92** (4), 489–93.

Bradley, P. (2004) *The Advanced Internet Searcher's Handbook*, 3rd edn, Facet Publishing.

Brecht, A. (1984/85) Changes in Legal Scholarship and Their Impact on Law School Library Reference Services, *Law Library Journal*, **77**, 157.

Breen, L. R. and Jenkins, A. (2002) Academic Research and Teaching Quality: the views of undergraduate and postgraduate students, *Studies in Higher Education*, **27** (3), 309–27.

Brindley, L. (2006) A World of Contrasts: information literacy in the digital age, *Lilac Conference held at the University of Leeds on 27–29 March 2006*.

Brittain, J. M. (1970) *Information and its Users: a review with special reference to the social sciences*, Oriel.

Broadbent, E. (1986) A Study of Humanities Faculty Library

Information Seeking Behavior, *Cataloging & Classification Quarterly*, **6**, 23–37.

Broadus, R. N. (1987) Information Needs of Humanities Scholars: a study of requests made at the National Humanities Center, *Library and Information Science Research*, **9** (2), 113–29.

Broadus, R. N. (1989) Use of Periodicals by Humanities Scholars, *Serials Librarian*, **16** (1–2), 123–31.

Broadus, R. N. (1990) The Range of Subject Literatures Used by Humanities Scholars, *Collection Management*, **12** (1/2), 61–8.

Brockman, W. S. et al. (2001) *Scholarly Work in the Humanities and the Evolving Information Environment*, Council on Library and Information Resources.

Brodie, M. (2000) The Impact of Change on Research Libraries: the State Library of New South Wales. In *ALIA 2000: proceedings of a conference held on 24–26 October 2000*.

Brophy, P. et al. (2004) *EDNER: Formative Evaluation of the Distributed National Electronic Resource: stakeholder consultation and analysis – user information needs. Deliverable MDA 3, EDNER Project, Manchester*, CERLIM (The Centre for Research in Library & Information Management).

Brown, C. D. (2001) The Role of Computer-Mediated Communication in the Research Process of Music Scholars: an exploratory investigation, *Information Research*, **6** (2), http://informationr.net/ir/6-2/paper99.html.

Brown, C. D. (2002) Straddling the Humanities and Social Sciences: the research process of music scholars, *Library and Information Science Research*, **24** (1), 73–94.

Brown, C. M. (1999) Information Seeking Behavior of Scientists in the Electronic Age: astronomers, chemists, mathematicians, and physicists, *Journal of the American Society for Information Science*, **50** (10), 929–43.

Budapest Open Archive Initiative (2002), www.soros.org/openaccess/read.shtml.

Budd, J. M. (1986) Characteristics of Research Materials Used by American Literature Scholars: a citation study, *DAI*, **46**, 3178A.

Budd, J. M. (1989) Research in the Two Cultures: the nature of scholarship in science and the humanities, *Collection Management*, **11** (3/4), 1–21.

Burchard, J. E. (1965) How Humanists Use a Library. In Overhage, C. F. J. and Harman, R. J., *Intrex: Report Conference of a Planning on Information Transfer Experiments*, MIT Press.

Burnette, M. et al. (1994) The Humanist and the Library: promoting new scholarship through collaborative interaction between humanists and librarians, *Reference Librarian*, **47**, 181–91.

Burton, M. P. and Phimister, E. (1995) Core Journals: a reappraisal of the Diamond List, *Economic Journal*, **105** (429), 361–73.

Byrnko, B. (2006) Of Millennials and Mashups, *Information Today,* **23** (4), 29.

Caldwell, T. (2005) Strategic Thinking, *Information World Review*, (Nov), 23.

California Digital Library (2006) *eScholarship Repository*, http://escholarship.cdlib.org.

Calman, S. and Gourlay, D. (2005) The Impact of the Freedom of Information Laws on Academic Research, *Freedom of Information*, **1** (4), 10–12.

Campbell, J. et al. (2003) *Supporting Research Staff: making a difference*, report of a project commissioned by HEFCE as part of its Good Management Practice Initiative, University of Sheffield.

Campbell, R. (2005) Open Access Institutional Repositories: the views of a learned-society publisher. In *Open Access Institutional Repositories (OAIRs): Leadership, Direction and Launch: proceedings of a conference held on 25–26 January 2005 at the University of Southampton*, www.eprints.org/events/jan2005/programme.html.

Candy, P. (2006) Running Amok with a Chainsaw: an unexpected perspective on information literacy, *Lilac Conference held at the University of Leeds on 27–29 March 2006*.

Cargille, K. et al. (1999) Electronic Journals and Users: three perspectives, *Serials Review*, **25** (3), 47–59.

Carpenter, E. (1977) The Literary Scholar, the Librarian, and the Future of Literary Research, *Literary Research Newsletter*, **2**, 143–55.

Carr, R. (2004) *The Challenge of E-science for Research Libraries: presentation to CURL Members' Meeting, Dublin, 26th March 2004,* www.bodley.ox.ac.uk/librarian/escience/escience.htm.

Case, D. O. (1986) Collection and Organization of Written Information by Social Scientists and Humanists: a review and exploratory study, *Journal of Information Science,* **12** (3), 97–104.

Case, D. O. (1991) The Collection and Use of Information by some American Historians: a study of motives and methods, *Library Quarterly,* **61** (1), 61–82.

Case, D. O. (2002) *Looking for Information: a survey of research on information seeking, needs, and behavior,* Academic Press.

Cássia, R. et al. (2003) *Competitiveness is Pushing Scientists to the Edge,* Science and Development Network, www.scidev.net/gateways/index.cfm?fuseaction=readitem&item=edito rletter&itemid=19&language=1&rgwid=1.

The Center for Academic Integrity (2006) *Center for Academic Integrity,* www.academicintegrity.org/.

Chen, C.-C. (1974) How Do Scientists Meet Their Information Needs? *Special Libraries,* **65**, 272–80.

Chikonzo, A. C. and Aina, L. O. (2001) The Information Environment of Veterinary Researchers at the University of Zimbabwe, *International Information and Library Review,* **33** (1), 97–111.

Choate, R. (1995) Library Support for Research: the view from Australia, *IATUL Proceedings, New Series,* **4**, 93–100.

Clapp, V. W. (1964) *The Future of the Research Library,* University of Illinois Press.

Clark, P. (1996) Disciplinary Structures on the Internet: linking library services to research practices, *Library Trends,* **44** (2), 226–38.

Clinch, P. (2001) FLAG Project: survey results, *Legal Information Management,* **1** (2), 45–58.

Cobbledick, S. (1996) The Information Seeking Behavior of Artists: exploratory interviews, *Library Quarterly,* **66** (4), 343–72.

Cohen, D. J. (1990) Scholarly Communication and the Role of Libraries: problems and possibilities for accessing journal articles, *Serials Librarian,* **17** (34), 43.

Colby, R. A. (1977) Literary Scholars, Librarians, and Bibliographical Systems, *Literary Research Newsletter*, **2**, 156–66.

Cole, C. (1997) Information as Process: the difference between corroborating evidence and 'information' in humanistic research domains, *Information Processing and Management*, **33** (1), 55–67.

Cole, C. (1998) Information Acquisition in History PhD Students: inferencing and the formation of knowledge structures, *Library Quarterly*, **68**, 33–54.

Cole, C. (2000) Inducing Expertise in History Doctoral Students via Information Retrieval Design, *Library Quarterly*, **70**, 86–109.

Copeland, S. and Penman, A. (2003) E-theses: recent developments and the JISC FAIR programme, *SCONUL Newsletter*, **28**, (Spring), 39–42.

Copeland, S., Penman, A. and Milne, R. (2005) Electronic Theses: the turning point, *Program*, **39** (3), 185–97.

Corkill, C. et al. (1981) *Doctoral Students in Humanities: a small-scale panel study of information needs and uses 1976–1979*, University of Sheffield Centre for Research on User Studies.

Corkill, C. M. and Mann, M. G. (1978) *Information Needs in the Humanities: two postal surveys*, University of Sheffield Centre for Research on User Studies.

Correia, A. M. R. and Teixeira, J. C. (2005) Reforming Scholarly Publishing and Knowledge Communication: from the advent of the scholarly journal to the challenges of open access, *Information Services & Use*, **25**, 13–21.

Coult, G. R. and Brindley, L. (2003) Lynne Brindley Explains the Way Ahead at the British Library, *Managing Information*, **10** (1) 4–6, 8.

Courant, P. (2005) Conservative Revolutionaries and Revolutionary Conservators: universities and scholarship in the digital age. In *Publication, the Public University and the Public Interest: conference held on 19 April 2005*, University of Minnesota Libraries.

Covi, L. M. (1996) Material Mastery: how university researchers use digital libraries for scholarly communication, *DAI*, **57**, 3727A.

Covi, L. and Kling, R. (1996) Organizational Dimensions of Effective Digital Library Use: closed rational and open natural systems models,

Journal of the American Society for Information Science, **47** (9), 672–89.

Cox, A. (2005) What are Communities of Practice? A comparative review of four seminal works, *Journal of Information Science*, **31** (6), 527–40.

Crawford, D. (1986) Meeting Scholarly Information Needs in an Automated Environment: a humanist's perspective, *College & Research Libraries*, **47**, 569–74.

Creaser, C., Maynard, S. and White, S. (2006) *LISU Annual Library Statistics*, LISU.

Cronin, B. and Overfelt, K. (1995) E–journals and Tenure, *Journal of the American Society for Information Science*, **46** (9), 700–3.

Cruickshank, J. (2002) The Role of Scientific Literature in Electronic Scholarly Communication, *Science and Technology Libraries*, **22** (3/4), 71–100.

Cude, W. (2001) *The PhD Trap Revisited*, Dundurn Press.

Curtis, K. L. et al. (1993) Information Seeking Behavior: a survey of health sciences faculty use of indexes and databases, *Bulletin of the Medical Library Association*, **81** (4), 383–92.

Curtis, K. L. et al. (1997) Information-Seeking Behavior of Health Sciences Faculty: the impact of new information technologies, *Bulletin of the Medical Library Association*, **85** (4), 402–10.

Dali, K. and Dilevko, J. (2004). Improving Collection Development and Reference Services for Interdisciplinary Fields through Analysis of Citation Patterns: an example using tourism studies, *College and Research Libraries*, **65** (3), 216–41.

Dalton, M. S. and Charnigo, L. (2004) Historians and Their Information Sources, *College & Research Libraries,* **65** (5), 400–25.

Davies, B. et al. (2000) We should Vet Together, *Library Association Record*, **102** (7) 390–1.

Davies, S. and Hosein, G. (2006) Hang Together – or We Will Hang Separately, *Times Higher Education Supplement*, (17 February), www.csrc.lse.ac.uk/idcard/TimesHigherArticle.pdf#search=%22times %20higher%20%22academic%20freedom%22%22.

de Jager, K. (1991) Researcher as Library User: a study of library support for successful research activities, *South African Journal of Library and Information Science*, **59** (2), 143–7.

de Tiratel, S. R. (2000) Accessing Information Use by Humanists and Social Scientists: a study at the Universidad de Buenos Aires, Argentina, *Journal of Academic Librarianship*, **26** (5), 346–54.

Department for Education and Skills (2003) *The Future of Higher Education*, Cm. 5735, The Stationery Office.

Department for Education and Skills (2006) *Reform of Higher Education Research Assessment and Funding: Consultation Paper*, DfES, www.dfes.gov.uk/consultations/downloadableDocs/consultationDocu ment%20jcutshall2.doc.

Department of Trade and Industry (2002) *Research Careers Initiative. Final Report 1997–2002*, DTI, www.universitiesuk.ac.uk/activities/RCIdownloads/RCI_final.pdf.

Dervin, B. and Nilan, M. (1986) Information Needs and Uses, *Annual Review of Information Science and Technology*, **21**, 3–33.

Dougherty, R. M. (1991) Needed: user-responsive research libraries, *Library Journal*, **116** (1), 59–62.

Dowler, L. (1997) *Gateways to Knowledge: the role of academic libraries in teaching, learning, and research*, MIT Press.

Downs, R. R. and Friedman, E. A. (1999) Digital Library Support for Scholarly Research, *Information Processing and Management*, **35** (3), 281–91.

Ducas, A. M. and Michaud-Oystryk, N. (2003) Toward a New Enterprise: capitalizing on the faculty-librarian partnership, *College and Research Libraries*, **64** (1), 55–74.

Duff, W. M. (2002) Accidentally Found on Purpose: information-seeking behavior of historians in archives, *Library Quarterly*, **72** (4), 472–96.

Dulle, F. W. et al. (2001) Researchers' Perspectives on Agricultural Libraries as Information Sources in Tanzania, *Library Review*, **50** (4), 187–92.

East, J. W. (2005) Information Literacy for the Humanities Researcher: a syllabus based on information habits research, *Journal of Academic Librarianship*, **31** (2), 134–42.

East, J. W. (2006) Subject Retrieval of Scholarly Monographs via Electronic Databases, *Journal of Documentation*, **62** (5), 597–605.

Economist (2006) *The World in 2007*, Economist Newspaper Ltd.

Ehrlich, E. (1991) *Amo, Amas, Amat and More*, Harper & Row.

Ellis, D. (1993) Modeling the Information-Seeking Patterns of Academic Researchers: a grounded theory approach, *Library Quarterly*, **63**, 469–86.

Ellis, D. and Haugan, M. (1997) Modelling the Information Seeking Patterns of Engineers and Research Scientists in an Industrial Environment, *Journal of Documentation*, **53** (4), 384–403.

Ellis, D. et al. (1993) A Comparison of the Information Seeking Patterns of Researchers in the Physical and Social Sciences, *Journal of Documentation*, **49** (4), 356–69.

Ellis, D. et al. (2002) Information Seeking and Mediated Searching, Part 5: User-intermediary interaction, *Journal of the American Society for Information Science and Technology*, **53** (11), 883–93.

Eprints UK (n.d.) The E-Prints UK Project, www.rdn.ac.uk/projects/eprints-uk.

Erens, B. (1996) *Modernizing Research Libraries: the effect of recent developments in university libraries on the research process*, Bowker Saur.

Ericson-Roos, C. (1997) The Journal in Focus: a report from an investigation of journal usage among Swedish researchers in the economic disciplines, *Inspel*, **31** (4), 213–26.

European Cultural Heritage Online (2002) *Charter of ECHO*, http://echo.mpiwg-berlin.mpg.de/heritage/oa_basics/charter.

Evans, S. M. and Line, M. B. (1973) A Personalized Service to Social Science Researchers: the experimental information service in the social sciences at the University of Bath, *Journal of Librarianship*, **5** (3), 214–32.

Fabian, B. (1986) Libraries and Humanistic Scholarship, *Journal of Librarianship*, **18** (2), 79–92.

Fagan, M. L. (1987) Practical Aspects of Conducting Research in British Libraries and Archives, *RQ*, **26** (3), 370–6.

Farrell, D. (1991) The Humanities in the 1990s: a perspective for research libraries and librarians, *Library Hi Tech*, **9** (1), 69–71.

Fidzani, B. T. (1998) Information Needs and Information-Seeking Behaviour of Graduate Students at the University of Botswana, *Library Review*, **47** (7), 329–40.

Fishenden, R. M. (1958) Methods by which Research Workers Find Information. In *Proceedings of an International Conference on Scientific Information held at the National Academy of Sciences on 16–21 November 1958 in Washington, D.C.*

Folster, M. (1989) A Study of the Use of Information Sources by Social Science Researchers, *Journal of Academic Librarianship*, **15** (1) 7–11.

Folster, M. B. (1995) Information Seeking Patterns: social sciences, *Reference Librarian*, **49/50**, 83–93.

Foxlee, R. and Borchardt, K. (2000) UQ Library's first CIS: towards customising information services at the University of Queensland Library, *IATUL Proceedings (New Series)*, **10**, CD-ROM Full Text Database.

Francis, H. (2005) The Information-Seeking Behavior of Social Science Faculty at the University of the West Indies, St Augustine Campus, *Journal of Academic Librarianship*, **31** (1), 67–72.

Frankel, M. (1998) *Freedom of Information and Universities*, Campaign for Freedom of Information, www.cfoi.org.uk/universities.html.

Franklin, B. and Plum, T. (2004) Library Usage Patterns in the Electronic Information Environment, *Information Research*, **9** (4), http://informationr.net/ir/9-4/paper187.html.

Friend, F. J. (2002) Creating Change in Europe: SPARC Europe and scholarly publishing, partnerships, consortia, and 21st century library service. In *Proceedings of the 23rd Annual IATUL Conference, 2–6 June 2002, Kansas City*, www.iatul.org/conference/proceedings/vol12/papers/friend.pdf.

Fulton, C. (1991) Humanists as Information Users: a review of the literature, *Australian Academic and Research Libraries*, **22** (3), 188–97.

Gardiner, D., McMenemy, D. and Chowdhury, G. (2006) Snapshot of Information Use Patterns of Academics in British Universities, *Online Information Review*, **30** (4), 341–59.

Garfield, E. (1980) Is Information Retrieval in the Arts and Humanities Inherently Different from that in Science? the effect that ISI's Citation Index for the Arts and Humanities is expected to have on future scholarship, *Library Quarterly*, **50**, 40–57.

Garvey, W. (1979) *Communication: the essence of science: facilitating information exchange among librarians, scientists, engineers and students*, Pergamon Press.

Gerhard, K. H. (2001) Challenges in Electronic Collection Building in Interdisciplinary Studies, *Collection Management*, **25** (2), 51–65.

Ghosh, S. (2003) Service Evaluation in a Special Library: supporting development research at the Institute of Social Sciences Library, New Delhi, *Library Review*, **52** (2), 76–83.

Glanville, J. and Smith. I. (1997) Evaluating the Options for Developing Databases to Support Research-Based Medicine at the NHS Centre for Reviews and Dissemination, *International Journal of Medical Informatics*, **47** (1/2), 83–6.

Glicksman, M. (1990) Changing Patterns of Scholarly Communications: implications for libraries, *Library Acquisitions*, **14** (4), 341–6.

Goddard, J. et al. (2003) *Learning Regional Engagement: a re-evaluation of the third role of Eastern Finland Universities*, Finnish Higher Education Evaluation Council.

Gorman, G. (1990) Patterns of Information Seeking and Information Use by Theologians in Seven Adelaide Theological Colleges, *Australian Academic and Research Libraries*, **21** (3), 137–56.

Gorman, M. (2000) *Our Enduring Values: librarianship in the 21st century*, American Library Association.

Gould, C. C. (1988) *Information Needs in the Humanities: an assessment*, Research Libraries Group.

Gould, C. C. and Handler, M. (1989) *Information Needs in the Social Sciences: an assessment*, Research Libraries Group.

Gould, C. C. and Pearce, K. (1991) *Information Needs in the Sciences: an assessment*, Research Libraries Group.

Gralewska-Vickery, A. (1976) Communication and Information Needs of Earth Science Engineers, *Information Processing and Management*, **12** (4), 251–82.

Gray, C. M. (1993) *Building Electronic Bridges between Scholars and Information: new roles for librarians. Designing Information: new roles for librarians*, Graduate School of Library and Information Science, University of Illinois at Urbana-Champaign.

Great Britain (1988). Education Reform Act, chapter 40,
www.opsi.gov.uk/acts/acts1988/Ukpga_19880040_en_1.htm.

Great Britain. House of Commons Science and Technology Committee
(2004) *Scientific Publications: free for all?* 10th report of session 2003–04,
www.publications.parliament.uk/pa/cm200304/cmselect/cmsctech/
399/399.pdf#search=%22%20%22Scientific%20publications%3A%2
0Free%20for%20all%3F%22%22.

Green, R. (2000) Locating Sources in Humanities Scholarship: the
efficacy of following bibliographic references, *Library Quarterly*, **70** (2),
201–29.

Grefsheim, S. et al. (1991) Biotechnology Awareness Study, Part 1:
where scientists get their information, *Bulletin of the Medical Library
Association*, **79** (1), 36–44.

Griffen-Foley, B. (2002) Confessions of a Library User Part 2. In
*Colloquium on Research Library Futures: strategies for action, State Library of
New South Wales 16–17 May 2002.*

Griffiths, M. (2000) The Role of the Education Librarian in Education
Research: a user's perspective, *Education Libraries Journal*, **43** (2), 5–12.

Grover, R. and Hale, M. L. (1988) Role of the Librarian in Faculty
Research, *College & Research Libraries*, **49** (1), 9–15.

Guest, S. (1987) The Use of Bibliographic Tools by Humanities Faculty
at the State University of New York at Albany, *Reference Librarian*, **18**,
157–72.

Hannabuss, S. (2001) Contested Texts: issues of plagiarism, *Library
Management*, **22** (6/7), 311–18.

Harley, S. (2003) Research Selectivity and Female Academics in UK
Universities: from gentleman's club and barrack yard to smart macho?
Gender and Education, **15** (4), 377–92.

Harnad, S. et al. (2004) The Access/Impact Problem and the Green and
Gold Roads to Open Access, *Serials Review*, **30** (4),
www.ecs.soton.ac.uk/%7Eharnad/Temp/impact.html.

Harrison, M. K. and Hughes, F. (2001) Supporting Researchers'
Information Needs: the experience of the Manchester Metropolitan
University Library, *The New Review of Academic Librarianship*, 7, 67–86.

Hartmann, J. (1995) Information Needs of Anthropologists, *Behavioral and Social Sciences Librarian*, **13** (2), 13.

Hatakenaka, S. (2005) *Development of Third Stream Activity: lessons from international experience*, Higher Education Policy Institute, www.hepi.ac.uk/downloads/Developmentofthirdstreamfunding-SachiHatakenaka.pdf.

Hatchard, D. B. and Crocker, C. (1990) Library Users – a psychological profile, *Australian Academic and Research Libraries*, **21** (2), 97–105.

Hatchard, D. B. and Toy, P. (1986) The Psychological Barriers Between Library Users and Library Staff: an exploratory investigation, *Australian Academic and Research Libraries*, **17** (2), 63–9.

Hayes, R. M. (1986) Strategic Planning for Information Resources in the Research University, *RQ*, **25** (4), 427–31.

Hazen, D. C. (1998) Understanding Research Agendas: explanations for change and the library response. In LaGuardia, C. and Mitchell, B. A. (eds), *Finding Common Ground: creating the library of the future without diminishing the library of the past*, Neal-Schuman Publishers.

HEFCE (2003) *Supporting Research Staff: making a difference*, Higher Educaton Funding Council for England, www.shef.ac.uk/~gmpcrs/index.html.

Hegarty, F. et al. (1995) Optimising the Provision of Information to Research Staff and Postgraduate Students in a New University of Technology, *IATUL Proceedings (New Series)*, **4**, 101–13.

Hendricks, R. (1992) *Latin Made Simple*, Doubleday.

Herman, E. (2001a) End-Users in Academia: meeting the information needs of university researchers in an electronic age, *Aslib Proceedings*, **53** (9), 387–401.

Herman, E. (2001b) End-Users in Academia: meeting the information needs of university researchers in an electronic age. Part 2, innovative information-accessing opportunities and the researcher: user acceptance of IT-based information resources in academia, *Aslib Proceedings*, **53** (10), 431–57.

Herner, S. (1958) The Information-Gathering Habits of American Medical Scientists. In *Proceedings of an International Conference on Scientific Information held at the National Academy of Sciences on 16–21 November 1958 in Washington, D.C.*

Hernon, P. (1984) Information Needs and Gathering Patterns of Academic Social Scientists, with special emphasis given to historians and their use of U.S. Government publications, *Government Information Quarterly*, **1** (4), 401–29.

Hertzum, M. and Pejterson, A. M. (2000) The Information-Seeking Practices of Engineers: searching for documents as well as for people, *Information Processing & Management*, **36** (5), 761–78.

HESDA (2003) *Career Paths of Academic Researchers*, Higher Education Staff Development Agency, www.hesda.org.uk/subjects/rs/case.html.

Hexham, I. (1999) *The Plague of Plagiarism*, Department of Religious Studies, The University of Calgary, http://c.faculty.umkc.edu/cowande/plague.htm#self.

Hey, J. M. N. and Simpson, P. (2004) Opening Access to Research with TARDis at Southampton University, *Assignation*, **21** (3), 19–22.

Hey, T. (2004) Why Engage in E-science? *Library & Information Update*, **3** (3), 25–7.

Hiller, S. (2002) How Different Are They? A comparison by academic area of library use, priorities, and information needs at the University of Washington, *Issues in Science and Technology Librarianship*, **33**, (Winter), www.istl.org/02-winter/article1.html.

Hirsch, S. and Dinkelacker, J. (2004) Seeking Information in Order to Produce Information: an empirical study at Hewlett Packard labs, *Journal of the American Society for Information Science and Technology Archive*, **55** (9), 807–17.

Hoch, P. K. (1988) The New Research Selectivity: frontier of advancement or managed contraction? *Physics in Technology*, **19** (4), 146–52.

Hogeweg de Haart, H. (1984) Characteristics of Social Science Information: a selective review of the literature, part II, *Social Science Information Studies*, **4**, 15–30.

Hogeweg de Haart, H. P. (1983) Social Science and the Characteristics of Social Science Information and its Users, *International Forum on Information Documentation*, **8** (1), 11–15.

Hoglund, L. and Wilson, T. (2000) *The New Review of Information Behaviour Research: studies of information seeking in context*, Taylor Graham.

Holland, M. P. and Powell, C. (1995) A Longitudinal Survey of

Information-Seeking and Use Habits of Some Engineers, *College and Research Libraries*, **56**, 7–15.

Hopkins, R. (1989) The Information Seeking Behaviour of Literary Scholars, *Canadian Library Journal*, **46** (2), 112–15.

Horner, J. and Thirlwall, D. (1988) Online Searching and the University Researcher, *Journal of Academic Librarianship*, **14** (4), 225–30.

Houghton, J. W., Steele, C. and Henty, M. (2004) Research Practices, Evaluation and Infrastructure in the Digital Environment, *Australian Academic and Research Libraries*, **35** (3), 161–76.

Hunt, T. (2006) Scholarly Squeeze: allowing undergraduates into the British Library's reading rooms has led to exclusion, not inclusion, *Guardian* (29 May), http://education.guardian.co.uk/higher/comment/story/0,,1785818,00.html.

Hurd, J. (1992) Interdisciplinary Research in the Sciences: implications for library organization, *College & Research Libraries*, **53**, 283–97.

Hurd, J. et al. (1992) Information Seeking Behavior of Faculty: use of indexes and abstracts by scientists and engineers. In *Proceedings of the 55th Annual Meeting of the American Society for Information Science*.

Hurd, J. et al. (1999) Information Use by Molecular Biologists: implications for library collections and services, *College and Research Libraries*, **60** (1), 31–43.

Hurych, J. (1986) After Bath: scientists, social scientists, and humanists in the context of online searching, *Journal of Academic Librarianship*, **12** (3), 158–65.

Ileperuma, S. (2002) Information Gathering Behaviour of Arts Scholars in Sri Lankan Universities: a critical evaluation, *Collection Building*, **21** (1), 22–31.

Information Commissioner (2005) *Information Intended for Future Publication*, FOIA Awareness Guidance 7, www.informationcommissioner.gov.uk/cms/DocumentUploads/ag%207%20info%20for%20fut%20pub.pdf.

Information Commissioner (2005) *The Public Interest Test*, FOIA Awareness Guidance 3, www.informationcommissioner.gov.uk/cms/DocumentUploads/ag%203%20-%20pub%20int%20reform%20may05.pdf.

Jacobs, N. et al. (2000) Using Local Citation Data to Relate the Use of Journal Articles by Academic Researchers to the Coverage of Full-Text Document Access Systems, *Journal of Documentation*, **56** (5), 563–81.

Jellinek, D. (2000) *Official UK: the essential guide to government websites*, HMSO.

Johnson, R. K. (2004) Open Access: unlocking the value of scientific research, *Journal of Library Administration*, **42** (2), 107–24, http:// eprints.rclis.org/archive/ 00005089/01/OA-Oklahoma_article.pdf.

Joint, N. (2005) Promoting Practitioner-Researcher Collaboration in Library and Information Science, *Library Review*, **54** (5), 289–94.

Joint Funding Bodies (2004) *Review of Research Assessment*, www.ra-review.ac.uk.

Joint Funding Councils' Libraries Review (Chair Professor Michael Anderson) (1995) *Report of the Group on a National/Regional Strategy for Library Provision for Researchers*, Higher Education Funding Council for England.

Joint Funding Councils' Report Group (Chair Sir Brian Follett) (1993) *Final Report*, Higher Education Funding Council for England.

Joint Information Systems Committee (n.d.) *EThOS project*, www.jisc.ac.uk/index.cfm?name=project_ethos.

Joint Information Systems Committee (n.d.) *JISC Digital Repositories Programme*, www.jisc.ac.uk/index.cfm?name=programme_digital_repositories.

Joint Information Systems Committee (n.d.) *JISCmail Discussion List on Defending Academic Freedom*, defending-academic freedom@jiscmail.ac.uk.

Joint Information Systems Committee (2006) *Plagarism Advisory Service*, www.jiscpas.ac.uk.

Joint Information Systems Committee Legal Information Service (2004) *Freedom of Information and Intellectual Property Rights*, www.jisclegal.ac.uk/publications/foidundaswilsonipr.htm.

Jones, R. (2004) Tapir: adding e-theses functionality to DSpace, *Ariadne*, **41** (October), www.ariadne.ac.uk/issue41/jones.

Jones, R. and Andrews, T. (2005) Open Access, Open Source and e-theses: the development of the Edinburgh Research Archive,

Program: Electronic Library and Information Systems, **39** (3), 198–212.

Joseph, H. (2005) The Scholarly Publishing and Academic Resources Coalition: an evolving agenda, *College and Research Libraries News*, **67** (2), www.ala.org/ ala/acrl/acrlpubs/crlnews/backissues2006/ february06/evolvingsparc.htm.

Jubb, M. (2005) The Research Libraries Network: some very initial thoughts. Address to CURL Members' Meeting, 17 March 2005, www.curl.ac.uk/members/documents/MJubbPres.doc.

Julien, H. (1995) Trends in the Recent Information Needs and Uses Literature: a content analysis. In *Connectedness: Information, Systems, People, Organizations: proceedings of the Third Annual Conference of the Canadian Association for Information Science (Association canadienne des sciences de l'information travaux), Alberta University, School of Library and Information Studies held on 7–10 June 1995.*

Kaniki, A. M. (1992) Meeting the Needs of Agricultural Researchers in Africa: the role of unpublished reports, *Information Development*, **8** (2), 83–9.

Katsirikou, A. (2003) 24th IATUL 2003 Conference: libraries and education in the networked information environment, *Library Hi Tech News,* **20** (8).

Kemoni, H. N. (2002) The Utilisation of Archival Information by Researchers in Kenya: a case study of the University of Nairobi, *African Journal of Library, Archives and Information Science*, **12** (1), 69–80.

Kesselman, M. and Watstein, S. B. (2004) Google Scholar and Libraries: point/counterpoint, *Reference Services Review*, **33** (4), 380–7.

King, D. W. et al. (1994) *Communication by Engineers: a literature review of engineers' information needs, seeking processes, and use*, Council on Library Resources.

King, J. B. (1994) History Research into the Twenty First Century, *Reference Librarian*, **22** (47), 89–108.

Knowles, M. S. (1978) *The Adult Learner: a neglected species*, Gulf Publishing.

Knowles, M. S. (1990) *The Adult Learner: a neglected species*, Gulf Publishing [updated].

Kock, N. and Davison, R. (2003) Dealing with Plagiarism in the Information Systems Research Community: a look at factors that drive plagiarism and ways to address them, *MIS Quarterly*, **27** (4), 511–32, www.tamiu.edu/~nedkock/Pubs/2003JournalMISQ/ KockDavison2003.pdf.

Korjonen-Close, H. (2005) The Information Needs and Behaviour of Clinical Researchers: a user-needs analysis, *Health Information and Libraries Journal*, **22** (2), 96–106.

Kwasitsu, L. (2003) Information-Seeking Behavior of Design, Process, and Manufacturing Engineers, *Library and Information Science Research*, **25** (4), 459–76.

LaGuardia, C. and Mitchell, B. A. (eds) (1998) *Finding Common Ground: creating the library of the future without diminishing the library of the past*, Neal-Schuman.

Lawlor, B. (2003) Abstracting and Information Services: managing the flow of scholarly communication – past, present, and future, *Serials Review*, **29** (3), 200–9.

Lawrence, P. A. (2003) The Politics of Publication: authors, reviewers and editors must act to protect the quality of research, *Nature*, **422**, 259–61.

Lawrence, S., Lee Giles, C. and Bollacker, K. (1999) Digital Libraries and Autonomous Citation Indexing, *IEEE Computer*, **32** (6), 67–71.

Layne, S. S. (1994) Artists, Art Historians and Visual Art Information, *Reference Librarian*, **47**, 23–36.

Lazinger, S. S. et al. (1997) Internet Use by Faculty Members in Various Disciplines: a comparative case study, *Journal of the American Society for Information Science*, **48** (6), 508–18.

Leckie, G. J. et al. (1996) Modeling the Information Seeking of Professionals: a general model derived from research on engineers, health care professionals, and lawyers, *Library Quarterly*, **66** (2), 161–93.

Lehmann, S. and Renfro, P. (1991) Humanists and Electronic Information Services: acceptance and resistance, *College & Research Libraries*, **52** (5), 409–13.

Lester, L. and Marshall, K. K. (1998) Traditional Library Services and the Research Process: are social sciences and humanities faculty getting what they need? In LaGuardia, C. and Mitchell, B. A. (eds), *Finding Common Ground: creating the library of the future without diminishing the library of the past*, Neal-Schuman.

Lester, R. (ed.) (2005) *The New Walford Guide to Reference resources, Vol. 1: Science, Technology and Medicine*, Facet Publishing.

Leung, Y. C. (2002) Always Yes, Never No, *Journal of Interlibrary Loan, Document Delivery and Information Supply*, **12** (3), 13–27.

Lewis, S. H. (2002) A Three-Tiered Approach to Faculty Services Librarianship in the Law School Environment, *Law Library Journal*, **94** (1), 89–100.

Libraries and Archives Canada (Bibliothèque et Archives Canada) (2006) *Theses Canada Portal*, www.collectionscanada.ca/thesescanada.

Lievrouw, L. A. (2004) *Bibliography: information seeking and use*, polaris.gseis.ucla.edu/ewhitmir/SeekList04LL.pdf.

Lin, N. (2002) Promise of an E-Future, *Library Journal Online*, 15 March, www.libraryjournal.com/article/CA200893.htm.

Line, M. B. (1969) Information Requirements in the Social Sciences: some preliminary considerations, *Journal of Librarianship and Information Science*, **1** (1), 1–19.

Line, M. B (1971) The Information Uses and Needs of Social Scientists: an overview of INFROSS, *ASLIB Proceedings*, **23** (8), 412–34.

Line, M. B. (1973) Information Needs of the Social Sciences, *INSPEL: International Journal of Special Libraries*, **8**, 29–39.

Line, M. B. (1999) Social Science Information: the poor relation. In *Proceedings of the IFLA Council and General Conference held in Bangkok 20–28 August 1999*, www.ifla.org/IV/ifla65/papers/030-150e.htm.

Line, M. B (2001) The Future Researcher and the Future Library: from the viewpoint of an independent user, *DF-Revy*, **24** (4), 103–8.

Line, M. B. et al. (1971) *Investigation into the Information Requirements of the Social Sciences: information requirements of researchers in social sciences*, Bath University Library.

Llull, H. P. (1991) Meeting the Academic and Research Information Needs of Scientists and Engineers in the University Environment, *Science & Technology Libraries*, **11** (3), 83–90.

Lonnquist, H. (1990) Scholars Seek Information: information-seeking behaviour and information needs of humanities scholars, *International Journal of Information and Library Research*, **2** (3), 195–203.

Lougee, W. P. et al. (1990) The Humanistic Scholars Project: a study of attitudes and behaviour concerning collection storage and technology, *College and Research Libraries*, **51** (3), 23–243.

Lyman, P. and Varian, H. (2003) *How Much Information 2003?* University of California at Berkeley, www2.sims.berkeley.edu/research/projects/how-much-info-2003.

Macmullen, W. J. et al. (2004) Planning Bioinformatics Education and Information Services in an Academic Health Sciences Library, *College and Research Libraries*, **65** (4), 320–33.

Mahé, A. (2004) Beyond Usage: understanding the use of electronic journals on the basis of information activity analysis, *Information Research*, **9** (4), http://informationr.net/ir/9-4/paper186.html.

Mahé A. et al. (2000) How French Research Scientists are Making Use of Electronic Journals: a case study conducted at the Pierre et Marie Curie University and Denis Diderot University, *Journal of Information Science*, **26** (5), 291–302.

Mallaiah, T. Y. and Badami, K. K. (1993) Library and Information Service Facilities in Mangalore University Library from the Research Scholars' Point of View: a survey, *Annals of Library Science and Documentation*, **40** (4), 155–65.

Markoff, J. (2004) Google Plans New Service for Scientists and Scholars, *New York Times*, (18 November), 11.

Marland, M. E. (1981) *Information Skills in the Secondary Curriculum*, Methuen Educational.

Maula, H. et al. (2004) Field Differences in the Use and Perceived Usefulness of Scholarly Mailing Lists, *Information Research*, **10** (1), http://informationr.net/ir/10-1/paper200.html.

McCulloch, E. (2006) Taking Stock of Open Access: progress and issues, *Library Review*, **55** (6), 337–43.

Meho, L. I. and Haas, S. W. (2001) Information-Seeking Behavior and Use of Social Science Faculty Studying Stateless Nations: a case study, *Library & Information Science Research*, **23** (1), 5–25.

Meho, L. I. and Tibbo, H. R. (2003) Modeling the Information-Seeking Behavior of Social Scientists: Ellis's study revisited, *Journal of the American Society for Information Science and Technology*, **54** (6), 570–87.

Meis, L. de, Carmo M. S. do and Meis, C. D. (2003) Impact Factors: just part of a research treadmill, *Nature*, **424**, 723.

Mendelsohn, S. (1999) Pharmaceutical Information: information sharing, *Information World Review*, **143**, 21–2.

Menzel, H. (1964) The Information Needs of Current Scientific Research, *Library Quarterly*, **34**, 4–19.

Menzel, H. (1966) Information Needs and Uses in Science and Technology, *ARIST*, **1**, 41–70.

Mercieca, P. (2006) Integration and Collaboration Within Recently Established Australian Scholarly Publishing Initiatives, *OCLC Systems & Services*, **22** (3), 149–54.

Milne, P. (1999) Electronic Access to Information and its Impact on Scholarly Communication. In *Strategies for the Next Millennium: proceedings of the Ninth Australasian Information Online & On Disc Conference and Exhibition held at Sydney Convention and Exhibition Centre, Sydney, 19–21 January 1999*.

Missingham, R. (1999) Science and Technology: a web of information: impact of the electronic present and future on scientists and libraries. In *Strategies for the Next Millennium: proceedings of the Ninth Australasian Information Online & On Disc Conference and Exhibition held at Sydney Convention and Exhibition Centre, Sydney, 19–21 January 1999*.

Moffat, M. (1997) A Glimpse at EEVL's Evaluation, *Ariadne*, **8**, www.ariadne.ac.uk/issue8/eevl-evaluation.

Monaghan, P. (1989) Some Fields are Reassessing the Value of the Traditional Doctoral Dissertation, *The Chronicle of Higher Education*, (March), A1.

Morton, H. C. and Price, A. J. (1989) *ACLS Survey of Scholars: a final report of views on publications, computers, and libraries*, American Council of Learned Societies

Mote, L. J. B. (1962) Reasons for the Variations in the Information Needs of Scientists, *Journal of Documentation*, **18** (4), 169–75.

Mueckenheim, J. K. (ed.) (2006) Gale Directory of Databases 2007, Thompson Gale.

Musumeci, D. (1997) *Role of Grammar in Communicative Language Teaching: an historical perspective*, McGraw Hill.

Nair, M. C. (1989) Social Science Information, Users, and Research Libraries: significance of organization of information, *IASLIC Bulletin*, **34** (3), 129–36.

National Library of Australia (2000) *A Review of Studies of Users of Scholarly Information*, Coalition for Innovation in Scholarly Communication.

Neway, J. (1982) The Role of the Information Specialist in Academic Research, *On-line Review*, **6**, 527–35.

Ngah, Z. A. and Sze, G. S. (1997) Information Needs and Use of Humanities Researchers: a bibliometric analysis and review of literature, *Kekal Abadi*, **16** (3), 1–15.

Nicholas, D., Huntington, P. and Rowlands, I. (2005) Open Access Journal Publishing: the views of some of the world's senior authors, *Journal of Documentation*, **61** (4), 497–519.

Nicholas, D. et al. (2005) Scholarly Journal Usage: the results of deep log analysis, *Journal of Documentation*, **61** (2), 248–80.

Noble, R. and Coughlin, C. (1997) Information-Seeking Practices of Canadian Academic Chemists: a study of information needs and uses of resources in chemistry, *Canadian Journal of Communication*, **20** (3/4), 49–60.

Notess, G. R. (2005) Scholarly Web Searching: Google Scholar and Scirus, *Information Today*, (July/August), www.infotoday.com/online/jul05/OnTheNet.shtml.

OAISTER (2006) *Oaister*, http://oaister.umdl.umich.edu/o/oaister/.

OECD (2002) *Benchmarking Industry–Science Relationships*, OECD.

OECD (2003) *Steering and Funding of Research Institutions: country report: United Kingdom*, OECD.

Office of Science and Technology (2002) *Knowledge Transfer/Exploitation Funding*, www.ost.gov.uk/enterprise/knowledge.

Olander, B. (1992) Applying Field Research in Information Science, *Svensk Biblioteks Forskning*, **4**, 3–11.

Open Access Team for Scotland (2004) *Scottish Declaration on Open*

Access, http://scurl.ac.uk/WG/OATS/ declaration.htm.

Open Archives Initiative (n.d.) *Open Archives Initiative*, www.openarchives.org.

Open Society Institute (n.d.) *Eprints UK Guide to Self-Archiving*, www.eprints.org/documentation/handbook.

Orbach, B. C. (1991) The View from the Researcher's Desk: historians' perceptions of research and repositories, *American Archivist*, **54**, 28–43.

Palmer, C. (1998) Ways of Working and Knowing Across Boundaries: research practices of interdisciplinary scientists. In LaGuardia, C. and Mitchell, B. A. (eds), *Finding Common Ground: creating the library of the future without diminishing the library of the past*, Neal-Schuman.

Palmer, C. L. (2005) Scholarly Work and the Shaping of Digital Access, *Journal of the American Society for Information Science and Technology*, **56** (11), 1140–53.

Palmer, C. L. and Neumann, L. J. (2002) The Information Work of Interdisciplinary Humanities Scholars: exploration and translation, *Library Quarterly*, **72**, 85–117.

Palmer, J. (1991a) Scientists and Information I. Using cluster analysis to identify information style, *Journal of Documentation*, **47**, 105–29.

Palmer, J. (1991b) Scientists and Information II. Personal factors in information behaviour, *Journal of Documentation*, **47**, 254–75.

Pankake, M. (1991) Humanities Research in the 90s: what scholars need; what librarians can do, *Library Hi Tech*, **9** (1), 9–15.

Park, J.-R. (2004) Language-Related Open Archives: impact on scholarly communities and academic librarianship, *Electronic Journal of Academic and Special Librarianship*, **5** (2/3), http://southernlibrarianship.icaap.org/content/v05n02/park_j01.htm.

Pat Wressell and Associates (ed.) (1997) *Library Service Provision for Researchers: proceedings of the Anderson Report Seminar organised by the Library and Information Co-operation Council (LINC) and the Standing Conference of National and University Libraries (SCONUL) held at Cranfield University on the 10–11 December 1996*, LINC.

Pechter, K. (2001) *Japanese Innovation Reform in the Light of Past Dialogue: conceptions of convergence as perspectives for comparative system assessment*, European Association of Evolutionary Political Economy, www.econ-pol.unisi.it/eaepe2001/EAEPE2001/Pechter.rtf.

Pencek, B. (2000) Internet Resources for Politics, Political Science, and Political Scientists, *Journal of Library Administration*, **30** (3/4), 293–334.

Perrow, C. (1989) On Not Using Libraries. In Lynch, B. P. (ed.), *Humanists at Work: disciplinary perspectives and personal reflections*, 29–42.

Pickering, B. (2006) RIN Plans Strategic Leadership, *Information World Review*, **220**, (January), 4.

Pinder, S. (2005) A Mandate to Self Archive? The role of open access institutional repositories, *Serials*, **18** (1), 30–4, http://eprints. nottingham.ac.uk/archive/00000152/01/mandate_to_archive.pdf.

Pinelli, T. and Kennedy, J. (1990) The Role of the Information Intermediary in the Diffusion of Aerospace Knowledge, *Science & Technology Libraries*, **11**, 59–76.

Pinelli, T. E. (1991) The Information-Seeking Habits and Practices of Engineers, *Science & Technology Libraries*, **11**, 5–25.

Pinelli, T. E. et al. (1993) Information Seeking Behavior of Engineers, *Encyclopedia of Library and Information Science*, 52 suppl. (15), 167–201.

Pinfield, S. (2003) Open Archives and UK Institutions: an overview, *D-Lib Magazine*, **9** (3), www.dlib.org/dlib/march03/pinfield/03pinfield.html.

Pinfield, S. (2005) Mandate to Self Archive? The Role of Open Access Institutional Repositories, *Serials*, **18** (1), 30–4.

Pocklington, K. and Finch, H. (1987) *Research Collections under Constraint: the effect on researchers – academics' perceptions of the impact on the research process of constraints to library budgets*, British Library Research Paper 36, British Library Research and Development Department.

Ponsati, A. and Baquero, M. (2005) An Analysis of the Use of Digital Collections in a Scientific Research Library Network: part two of a case study from CSIC, Madrid, Spain, *Serials*, **18** (1), 51–8.

Porter, S. (2003) *Reports from the Front: six perspectives on scholar's information requirements in the digital age*, www.ahds.ac.uk/old/public/uneeds/un4.html.

Posner, R. A. (1999) *Encyclopedia of Law and Economics*, http://encyclo.findlaw.com/foreword.html.

Poulter, A., McMenemy, D. and Hiom, D. (2005) *The Library and Information Professional's Internet Companion*, Facet Publishing.

Price, G. (1999) User Education in Higher Education: helping academics join the learning environment, *IATUL Proceedings (New Series)*, **9**, CD-ROM Full Text Database.

Prosser, D. C. (2004) Fulfilling the Promise of Scholarly Communication – a comparison between old and new access models. In Nielsen, E. K., Saur, K. G. and Ceynowa, K. (eds), *Scholarly Journal Prices: selected trends and comparisons*, KG Saur, http://eprints.rclis.org/archive/00003918/01/mittler_Paper.doc.

Publicker, S. and Stoklosa, K. (1999) Reaching the Researcher: how the National Institutes of Health Library selects and provides e-journals via the world wide web, *Serials Review*, **25** (3), 13–23.

Qayyum, M. A. (2002) Internet Reference Services and the Reference Desk: does the nature of a user's query really change, *Internet Reference Services Quarterly*, **7** (3), 15–22.

Quigley, J. et al. (2002) Making Choices: factors in the selection of information resources among science faculty at the University of Michigan; results of a survey conducted July–September, 2000, *Issues in Science and Technology Librarianship*, (Spring), www.istl.org/02-spring/refereed.html.

Quint, B. (2004) Google Scholar Focuses on Research-Quality Content, *Information Today*, (November), www.infotoday.com/newsbreaks/nb041122-1.shtml.

Ranganathan, S. R. (1931) *The Five Laws of Library Science*, Madras Library Association.

Reddick, M. J. (1998) Changing Face of Social Science Research: building and protecting gateways between the past and the future. In LaGuardia, C. and Mitchell, B. A. (eds), *Finding Common Ground: creating the library of the future without diminishing the library of the past*, Neal-Schuman.

Reed, B. and Tanner, D. R. (2001) Information Needs and Library Services for the Fine Arts Faculty, *Journal of Academic Librarianship*, **27**, 229–33.

Reeves, S., Hagen, J. and Jewell, C. (2006) Unlocking Scholarly Access:

ETDs, institutional repositories and creators: highlights of ETD 2006, the 9th International Symposium on Electronic Theses and Dissertations, *Library Hi Tech News*, **23** (7), 12–15.

Reid, D. (2006) The National Library of New Zealand as a Sun Centre of Excellence, *Electronic Library*, **24** (4), 429–33.

Research Councils and Arts and Humanities Research Board (2001) *Joint Statement of Skills Training Requirements of Research Postgraduates*, www.grad.ac.uk/jss.

Research Information Network (2006) *Researchers and Discovery Services: behaviour, perceptions and needs*, Research Information Network.

Research Information Network and Consortium of Research Libraries (2006) *The Future of Your Research Library* [personal communication], 13 December.

Research Support Libraries Group (2003) *Final Report*, Higher Education Funding Council for England, www.rslg.ac.uk/final/final.pdf.

Research Support Libraries Programme (2002) *About RSLP*, www.rslp.ac.uk.

Rice, R. E and Tarin, P. (1993) Staying Informed: scientific communication and the use of information sources within disciplines. In *Proceedings of the 56th Annual Meeting of the American Society for Information Science*, Learned Information.

Richardson, J. (1991) Library User Trials with a CD-ROM database, *Computers in Libraries*, **11** (4), 28–34.

Roberts, P. (1960) *Understanding English*, Harper & Row.

Robertson, A. (1974) Behavior Patterns of Scientists and Engineers in Information Seeking for Problem Solving, *ASLIB Proceedings*, **26**, 384–90.

Robertson, M. and Young, C. (2003) Information Needs of QUT Researchers – a report on focus group research conducted in 2002 by QUT Library, Queensland University of Technology, www.library.qut.edu.au/pubspolicies/information_needs.jsp.

Roderer, N. K. and Aguirre, A. (1991) User Response to the Columbia IAIMS. In *National Online Meeting 1991: proceedings of the Twelfth National Online Meeting, New York*, Learned Information.

Rolinson, J. et al. (1996) Information Usage by Biological Researchers, *Journal of Information Science*, **22** (1), 47–53.

Row, J. et al. (2001) Across the Disciplines: does subsidized document delivery meet the challenges?, *Collection Management*, **26** (2), 13–29.

Rowland, J. F. B. (1982) The Scientist's View of his Information System, *Journal of Documentation*, **38**, 38–42.

Rowlands, I. and Nicholas, D. (2005) Scholarly Communication in the Digital Environment: the 2005 survey of journal author behaviour and attitudes, *Aslib Proceedings*, **57** (6), 481–97.

Rudd, E. (1985) *A New Look at Postgraduate Failure*, Society for Research into Higher Education.

Rumsey, S. (2006) Purpose of Institutional Repositories in UK Higher Education: a repository manager's view, *International Journal of Information Management*, **26**, 181–6.

Rusch-Feja, D. (1996) New Roles for Librarians in Supporting Researchers in the Social Sciences: the impact of new technology, *INSPEL*, **30** (4), 324–34.

Russell, J. M. (2001) Scientific Communication at the Beginning of the Twenty-First Century, *International Social Science Journal*, **53**, (168), 271–82.

Rutledge, J. (1999) Ulrich Ammon's 1st Deutsch Noch Internationale Wissenschaftssprache? *WESS Newsletter*, **22** (2), www.dartmouth.edu/~wessweb/nl/Spring99/AmmonS99.html.

Salmon, G. (2000) *E-moderating*, Kogan Page.

Samimi, M. (1976) *Library Use and Academic Research in Iran in the Sciences, Social Sciences, and Humanities*, School of Graduate Studies, Pahlavi University, Iran.

Sano, H. (1986) Information Needs of Agricultural Researchers and Online Searching: cases of University of Osaka Prefecture [in Japanese], *Online Kensaku*, **7** (4), 164–71.

Saule, M. R. (1992) User Instruction Issues for Databases, *Library Trends*, **40** (4), 596–613.

Schmidt, J. (1999) Coping with Changes in Scholarly Communication at the University of Queensland Library, *Australian Academic & Research Libraries*, **30** (2), 89–94.

Scholman, B. (2005) Google Extends its Reach, *Online Journal of Issues in Nursing*, (14 February),
www.nursingworld.org/ojin/infocol/info_16.htm.

Schreuder, D. (2002) Webs of Knowledge, Australian Information Needs and 21st Century Research, *LASIE*, **33** (1), 35–47.

Schwartz, J. (2002) Internet Access and End-User Needs: computer use in an academic library, *Reference and User Services Quarterly*, **41** (3), 253–63.

Seaman, G. (1975) Experiences of a Professional Musicologist with the New Zealand Library System, *New Zealand Libraries*, **38** (3), 148–57.

Searing, S. E. (1996) Meeting the Information Needs of Interdisciplinary Scholars: issues for administrators and large university libraries, *Library Trends*, **45** (2), 315–42.

Selden, L. (2001) Academic Information Seeking: careers and capital types, *New Review of Information Behaviour Research*, **2**, 195–215.

Semra, H. (1986) Documenting Practices and Needs of Geographers Specializing in the Maghreb, *Inspel*, **20** (3), 168–73.

Shaugnessy, T. W. (1989) Scholarly Communication: the need for an agenda for action – a symposium, *Journal of Academic Librarianship*, **15** (2), 68.

Shaw, W. (2000) The Use of the Internet by Academics in the Discipline of English Literature: research in progress, *Computers & Texts*, **18–19**, 8–9.

Shaw, W. (2001) The Use of the Internet by Academics in the Discipline of English Literature: a quantitative and qualitative approach, *Information Research*, **6** (2), http://informationr.net/ir/6-2/ws8.html.

Shearer, K. and Birdsall, W. F. (2005) A Researcher's Research Agenda for Scholarly Communication in Canada, *New Review of Information Networking*, **11** (1), 99–108.

Shepherd, J. (2006) Staff are Silenced by Fear of Reprisals, *Times Higher Education Supplement* (4 August).

SHERPA: Securing a Hybrid Environment for Research Preservation and Access project (n.d.), *SHERPA*, www.sherpa.ac.uk.

SHERPA Romeo (n.d.) *Publisher Copyright Policies and Self-Archiving*, www.sherpa.ac.uk/romeo.php.

Shoham, S. (1998) Scholarly Communication: a study of Israeli academic researchers, *Journal of Librarianship and Information Science*, **30** (2), 113–21.

Siegfried, S. et al. (1993) A Profile of End-User Searching Behavior by Humanities Scholars, Getty Online Searching Project Report No. 2, *Journal of Academic Librarianship*, **44** (5), 273–91.

Sife, A. S. (2004) Information Needs and Seeking Behaviour of Tanzanian Forestry Researchers in the Electronic Environment, *University of Dar es Salaam Library Journal*, **6** (1), 78–89.

Skelton, B. (1973) Scientists and Social Scientists as Information Users: a comparison of results of science user studies with the investigation into information requirements of the social sciences, *Journal of Librarianship*, **5**, 138–56.

Slater, M. (1988) Social Scientists' Information Needs in the 1980s, *Journal of Documentation*, **44** (3), 226–37.

Slater, M. (1989) *Information Needs of Social Scientists: a study by desk research and interview*, British Library.

Slatta, R. W. (1986) Telecommunications for the Humanities and Social Sciences, *Microcomputers for Information Management*, **3** (2), 91–110.

Slutsky, B. (1991) How to Avoid Science Anxiety Among Science Librarians, *Science & Technology Libraries*, **12** (1), 11–19.

Smith, B. (1985) Library Support of Faculty Research: an investigation at a multicampus university, *Advances in Library Administration and Organization*, **4**, 111–20.

Smith, J. (2003) Testing the Assumption that End-User Input into the Design of an Academic Library Catalogue Makes the Catalogue a Better Information Resource, *Canadian Journal of Information and Library Science*, **27** (4), 89–91.

Snow, C. (1975) Architects' Wants and Needs for Information, Demonstrated Through a University-Based Information Service, *ASLIB Proceedings*, **27**, 112–23.

Society of College, National and University Libraries (2005) *SCONUL Vision: academic information services in the year 2010*, www.sconul.ac.uk/pubs_stats/pubs/vision%202010.

Somerville, A. (1986/7) Information Services to the Academic Scientific Community in the 1980s, *Reference Librarian*, **16**, 125–39.

SPARC Europe (2006) *SPARC Europe*, Association of Research Libraries, www.sparceurope.org.

Spurr, S. H. (1958) Requirements of Forest Scientists for Literature and Reference Services. In *Proceedings of the International Conference on Scientific Information, Washington DC, National Academy of Sciences*, National Research Council.

Stam, D. C. (1984) Art Historians Look for Information, *Art Documentation*, **3**, 117–19.

Stam, D. C. (1989) Tracking Art Historians: on information needs and information-seeking behaviour, *Art Libraries Journal*, **14** (3), 13–16.

Steele, C. (2003) New Models of Academic Publishing, *Information Management Report*, 1–7.

Steele, T. W. and Stier, J. C. (2000) The Impact of Interdisciplinary Research in the Environmental Sciences: a forestry case study, *Journal of the American Society for Information Science*, **51** (5), 476–84.

Steinke, C. A. (1991) *Information Seeking and Communicating Behavior of Scientists and Engineers*, Haworth Press.

Steinwedel, S. (1999) The Information Seeking Behavior of Theologians as Humanists: a review, www.geocities.com/sjsteinwedel/theolog.htm.

Stewart, T. (1996) The Invisible Key to Success, *Fortune Magazine*, (5 August), http://money.cnn.com/magazines/fortune/fortune_archive/1996/08/05/215440/index.htm.

Stieg, M. F. (1981). The Information Needs of Historians, *College and Research Libraries*, **42**, 549–60.

Stoan, S. (1991) Research and Information Retrieval among Academic Researchers: implications for library instruction, *Library Trends*, **39** (3), 238–58.

Stokker, J. (1998) A Researchers' Centre: one library's experience in meeting the needs of research level students and academic staff, *Australian Academic and Research Libraries*, **29** (4), 190–9.

Stone, S. (1982) Humanities Scholars: information needs and uses, *Journal of Documentation*, **38** (4), 292–313.

Styvedaele, B. J. H. V. (1977) University Scientists as Seekers of Information: sources of references to periodical literature, *Journal of Librarianship and Information Science*, **9** (4), 270–77.

Subrahmanyam, T. (1983) Study of Information Seeking Behavior of Doctoral Candidates in Social Sciences, *Herald of Library Science*, **22** (3), 200–4.

Sukovic, S. (2000) Humanities Researchers and Electronic Texts, *LASIE*, **31** (3), 5–29.

SURF (n.d.) *SURF*, www.surf.nl/en/home/index.php.

Swan, A. and Brown, S. (2004) JISC/OSI Journal Authors Survey Report, Key Perspectives, www.jisc.ac.uk/uploaded_documents/JISCOAreport1.pdf.

Swan, A. et al. (2005) Developing a Model for E-Prints and Open Access Journal Content in UK Further and Higher Education, *Learned Publishing*, **18** (1), 25–40, www.thes.co.uk/current_edition/story.aspx?story_id=2031645.

Swank, R. (1945) Organization of Library Materials for Research in English Literature, *Library Quarterly*, **15,** 49–74.

Swinburne, J. K. (1983) Information Use and Transfer by British and French Scientists: a study of two groups, *Journal of Information Science*, **6**, 75–80.

Symons, J. (1996) Management Researchers Don't Need Libraries Do They? *Managing Information*, **3** (3), 39–41.

Sze, G. S. and Ngah, Z. A. (1997) Postgraduate Research in the Humanities at the University of Malaya, *Malaysian Journal of Library and Information Science*, **2** (1), 71–80.

Tennant, M. R. (2005) Bioinformatics Librarian: meeting the information needs of genetics and bioinformatics researchers, *Reference Services Review*, **33** (1), 12–19.

Tenopir, C. (2005) Google in the Academic Library, *Library Journal*, (1 February), www.libraryjournal.com/article/CA498868.html?display=Online+Dbs News&industry=Online+Dbs&industryid=3761&verticalid=151.

Thaxton, L. (1985) Dissemination and Use of Information by Psychology Faculty and Graduate Students: implications for bibliographic instruction, *Research Strategies*, **3**, 116–24.

Thomson Gale (2004) *Péter's Digital Reference Shelf*, (December), Google Scholar Beta,

www.galegroup.com/servlet/HTMLFileServlet?imprint=9999&region
=7&fileName=/reference/archive/200412/googlescholar.html.

Tibbo, H. R. (2002) Primarily History: historians and the search for primary source materials: International Conference on Digital Libraries archive. In *Proceedings of the 2nd ACM/IEEE-CS Joint Conference on Digital Libraries, Portland, Oregon, USA*, Association for Computing Machinery.

Torma, S. and Vakkari, P. (2004) Discipline, Availability of Electronic Resources and the Use of Finnish National Electronic Library: FinELib, *Information Research*, **10** (1).

Tornudd, E. (1959) Study on the Use of Scientific Literature and Reference Services by Scandinavian Scientists and Engineers Engaged in Research and Development. In *Proceedings of the International Conference on Scientific Information*, http://listserv.utk.edu/ cgi-bin/wa?A2=ind0404&L=sigmetrics&P=5067.

Treasury (2003) *SET for Success: final report of Sir Gareth Roberts' Review*, Treasury, www.hm treasury.gov.uk/Documents/Enterprise_and_ Productivity/Research_and_Enterprise/ent_res_roberts.cfm.

Tsai, F. Y. (1987) Technical and Reader Services for the Research Library – the challenge in the next decade, *Journal of Library and Information Science*, **13** (1), 43–61.

Ucak, N. O. and Kurbanoglu, S. S. (1998) Information Need and Information Seeking Behavior of Scholars at a Turkish University. In *Proceedings of the 64th IFLA General Conference, August 16–21 in Amsterdam*.

Unsworth, J. (1997) Some Effects of Advanced Technology on Research in the Humanities. In Dowler, L. (ed.), *Gateways to Knowledge: the role of academic libraries in teaching, learning, and research*, MIT Press.

Uva, P. A. (1977) *Information Gathering Habits of Academic Historians: report of the pilot study*, Syracuse University of New York, Upstate Medical Center Library.

Vakkari, P. et al. (1997) Information Seeking in Context. In *Proceedings of an International Conference on Research in Information Needs, Seeking and Use in Different Contexts, August 14–16 in Tampere, Finland*, Taylor Graham.

van Bentum, M. and Braaksma, J. (1999) The Future of Libraries and Changing User Needs: general concepts and concrete developments, *IATUL Proceedings (New Series)*, **9**, CD-ROM Full Text Database.

Varlejs, J. (1987) Information Seeking: basing services on users' behaviors. In *Proceedings of the Twenty-Fourth Annual Symposium of the Graduate Alumni and Faculty of The Rutgers School of Communication, Information and Library Studies*, McFarland.

Vine, R. (2006) Google Scholar: review, *Journal of the Medical Library Association*, **94** (1), 97–9.

Voigt, M. J. (1959) The Researcher and His Sources of Scientific Information, *Libri*, **9** (3), 177–93.

Voigt, M. J. (1961) *Scientists' Approaches to Information*, American Library Association.

Voorbij, H. and Ongering, H. (2006) Use of Electronic Journals by Dutch Researchers: a descriptive and exploratory study, *Journal of Academic Librarianship*, **32** (3), 223–37.

Voorbij, H. J. (1999) Searching Scientific Information on the Internet: a Dutch academic user survey, *Journal of the American Society for Information Science*, **50** (7), 598–615.

Wainwright, E. J. (2005) Strategies for University Academic Information and Service Delivery, *Library Management*, 26 (8/9), 439–56.

Walker, T. J. (2002) Two Societies Show How to Profit by Providing Free Access, *Learned Publishing*, **15** (4), 279–84.

Waller, J. H. (2005) Evaluating Scholarly Communication, *Collection Management*, **30** (2), 45–57.

Ward, A. W. and Waller, A. R. (eds) (1907–21) *Cambridge History of English and American Literature, Volume III, Renascence and Reformation*, Cambridge University Press, www.bartleby.com/213/index.html.

Warner, S. (2005) Transformation of Scholarly Communication, *Learned Publishing*, **18**, 177–85.

Watson, L. (2004) Digital Reference Services for Social Scientists: SLIS capping exercise, www.slis.ualberta.ca/cap04/lisa/lw%20capping%202004%20intro.htm.

Watson-Boone, R. (1994) The Information Needs and Habits of Humanities Scholars, *RQ*, **34** (2), 203–16.

Webb, J. and Powis, C. (2004) *Teaching Information Skills: theory and practice*, Facet Publishing.

Weintraub, K. J. (1980) The Humanist Scholar and the Library, *Library Quarterly*, **50** (1), 22–39.

Wenger, E. (1998) *Communities of Practice: learning meaning and identity*, Cambridge University Press.

Westbrook, L. (1997) Information Access Issues for Interdisciplinary Scholars: results of a Delphi study on women's studies research, *Journal of Academic Librarianship*, **23** (3), 211–16.

Westbrook, L. (1999) *Interdisciplinary Information Seeking in Women's Studies*, McFarland & Company.

Westbrook, L. (2003) Information Needs and Experiences of Scholars in Women's Studies: problems and solutions, *College and Research Libraries*, **64** (3), 192–209.

Wiberley, S. E. (1991) Habits of Humanists: scholarly behavior and new information technologies, *Library Hi Tech*, **9** (1), 17–21.

Wiberley, S. E. and Jones, W. G. (1989) Patterns of Information Seeking in the Humanities, *College and Research Libraries*, **50** (6), 638–45.

Wiberley, S. E. and Jones, W. G. (2000) Time and Technology: a decade-long look at humanists' use of electronic information technology, *College & Research Libraries*, **61**, 421–31.

Wilson, K. B. and Eustis, J. D. (1981) The Impact of User Frustration on Humanities Research, *College & Research Libraries*, **42**, 361–65.

Wilson, T. D. (1994) *Information Needs and Uses: fifty years of progress? Fifty years of information progress: a Journal of Documentation review*, Aslib.

Wilson, T. D. (1997) Information Behaviour: an interdisciplinary perspective, *Information Processing and Management*, **572** (33), 551–72.

Wilson, T. D. and Allen, D. K. (1999) Exploring the Contexts of Information Behaviour. In *Proceedings of the 2nd International Conference on Research in Information Needs, Seeking and Use in Different Contexts, August 13–15 1998, held in Sheffield*, Taylor Graham.

Wisneski, R. (2005) Investigating the Research Practices and Library Needs of Contingent, Tenure-Track, and Tenured English Faculty, *Journal of Academic Librarianship,* **31** (2), 119–33.

Withnall, M. (2000) Need to Attract and Retain the Best Young Bioscientists, *Seb Bulletin*, www.sebiology.org/Bulletin/Jan2000/news.htm.

Wittenberg, K. (2004) Collaborators in Communication, *Educause Review*, (Nov/Dec), 64–76.

Yakoubi, B. (1987) User Education at the Oran University of Science and Technology, *IATUL Quarterly*, **1** (1), 63–7.

Yang, J. and Frank, D. (1999) Working Effectively with Scholars: a key to academic library success, *Georgia Library Quarterly*, **36** (2), 10.

Yarfitz, S. and Ketchell, D. S. (2000) A Library-Based Bioinformatics Services Program, *Bulletin of the Medical Library Association*, **88** (1), 36–48.

Yerbury, D. (1993) Issues for the Humanities. In Mulvaney, J. and Steele, C. (eds), *Changes in Scholarly Communication Patterns: Australia and the electronic library*, Highland Press.

Yitzhaki, M. and Hammershlag, G. (2004) Accessibility and Use of Information Sources among Computer Scientists and Software Engineers in Israel: academy versus industry, *Journal of the American Society for Information Science and Technology*, **55** (9), 832–42.

Young, J. (2005) More than 100 Colleges Work with Google to Speed Campus Users to Library Resources, *The Chronicle of Higher Education*, 11 May, http://chronicle.com/free/2005/05/2005051101t.htm.

Zacharov, A. G. (1986) Information Needs of Scientists, *Kniznice a Vedecke Informacie*, **17** (5), 209–21.

Useful websites

AbeBooks
    www.abebooks.co.uk
ACLS History Project
    www.historyebook.org/intro.html
ACQWEB
    http://acqweb.library. vanderbilt.edu
Agriculture Network Information Center
    www.agnic.org
Alibris
    www.alibris.com
All conferences.com
    www.allconferences.com
Berlin Declaration (2003)
    www.zim.mpg.de/openaccess-berlin/berlin_declaration.pdf
Bibliofind
    www.bibliofind.com
Books for Academics
    www.services.ex.ac.uk/bfa
BookWire (USA)
    www.bookwire.com
BOPCRIS
    www.bopcris.ac.uk

BRENDA
    www.brenda.uni-koeln.de

British Library integrated catalogue
    http://catalogue.bl.uk

British Library National Reports Collection
    www.bl.uk/services/document/reportsuk.html

Budapest Open Archive Initiative (2002)
    www.soros.org/openaccess/read.shtml

Cabell's directories
    www.cabells.com

California Digital Library eScholarship Repository
    http://escholarship.cdlib.org

Census Registration Service
    http://census.data-archive.ac.uk

Center for Academic Integrity
    www.academicintegrity.org

Charter of ECHO (2002)
    http://echo.mpiwg-berlin.mpg.de/heritage/oa_basics/charter

Chartermark
    www.cabinetoffice.gov.uk/chartermark/index.asp

Citeseer
    http://citeseer.ist.psu.edu

Clique
    www.clique.co.uk

COPAC
    http://copac.ac.uk

COS Expertize
    www.cos.com

Current Contents Connect (CCC)
    http://scientific.thomson.com/products/ccc

Current Serials Received
    www.bl.uk/serials

Early English Books Online (EEBO)
    http://eebo.chadwyck.com/home

Eighteenth Century Collections Online (ECCO)
   www.nls.uk/collections/rarebooks/ecco.html
eBook Library from Dawsons
   www.dawsonbooks.co.uk/services/e-books.html
Ebrary
   www.ebrary.com
EEVL
   www.eevl.ac.uk
Emerald
   www.emeraldinsight.com/info/about_emerald/overview/index.jsp
EngNetBase
   www.engnetbase.com
Entrez
   www.ncbi.nlm.nih.gov/Entrez
Eprints UK
   www.rdn.ac.uk/projects/eprints-uk
Eprints UK guide to self-archiving
   www.eprints.org/documentation/handbook
Esp@cenet
   www.espacenet.com
EThOS project
   www.jisc.ac.uk/index.cfm?name=project_ethos
European Archival Network
   www.european-archival.net/ean
European Bioinformatics Institute
   www.ebi.ac.uk
European Library
   www.theeuropeanlibrary.org
FirstGov (the US Government's web portal)
   www.firstgov.gov
FreePint
   www.freepint.com
Gale Directory of Databases, Thomson Gale 2007
   www.galegroup.com

GenomNet Japan
    www.genome.ad.jp/dbget
Google Scholar
    www.scholargoogle.co.uk (also harvests IR material)
GrayLIT Network
    www.osti.gov/graylit
Greynet
    www.greynet.org/greysourceindex.html
HERO gateway
    www.hero.ac.uk/uk/reference_and_subject_resources/
    purchase_and_supply/bookshops_and_publishers3803.cfm
HERO website
    www.hero.ac.uk/niss/niss_library4008.cfm
HESDA
    www.hesda.org.uk/subjects/rs/case.html
Higher Education Archives Hub
    www.archiveshub.ac.uk
Highwire Press
    http://highwire.stanford.edu
Index to Theses
    www.theses.com
Ingenta
    www.ingentaconnect.com/;jsessionid=6ttpgk1ob3aeh.victoria
Internet Resources Newsletter
    www.hw.ac.uk/libwww/irn/irn.html
Intute service
    www.intute.ac.uk
JISC Collections Portfolio of Online Resources
    www.jisc.ac.uk/index.cfm?name=coll
JISC Digital Repositories Programme
    www.jisc.ac.uk/index.cfm?name=programme_digital_repositories
JISCmail
    www.jiscmail.ac.uk
JISCmail discussion list on Defending Academic Freedom
    DEFENDING-ACADEMIC-FREEDOM@JISCMAIL.AC.UK

JISCPAS
    www.jiscpas.ac.uk
Journal Citation Reports
    http://portal.isiknowledge.com/portal.cgi
JustBooks (Europe)
    www.justbooks.co.uk
LibQual
    www.libqual.org
Knovel
    www.knovel.com
Listserve
    www.listserve.com
Metalib from Ex Libris
    www.exlibrisgroup.com/metalib.htm
National Archives
    www.nationalarchives.gov.uk
National Digital Archive of Datasets
    www.ndad.nationalarchives.gov.uk
National Student Survey
    www.hefce.ac.uk/NEWS/HEFCE/2006/survey.htm
OAISTER
    http://oaister.umdl.umich.edu/o/oaister
Online Books Page
    http://onlinebooks.library.upenn.edu
Open Access Team for Scotland Declaration (2004)
    http://scurl.ac.uk/WG/OATS/declaration.htm
Open Archives Initiative movement
    www.openarchives.org
Preprint archive
    http://xxx.soton.ac.uk
Project Gutenberg
    www.gutenberg.org
Project Romeo
    www.sherpa.ac.uk/romeo.php

ProQuest Digital Dissertations
   wwwlib.umi.com/dissertations
Resource shelf
   www.resourceshelf.com
RLG
   www.rlg.org
ROAR (Registry of Open Access Repositories)
   http://archives.eprints.org/index.php?action=browse
ScienceDirect
   www.sciencedirect.com
Sconul Research Extra (SRX)
   www.sconul.ac.uk/use_lib/srx
Scopus, from Elsevier
   www.info.scopus.com
SCoRe
   www.score.ac.uk
SHERPA project
   www.sherpa.ac.uk
SHERPA Romeo project
   www.sherpa.ac.uk/romeo.php
SPARC Europe
   www.sparceurope.org
SpringerLink
   www.springerlink.com/home/main.mpx
SURF
   www.surf.nl/en/home/index.php
Swetswise
   https://www.swetswise.com/public/login.do
Theses Canada Portal
   www.collectionscanada.ca/thesescanada
Thomson Scientific Research Services Group
   http://scientific.thomson.com/products/rsg
UK Data Archive
   www.data-archive.ac.uk

UKeIG website
    http://ukeig.xwiki.com/xwiki/bin/view/Main
Ulrich's Periodicals Directory
    www.ulrichsweb.com/ulrichsweb
UnCover Reveal
    www.ulib.iupui.edu/erefs/reveal.html
USPTO (US Patent and Trademark Office)
    www.uspto.gov/patft
Wikipedia
    http://en.wikipedia.org/wiki
Worldcat
    http://firstsearch.uk.oclc.org/i
WSSN
    www.wssn.net
ZETOC Alert
    http://zetoc.mimas.ac.uk/alertguide.html

Index